PRAISE FOR *AQUINAS ON BEATIFIC CHARITY AND THE PROBLEM OF LOVE*

"In *Aquinas on Beatific Charity and the Problem of Love*, Chris Malloy tackles head on an apparent dilemma that has long tormented Western consciousness: Can I truly love God for Himself and above all created things if I search in Him my own happiness? His sound answer is based on a close analysis of St. Thomas Aquinas's texts, in constant dialogue with the best contemporary scholars. It illuminates the non-competitive conception of love for God and self-love in the light of the metaphysical doctrine of participation and in the context of the Thomist conception of the harmonious articulation between nature and grace. By focusing on charity in its glorious phase, Malloy opens a fresh perspective on an old problem."

Serge-Thomas Bonino, O.P.,
President of the Pontifical Academy of Saint Thomas

"Christopher Malloy's study belongs to the highest level of contemporary scholarship concerning what Pierre Rousselot influentially describes as the problem of love. The problem concerns both the interpretation of medieval debates and the perennial importance of these debates for our understanding of charity. Professor Malloy is keenly aware of these two facets of the problem and handles them deftly. His analysis of Thomas Aquinas's theology of love engages the best of the secondary literature and outlines the contemporary interest of Aquinas's theology. The book is a welcome addition to scholarly debates on this problem."

Michael Sherwin, O.P.
University of Fribourg

"A worthy addition to this series! The topic of this book is important, and throughout Malloy is attentive to the key claims offered by Aquinas about love and charity, unpacking them in methodical fashion in the company of such stalwarts as Mansini, Sherwin, and Gallagher. Where need be Malloy, himself a systematic theologian, can engage as well in speculation, but he is, as is appropriate, unfailingly modest and reserved in thus moving the argument forward, always seeking to be faithful to Aquinas. Readers may well disagree with specific points of exegesis; but all will benefit from this sustained reflection about the compatibility of the 'love of beatitude' and the love of God above all things, for God's sake."

Joseph Wawrykow
University of Notre Dame

To My Father, Timothy Joseph Malloy

TABLE OF CONTENTS

Acknowledgments xiii
Abbreviations xv
Introduction 1
Chapter 1: Love in General and the Order of the Passions 9
Chapter 2: Rational Love: In Itself, Natural Dilection as a Root of Choice, and Love's Twofold Structure 35
Chapter 3: Twofold Beatitude and the Love Thereof 71
Chapter 4: Dilection for Others 87
Chapter 5: Charity and Love of Beatitude 133
Chapter 6: Charity in Faith 167
Chapter 7: Charity in Glory 193
Chapter 8: An Aporia? 217
Chapter 9: Towards a Resolution 233
Conclusion 251
Bibliography 255
Index 265

Acknowledgments

I CANNOT POSSIBLY GIVE DUE CREDIT to all who have helped me to produce this monograph. Above all, I would like to thank my wonderful wife Flory for her encouragement, sacrifices, and generosity. Several colleagues deserve thanks for convincing me to publish this work: Matthew Levering, Michael Sirilla, Guy Mansini, and Peter Kwasniewski. After completing my dissertation on beatific charity in Aquinas as it concerns the "problem of love," I abandoned the topic in order to produce a monograph on the Catholic-Lutheran dialogue concerning justification. I attempted to return to Aquinas on charity during my sabbatical in 2007–2008, but the issues involved seemed insoluble. Alas, they remain so—simple and subtly difficult at once. Various intellectuals and Thomistic interpreters strive from diverse sides towards a summit, where the fire and the rose are one. Hence, disagreements exhibit the complex simplicity of the issues and the goodwill of participants. Still, certain positions have deleterious ramifications. The stakes are high. I offer here a proposal, exegetical and speculative. The title implicitly bears the word "Towards." One item requiring further integration is Thomas's thought on the common good and on God as the supreme common good.

 I would also like to thank The University of Dallas for its generous Summer Grant of 2017 to aid me in completion of the work. The library staff at my university has been helpful. I would like to single out, especially, Alice Puro, through whose indefatigable assistance I procured many works from other libraries. Dr. Shannon Valenzuela has given invaluable editorial help. Matthew Levering and Chris Erickson have been supportive.

 I must not forget my dissertation director Peter Casarella, a champion of the student, a fine mentor, and a friend. With my own thesis students, I attempt to pay the thanks I owe him for his incredible labor and patience with the several drafts submitted during the dissertation process. Last but

Acknowledgments

not least, I owe a debt of thanks to David Gallagher, who permitted me to attend his splendid doctoral seminar on this topic at The Catholic University of America. His insights are lucid and profound.

ABBREVIATIONS FOR WORKS OF AQUINAS

Ad Col.	/	*Super Epistolam ad Colossenses Lectura* (1265–68)
Ad 1 Corin.	/	*Super Primam Epistolam ad Corinthios Lectura* (1265–68)
Ad Eph.	/	*Super Epistolam ad Ephesios Lectura* (1265–68)
Ad Gal.	/	*Super Epistolam ad Galatas Lectura* (1265–68)
Ad Hebr.	/	*Super Epistolam ad Hebraeos Lectura* (1265–68)
Ad Phil.	/	*Super Epistolam ad Philippenses Lectura* (1265–68)
Ad Rom.	/	*Super Epistolam ad Romanos Lectura* (1272–73)
Comp.	/	*Compendium theologiae* (*Prima* 1265–67; *Secunda* 1272–73)
DA	/	*Sententia Libri De Anima* (1267–68)
DC	/	*Quaestio disputata De caritate* (1271–72)
DDN	/	*In Librum Beati Dionysii De divinis nominibus* (Either 1261–65 or 1265–68)
De perf.	/	*De perfectione spiritualis vitae* (1269–70)
DM	/	*Quaestiones disputatae De malo* (Qq. 1–15 in 1270; Q. 16 in 1272)
DP	/	*Quaestiones disputate De potentia Dei* (1265–66)
DS	/	*Quaestio disputata De spe* (1271–72)
DT	/	*Expositio super librum Boethii De trinitate* (1257–58)
DV	/	*Quaestiones disputatae De veritate* (1256–59)

ABBREVIATIONS

Eth.	/	*Sententia Libri Ethicorum (1271–72)*
In Ioan.	/	*Super evangelium S. Ioannis lectura (1270–72)*
Psalm.	/	*Postilla super Psalmos* (1273)
Quodl.	/	*Quaestiones de quodlibet* (Qq. 1–6 and 12 from 1268–72)
SCG	/	*Summa contra Gentiles (1260–65)*
Sent.	/	*Scriptum Super libros Sententiarum (1252–56)*
ST	/	*Summa theologiae* (*Prima* 1266–68; *Secunda* 1271–72; *Tertia* 1272–73)

*Dates taken from Gilles Emery's catalogue in J.-P. Torrell's biography of Aquinas.[1]

---

[1] J.-P. Torrell, *Saint Thomas Aquinas*, 2 vols., rev. ed., trans. Robert Royal (Washington, DC: The Catholic University of America Press, 2005).

Introduction

TWO OPPOSING LOVES, Augustine holds, establish two opposed cities: "The love of self unto the contempt of God" founds the city of man, while "the love of God unto the contempt of self" founds the city of God.[1] Are we confronted with an absolute disjunct between two opposed loves, self-love and love of God? And is nature opposed to grace, man to God? Given that love of beatitude is integral to self-love, is Augustine, otherwise a great proponent of true happiness, proposing a love of God unto contempt of beatitude? These questions point to what is called "the problem of love."

In the twentieth century, Pierre Rousselot summed up the problem in two questions: "Is a love that is not egoistic possible? And if it is possible, what is the relation between this pure love of the other and the love of self that seems to be the basis of all natural tendencies?"[2] In his introduction to the English translation of this classic, Alan Vincelette boils it down to one question: "Whether and how there can be a self-denying and sacrificial love for others which is at the same time fulfilling and perfective of oneself."[3] On the one hand, few will contest that the desire for happiness motivates many actions. Indeed, by grasping an action as conducive to happiness, one has sufficient explanation for the action. On the other hand, if all free action is rooted in the desire for happiness, how is love of the other possible? It would seem that either there is a foundation for all free action, the desire for happiness, in which case genuine love of another is eclipsed from the start, or that genuine love of another is possible, and

---

[1] Augustine, *City of God*, XIV, chap. 28 (CCL 48, p. 451:37–39).
[2] Pierre Rousselot, *The Problem of Love in the Middle Ages: An Historical Contribution*, trans. Alan Vincelette, vol. 2, *Collected Philosophical Works of Pierre Rousselot*, no. 24, Marquette Studies in Philosophy (Milwaukee: Marquette University Press, 2002), 1.
[3] Alan Vincelette, introduction to Rousselot, *The Problem of Love*, 13.

so lacks any explanatory foundation other than itself. The alternatives are unappealing.

As Vincelette notes, variations of this question have arisen time and again through the ages and not just in religious circles. Debates arose with vehemence in the Middle Ages, although it was not until later that answers grew starker. Even so, neat paradigms, although tempting, often fail their mark. As Thomas Osborne, Jr., has shown, Catholic theologians from Augustine through Thomas Aquinas (1225–1273), not excluding John Duns Scotus (1265/66–1308), despite their many and sometimes deep differences, defended a harmony between the love of self and the love of God for His own sake. Still, there were serious differences. These differences constitute at least in part the roots of subsequent, more radical divergences. On the one hand, there was the Dominican emphasis on virtue as right living that leads to beatitude; on the other hand, there was the later Franciscan call to a life of selfless love in accordance with God's will.[4] Nonetheless, according to Osborne, ancient and medieval Christians shared a "broadly eudaimonistic" outlook on ethics.[5] "Eudaimonism" in this context means that happiness plays a significant, positive role in motivating moral or ethical action. Extreme approaches to the relationship between love of self and love of God ripened several centuries later.

After the high Middle Ages, we encounter some portraits of love exhibiting suspicion regarding the love of beatitude. Martin Luther is a significant case in point. Luther rejected a "theology of glory" wedded to the notion that the will is inclined to the fitting good (*sibi conveniens*), repelled by what is opposed to that good, and thus attracted to God as the greatest, most fitting good.[6] For Luther, in our present condition and without grace, we are enslaved to an egocentrism and for this reason damnable in all we do. For Luther, what Catholics proclaim about God's liberating work is false. Catholics hold that God infuses the charity whereby the justified person is able to fulfill the law, obedience to which remains a condition for salvation. According to Luther, if the Catholic opinion were true,

---

[4] Servais Pinckaers's famous study on ethics traces a fundamental divide between Aquinas and William of Ockham. Scotus's position, although not as a radical as that of Ockham, lurks in the background. See Servais Pinckaers, *The Sources of Christian Ethics*, trans. Mary Thomas Noble (Washington, DC: Catholic University of America Press, 1995).

[5] Thomas Osborne, Jr., *Love of Self and Love of God in Thirteenth-Century Ethics* (Notre Dame: University of Notre Dame Press, 2005), 1.

[6] See Martin Luther, *Explanations of the Ninety-Five Theses*, 58th Thesis (LW 31:227; WA 1.614.17–22).

one would remain radically enslaved in selfishness. The motive to obey the law would remain the same, for example, attainment of happiness. This motive Luther condemns as sinful; thus, for him, the Catholic conception is of a charity that instrumentally serves sin. On this view, one could not love God and neighbor except instrumentally. How to be freed from this radical enslavement? For Luther, only justification by faith alone can free the sinner from self-centeredness. In mercy, God does not oblige the justified person to fulfill the law as a way or condition of salvation. Salvation is a pure gift received in faith, itself also a gift, the gift of receptivity to God's giving. Not obliged to do anything for the attainment of salvation, the justified person is filled with joy. This grateful joy leads to free love of God and neighbor. The foregoing is, arguably, a defensible account of a theological motive for Luther's theory of justification. Such a reading has a number of significant supporters. The great Finnish Lutheran theologian Simo Peura, for example, writes, "Luther's entire theological work can be viewed as an attempt to solve the problem of self-serving love."[7] Respected Catholic ecumenist Peter Manns held a similar view.[8]

Luther's thesis, however, is not systematically coherent. His solution to the problem of love is premised on a promise: the Gospel. Now, the Greek word "Gospel" (*euangelion*) means "news that is good." Why is the news of salvation from eternal punishment and for eternal life "good"? The news is good precisely because of the love of happiness. If the Gospel is good in view of the love of happiness, surely the love of happiness must be good, not evil. But if the love of happiness is good, surely man does not sin in every action. Luther's dilemma, however, is predicated on the thesis that desire for happiness is sinful. If the love of happiness is sinful, then faith securing the end of that love serves sin. Luther's solution proposes that the desire for happiness is the reason that promised salvation is good news. If the solution is correct, the dilemma as Luther constructs it crumbles, and sin is not as ubiquitous as he feared. If the dilemma holds good, the proposed solution does not liberate one from sin.[9] Luther must choose:

---

[7] Simo Peura, "What God Gives Man Receives: Luther on Salvation," in *Union with Christ: The New Finnish Interpretation of Luther*, ed. and trans. Carl E. Braaten and Robert W. Jenson (Grand Rapids: Eerdmans, 1998), 78.

[8] See Peter Manns, "Absolute and Incarnate Faith – Luther on Justification in the Galatian's Commentary of 1531–1535," in *Catholic Scholars Dialogue with Luther*, ed. Jared Wicks (Chicago: Loyola University Press, 1970), 146.

[9] I have developed this critique of Luther in two works: Christopher Malloy, "Thomas More on Luther's *Sola Fide*: Just or Unjust?," *The Angelicum* 90 (2013): 761–798 and "*Sola salus*, Or *Fides caritate formata*: The Premised Promise of Luther's Dilemma,"

either the goodness of the Gospel or the inveterate sinfulness of the desire for happiness. Should he choose the latter, he condemns even faith itself. Should he choose the former, he must abandon the pessimism that colored man as totally depraved. Further, Luther must revisit his "pure" reading of the first and greatest commandment, which does not condemn as sin everything short of perfection and which does not condemn as sin the very love of happiness that is nature's thirst. If Luther's legacy is a deep pessimism concerning the love of happiness, certain quietists would carry the thesis even further.

Whereas uneasiness with love of happiness might not seem strange to some, it understandably seemed irrational and destructive to others. The complaints of Ludwig Feuerbach and Friedrich Nietzsche can be read as visceral reactions opposed to the anti-happiness distortions of religious piety. More recently, Lutheran theologian Anders Nygren has defended a view of disinterested love, the divine "*agape*," against interested love or "*eros*."[10] With an antithetical and roughly contemporaneous view, the secularist Ayn Rand portrayed human relations as essentially self-centered.

Some see the debate as dividing neatly between religious and secularist perspectives; thus, the former would defend pure love and scorn the love of happiness, while the latter would do the opposite. The debate, however, cuts through both religious and secular points of view. First, as noted above, there had been widespread endorsement of a "broadly eudaimonistic" view in the first twelve centuries of Christianity. Second, one can mount a secularist charge that Christianity endorses the most radically egocentric approach to life, a hypocritical "delayed gratification" scheme.[11] Third, while some Catholics have espoused views antithetical to eudaimonism, the Catholic Church has consistently taught the glory of God to be the ultimate end of all while defending legitimate self-love as integral to and good for the ethical life. The Catholic Church rejects the rejection of happiness.[12] Fourth, polar oppositions have appeared also in

---

Fides Catholica 2 (2008): 375–432.

[10] Anders Nygren, *Agape and Eros: The Christian Idea of Love*, trans. Philip Watson (Chicago: The University of Chicago Press, 1953; reprint, 1982).

[11] See Vincelette's remarks in Rousselot, *Problem*, 26ff.

[12] The Catholic Magisterium defends the goodness and value of genuine self-love, which includes the desire for beatitude and the fear of punishment, especially of hell. See Denzinger-Schönmetzer 958, 964, 965, 1456, 1489, 1539, 1576, 1581, 1705, 2207, 2212, 2216, 2309, 2310, 2313, 2314, 2315, 2351–73, 2455, 2457, 2460, 2462, and 2625. More recently, John Paul II defended the foundations of the moral life in terms of the desire for happiness in his *Veritatis splendor* (1993), arts. 9, 30, and 72–73. Most recently, Pope

"purely" ethical or philosophical contexts. Thomas Hobbes (1588–1679) represents the love of self to the neglect of the object loved:

> Whatsoever is the object of any man's Appetite or Desire; that is it, which he for his part calleth *Good*: And the object of his Hate, and Aversion, *Evill*.... For these words of Good, Evill... are ever used with relation to the person that useth them: There being nothing simply and absolutely so; nor any common Rule of Good and Evill, to be taken from the nature of the objects themselves.[13]

The solipsism represented here forebodes the modern ailment of selfish isolation. Equally and oppositely extreme is the moralism of Immanuel Kant (1724–1804):

> Only something which is conjoined with my will solely as a ground and never as an effect—something which does not serve my inclination, but outweighs it or at least leaves it entirely out of account in my choice—and therefore only bare law for its own sake, can be an object of reverence and therewith a command.[14]

Finally, in the midst of the present, self-absorbed age, postmodern thinkers and students torment themselves about whether or not one can really give a gift.[15]

Against the backdrop of recent disputes about this classical problem, Pope Benedict XVI issued an unexpected inaugural encyclical in an attempt to navigate a middle path between the dialectical polarities. As can only be the case in a Christian approach or in a true humanism, the balance of the middle path involves not mere juxtaposition of the extremes but synthesis. Hence, Benedict did not simply approve of both self-love and love of God; he undertook to portray their hierarchically structured harmony. There cannot be two final ends but only one. So, one end must be ordered

---

Benedict XVI has defended the integral unity of *eros* and *agape* in his encyclicals *Deus caritas est* (2005), arts. 3–8, and *Spe salvi* (2007), arts. 11–12.

[13] Thomas Hobbes, *Leviathan* (New York: Penguin, 1968), 120.

[14] Immanuel Kant, *Groundwork of the Metaphysic of Morals*, trans. H. J. Paton (New York: Harper & Row, 1964), 68.

[15] Jacques Derrida (1930–2004) writes, "I perjure myself like I breathe." Jacques Derrida, "To Forgive: The Unforgivable and the Imprescriptible," trans. Elizabeth Rottenberg, in *Questioning God*, ed. John Caputo, Mark Dooley, and Michael Scanlon (Bloomington: Indiana University Press, 2001), 49.

to another. God must be loved above all, yet the natural drive for happiness and fulfillment is not thereby excluded but rather perfected.[16]

Although desirable, articulation of the hierarchical harmony of love of God and love of beatitude is quite difficult. It may be asked whether anyone has successfully accomplished such a feat. Thomas Aquinas attempted to do so in the overall product of his corpus. Of course, some denigrate his achievement as merely egocentric, citing his claim that all free actions are rooted in an ineluctable desire for the lover's happiness.[17] Others applaud him for teaching what they consider to be a true "eudaimonism," according to which the lover's love of beatitude is almost indistinguishable from the love of God.[18] Whether fan or critic, many a thinker finds grounds

---

[16] Pope Benedict XVI, *Deus caritas est*, arts. 7–8. A Thomistic evaluation of Benedict's encyclical can find this basic strategy to be sound and some of its details flawed.

[17] Hans Reiner, for instance, holds that for Thomas "*all* men [strive] after their own beatitude as their *single*, ultimate *end*." Hans Reiner, "Beatitudo und Obligatio bei Thomas von Aquin: Antwort an P. Pinckaers," in *Sein un Ethos: Untersuchungen zur Grundlegung der Ethik*, ed. Paulus Engelhardt, Philosophische Reihe (Mainz: Matthias-Grünewald, 1963), 309. Nygren claims the same: "Self-love properly understood must drive us to love God who, as the highest good, includes all that concerns our happiness. The reason why we love God at all is that we need Him as our bonum (sic). . . . The good know that the chief part of their nature is reason (ratio) (sic), and that this finds full satisfaction and perfection only in the blessed contemplation of God (visio Dei) (sic)" (Nygren, *Agape*, 642–43).

[18] Paul Wadell helpfully stresses man's neediness and rightly reads Aquinas as maintaining that pursuit of goods answering to that neediness is a good activity. Wadell tends, however, to read Aquinas too much within this framework, allowing insufficient room for the hierarchical supremacy of love of God: "Our lives are strategic endeavors to be united to what we think will bring us to completion, and whatever that is will be our ultimate end." Paul Wadell, *The Primacy of Love: An Introduction to the Ethics of Thomas Aquinas* (New York: Paulist Press, 1992), 37.

Although this text is introductory, the passage cited sums up a consistent theme in Wadell's reading of Aquinas. In his most important text, Wadell writes, "Thomas suggests we love whatever makes us happy, and we love most whatever offers us the greatest happiness. What not only causes but also makes possible the special friendship of charity is that God who is perfect happiness offers us a sharing in what accounts for God's happiness; and since we love whatever makes us happy, Thomas says we love God, who is the source of this happiness, as happiness itself." Paul Wadell, *Friends of God: Virtues and Gifts in Aquinas*, no. 76, Theology and Religion, American University Studies, series 7 (New York: Peter Lang, 1991), 15–16. See also, *Friends of God*, 55–57.

Christopher Toner interprets *ST* 1-2.1.6 as teaching that "everything a rational agent wills is willed for the sake of his perfection." Christopher Toner, "Angelic Sin in Aquinas and Scotus and the Genesis of Some Central Objections to Contemporary Virtue Ethics," *The Thomist* 69 (2005): 97. However, Toner does not read Thomas as an "egoist" but distinguishes the search for perfection (perfectionism) from the search for

in Thomas for such readings. Some offer the rarer reading of Thomas as proposing a purely disinterested love.[19] Thomas's own thought is rather subtle. Nor is this surprising, since Thomas was a realist, and the matter at hand is intricate.

The task of this book is to articulate, on Thomas's principles, the relationship between love of beatitude and love of God for His own sake, especially as this relationship comes to fruition with respect to beatific charity and the vision of God. Some remarks about the contents and structure are in order. First, we must begin with matters closer and simpler to us although we endeavor to rise to matters more excellent and unified in themselves.[20] Although more knowable in itself because more actual, beatific charity is less knowable to us than is charity in the state of pilgrimage. Further, charity is a supernatural love, the further actualization of natural dilection or rational love, which is closer to our capacity to understand. Finally, rational love is best understood on the basis of a grasp of love in general, which in some ways is more evident on the sensible plane with the passion of love. Accordingly, Chapter One examines love in general (*amor*) approached from its embodiment as a passion. It also treats the order of three foundational passions: love, desire, and delight. Chapter Two examines rational love or dilection (*dilectio*), its natural and elected acts, and the

---

one's *own* good *qua* one's own (egoism). See Toner, "Angelic Sin," 83ff, and Christopher Toner, "Was Aquinas an Egoist?," *The Thomist* 71 (2007): 578–84.

This distinction allows Toner to include obedience to God as integral to human perfection; therefore, according to Toner, one need not seek refuge in a dualism of volitional principles (Toner, "Angelic Sin," 109–11). Both Toner and Wadell speak of love of God and neighbor for their own sakes (Toner, "Egoist?," 586ff and 601ff; Wadell, *Friends*, 3; Wadell, *Primacy*, 51 and 66; and Wadell, "Charity as Friendship with God and Form of the Virtues: An Interpretation of the Christian Moral Life according to St. Thomas Aquinas" [PhD diss., Notre Dame, 1983], 177).

Finally, both rightly highlight the integrity of love for Aquinas. One who loves wishes to be united with what he loves (see Wadell, "Charity as Friendship," 47 and 50). For Aquinas, it is unthinkable that one who truly loves another would not by that very love be impelled towards union with that beloved. Still, I think that neither Toner nor Wadell has dealt sufficiently with the difficulties of love of God for His own sake.

[19] See, for example, Louis-B. Geiger, *Le problème de l'amour chez Saint Thomas d'Aquin* (Montréal: Institut d'Études médiévales, 1962); Avital Wohlman, "Amour du bien propre et amour de soi dans la doctrine thomiste de l'amour," *Revue thomiste* 81 (1981): 205–34; and Wohlman, "L'élaboration des éléments aristotéliciens dans la doctrine thomiste de l'amour," *Revue thomiste* 82 (1982): 247–69. Perhaps the earliest such reading of Thomas was that of François Fénelon (1651–1715). Diametrically opposed to his reading was that of Jacques-Bénigne Bossuet (1627–1704).

[20] See *DV* 10.12; *Sententia super Physicam* 1.1.8; *ST* 1.2.2; 1-2.57.2; and *ST* 2-2.27.4.

twofold structure of its act as targeting a person and his perfecting good. Chapter Three treats the twofold character of beatitude as object and attainment as well as the love thereof. Chapter Four treats dilection of others, especially of God. Chapter Five introduces charity as a friendship of man for God founded on the communication of supernatural goods. This chapter also discusses the various relations of charity to love of beatitude. Chapter Six treats the limitations of charity connected with the pilgrim state of the believer. Chapter Seven treats the corresponding perfections in beatific charity. Both of these chapters focus on the relation of charity, in its two states, to love of beatitude. The upshot of the examination at this point is that Aquinas's thought is eudaimonistic without compromising love of God for His own sake. Chapter Eight raises a radical difficulty or *aporia* concerning the consistency of Aquinas's positions. Chapter Nine suggests a resolution to this difficulty.

The *aporia* treated in Chapter Eight regards the ultimate import of Aquinas's principles and texts on the relationship between love of beatitude, as the ineradicable principle of all freely chosen loves, and love of God above self. The *aporia* can be stated as a question: can Thomas consistently maintain both (a) that a man ought to love God more principally than himself, and for God's sake, and (b) that a man chooses everything he chooses out of an ineradicable, primordial love of beatitude? Resolution of this difficulty would seem to demand either sliding into a voluntarism that opposes eudaimonism—as seems to have happened in the later Franciscan tradition—or foregoing the attempt to articulate satisfactorily how God is loved truly for His own sake and not simply as ultimate object desired (*concupitum*). If Thomas does not explicitly treat the difficulty in this manner, his texts leave us with it. Further, it is an heirloom from the tradition and a question of interest *per se*. The suggested resolution returns to a consistent theme in Thomas's corpus, developed earlier in the monograph: Every lover thirsts for union with his beloved. This thirst, grounded in genuine love of the other for the other's sake, can be styled an "ecstatic attraction." The thirst for God as supernatural friend and covenantal Triune God, rooted in the love of charity, can be satisfied only in the vision of God, and this thirst for the vision arises precisely from a love of God for His own sake.

CHAPTER 1

Love in General and the Order of the Passions

THIS CHAPTER EXPOUNDS Thomas's definition of love in general, gathering the elements of this definition with regard to love's realization as a sensible passion. Love is a cognitive being's affective or appetitive proportioning to something it perceives as good. On the basis of this being proportioned, the lover either desires—inclines appetitively towards possession of the loved good—or delights—rests appetitively in the possession of the good. Clearly, desire and delight do not determine the possession or non-possession of the good; they are, rather, determined by the possession or non-possession of the good. Since love is more primordial than desire and delight, the foundation of both, it regards the good whether possessed or not possessed. Thus, none of these three passions constitutes the possession of or union with the good. As can be shown, all other passions can be traced back to one or more of these three passions as foundation. Hence, no passion or appetitive movement can constitute union with the good.

While this summary is clear and straightforward, Thomas struggled to achieve this understanding of the order of the passions. His very struggle sets in relief his argument and ultimate claim that no appetitive movement constitutes the presence of the good, at least as regards sensitive love. I will first sketch Thomas's mature understanding of love and its relation to desire and delight; I will then study his struggle.

APPETITE

Thomas discusses the passions in light of the world in motion, various things variously acting. Always or for the most part, each thing tends towards its good as its goal or end.¹ As the goals or ends are distinctive, so are the natures. Since the principle determinate of nature is form, different ends correspond to different forms. As these ends are achieved by proper operations or acts, a proper operation corresponds to each form. Just as each thing has its proper end as the goal of its activity, so it has an inclination to the operation by which it can achieve that end. Thus, inclination to operation follows form (taken in the sense of essence).

Natural Inclination

Since operation follows form, diverse kinds of form exhibit diverse kinds of inclination. A physical thing whose form is not receptive of other forms, a physical thing that simply exists in itself, has only one proper operation, which is constant in certain environing conditions. A fire kindled on earth, for instance, steadily tends upwards, while a block of sodium explodes in water. The invariant tendency of any form to its proper operation Aquinas names "natural inclination."

To be sure, he uses the phrase "natural inclination" in extended senses as well.² More complex things often have various operative powers, each of which is in a certain way a "form" having its own proper operation. Since each has its own proper operation with its own proper object, each of these powers (sub-forms) has its natural inclination. So, "natural inclination" is found in various ways, not just in simple physical substances. The faculty of eyesight, for instance, tends to the colored within a certain light spectrum and intensity. Objects within these parameters attract the faculty and objects outside these parameters either fail to attract (ultraviolet, the audible as such) or cause pain (naked sunlight) or strain (dim light). Whereas we first achieve insight into natural inclination with regard to

---

[1] Of course, Thomas's actual interest is human finality. Thus, he treats the passions in the context of the virtues in *Sent*. 3. He discusses the passions in *DV* 26 after treating the universal tendency of things to the good and to God in *DV* 22. *DM* 1.3 and 1.4 touch on the passions in the context of the continual reference to human finality in *DM* 1. The *Summa theologiae* treats the passions (*ST* 1-2.22 through *ST* 1-2.48) after examining beatitude (*ST* 1-2.1 through 1-2.5).

[2] In *DS* 3, Aquinas uses "natural inclination" for the inclination in things *qua* not following cognition, whereas he uses "natural appetite" for the inclination that follows cognition. Elsewhere, he uses the terms less strictly: see *DV* 22.1; *ST* 1.80.1; and *ST* 1-2.26.1. My practice, following Aquinas, is to commence with or strive towards a strict definition of terms and to develop extended senses of a term in light of this strict sense. Thomas's expressions are flexible, but his thought is crisp, and we highlight that crispness if we follow this course.

simple physical items such as rocks, which when dropped from a height tend downwards, we analogically apply this notion to any form insofar as it has a constant or invariant inclination (given certain conditions) to some proper operation.[3]

Natural inclination has a peculiar twofold property. On the one hand, as natural, it is a principle of motion and rest internal to the being so inclined; so, the inclination is not violent but intrinsic. Uranium's way of being *is* to radiate energy rapidly. This tendency is intrinsic to its makeup. On the other hand, this tendency is not under the dominion of the being so inclined but is, as it were, stamped upon it from without. Arguably, only the cause of nature could be the sufficient and necessary explanation of a stable interior inclination to the good not at the disposition of the thing inclined. Such is Thomas's claim, and he establishes it as follows. Some non-cognitive creatures have invariant proper operations following their form. Now, what occurs always or for the most part occurs not by chance but for an end. Hence, the proper operation of such non-cognitive beings is for an end. However, only that which knows can direct what is for the end to the end. Non-cognitive beings lack cognition by definition and thus cannot direct themselves to their ends. Hence, a natural inclination in a non-cognitive being must be authored from without by the very author of the nature directing it to its end. Aquinas ultimately argues that this inclination is produced by the Divine Author directing each thing fittingly towards its proper operation.[4]

Having sketched the invariant character of natural inclination, I should now make a qualification. Insofar as a thing is in potency, it is not necessarily always in act.[5] Hence, if one ascribes a natural inclination to a thing of such-and-such nature as always present to it, in this respect one seems to be identifying the *relation* of the thing (or its power) to its proper operation with its proper object. This relation, not necessarily the operation, is what remains invariant.

Natural Appetite

Cognitive things, by contrast, are not restricted to the possession of only

---

[3] See *ST* 1.78.1, ad 3; *ST* 1-2.10.2; and *DM* 6.
[4] See *DV* 22.1 and *ST* 1.2.3. The dialectical argument has roots in Aristotle's *Physics* 2.8 (198b17–199b32). I hold that Aquinas's further argument is strictly demonstrative, although not necessarily as explicitly laid out in the *Prima pars*, much less as summarily sketched above.
[5] See *ST* 1-2.10.2, ad 2.

one form in the manner above. Of course, each thing has but one substantial form and has necessarily only those "forms" that can be considered proper accidents, such as, for man, the faculty of sight and the intellect. Further, each of these "forms" as such (the substantial, the faculty of sight, the intellect, etc.) has the aforesaid constant or invariant natural inclination. These are not the only inclinations cognitive things have.

Remarkably, things whose substantial forms give rise to cognitive powers, whether dependent on bodily organs or not, are intentionally receptive of other forms. Through cognition or apprehension, one being receives something of the intelligible structure of some aspect of an external object into itself, so to speak. However, cognition is cognition of the known thing; so, it is better to say that through its apprehensive powers, the knowing thing becomes the known intentionally, that is, by an act of cognitive targeting. (This is not a volitional or moral "intention.") The principle of this cognitive targeting is the apprehensive power's reception of the intelligibility of the known.

Now, a cognitive being's *susceptibility* to a variety of forms entails that it can have variable inclinations. It does not always have the same intentional form. Even if sight is always inclined to the visible, the visible may be green or blue, and the animal can close its eyes. Hence, the inclination of sight is significantly different from the downward inclination of the heavy object. Cognition entails greater variability of inclinations to operations. Even a clam that can only taste and touch encounters some objects to which it is indifferent, others to which it is attracted, and still others by which it is repulsed. In short, we find in cognitive beings an internal principle for variability of inclination. It is almost as though the clam judges the suitability of various objects it encounters. Of course, this judgment is so singly determined by one sensitive power that it almost appears to be the judgment simply of that organic power.

Some cognitional beings exhibit higher levels and greater variety of cognitive power and correspondingly higher levels of variability in inclination. An animal with such powers seems able to grasp the suitability of an external object with regard to itself as a whole rather than merely the suitability of an object with respect to one sensitive power or another. The wolf is pleasantly grey, and even its growl is neither deafening nor painful. If only its individual senses were to judge concerning the wolf, the lamb might not flee. That lambs do flee wolves indicates that lambs make cognitive judgments about wolves. A judgment of this sort regards a wolf's relation to a lamb as a whole, namely, that the wolf is a vital threat to the lamb. An animal's cognitive judgment about the suitability of some external thing for itself (the one judging) as a whole is the basis for an inclination proper to animals. Aquinas names "appetite" the power and the act of an inclination grounded in the cognitive judgment of the thing inclined.

So, Thomas finds appetite and apprehension to constitute the two irreducible yet ordered manners in which a cognitive thing is related to other things. In apprehension, it takes something of the intelligibility of the other into itself, targeting the known thing intentionally or apprehensively. If, further, this other thing is apprehended as good or as evil, appetite emerges. By its appetite, the sensitive thing inclines towards or away from that which it judges good or evil, respectively.[6] Clearly, appetite follows or depends upon apprehension, because a thing cannot itself be the proximate cause of its tending towards the other as good unless it judges the other as good for it, and judgment requires apprehension. Indeed, apprehension is universally prior to inclination. In things without cognition, the apprehension belongs to the Author of nature; with regard to appetite, apprehension belongs to the thing inclined.

Elicited Acts

It is fitting to broach here one further set of distinctions. Natural inclination of a power is distinguished from elicited movements or acts of a power. Every power is a certain "form" and so has a certain (relatively) invariant inclination to its proper object. The appetite is such a form. (As we shall see, so is the will.) The natural inclination that every power has is distinguished from the distinct acts or movements of that power.[7] Such acts or movements are "drawn out" of the power as the power is "reduced to act." Eyesight always inclines to the visible, but one sees only at this or that time. When daylight streams through the window, a distinct and specific act is "drawn out" of the power, or, rather, the power is actualized ("reduced to act"). Thomas thus distinguishes the natural inclination that is invariant, constituting a fundamental orientation of the power to its proper acts, from the acts themselves. Reflective of his thought, his commentators name acts that are drawn out "elicited acts." Thus, the first distinction we should appreciate, in order to understand Thomas's thought,

---

[6] See *DV* 22.10; *DDN* 4.10 (par. 427); and *ST* 1.81.1.

[7] Daniel Shields stresses this distinction. As I understand him, he holds the natural inclination to be the very relation of fittingness that the power has for its object. See Daniel Shields, "Aquinas on Will, Happiness, and God: The Problem of Love and Aristotle's *Liber de Bona Fortuna*," *American Catholic Philosophical Quarterly* 91 (2017): 121–25.

is that between natural inclination and elicited act.

Lawrence Feingold helpfully identifies three elements of this distinction as it applies to the appetitive powers. First, in an elicited act, our power is the source of the act and not simply something moved. By contrast, the natural inclination is authored by the Author of nature, inclining the power to its proper acts. Second, elicited acts of appetite follow knowledge. By contrast, the natural inclination is an ordering of the power to its proper act that is not occasioned by a particular act of knowledge in the thing inclining. Third, an elicited act is an act or movement of the power, whereas the natural inclination seems to be the very relation or proportion of the power to its proper operation and object.[8]

I risk a brief comment on the natural inclination before proceeding to the other meaning of "elicited acts." If the power is the potency and the movement of the power is its act, what *is* the natural inclination? As Daniel Shields notes, the natural inclination is not itself an act, for one must distinguish acts (elicited acts) from the natural inclination.[9] Is the natural inclination, then, simply the pure relation in which the power stands to its possible objects, as Scotus came to think?[10] It seems unlikely that such would be the understanding of Thomas, for whom the Augustinian sense of *gravitas* (heaviness, downwardness) is so illustrative of the natural inclination of rocks. The downward inclination of a rock is not a mere relation to the earth. However, if the natural inclination is not merely a relation, is it then an act? It cannot be, or else the power would invariably be in act.

Perhaps the solution may be discovered by adverting to Thomas's notion of abstraction. Thomas's moderated realism appreciates that we truly know the real and yet differentiates the manner of being of the real from the manner of being of the known as known. In less moderated realism, there is more pressure to verify the distinctly known *as* existing distinctly. Supposing a less moderated realism, then, one might think as follows: if what exists distinctly is (a) a power with its pure relation to (order to) an object and (b) the act of that power, then only these (the power with its relation and the act) can be known. With moderate realism, something further may be said. We might make the claim that the act itself, the elic-

---

[8] Lawrence Feingold, *The Natural Desire to See God According to St. Thomas Aquinas and His Interpreters* (Naples, FL: Sapientia Press, 2010), 14–16.

[9] Daniel Shields, "On Ultimate Ends: Aquinas's Thesis that Loving God is Better than Knowing Him," *The Thomist* 78 (2014): 122.

[10] See Duns Scotus, *Scotus on the Will and Morality*, selected and trans. by Allan B. Wolter, ed. by William A. Frank (Washington, DC: The Catholic University of America Press, 1997), 43.

ited act, exhibits—or structurally has—that which is known as "natural inclination" even though this inclination does not *distinctly* exist. The claim would be that in the elicited act itself there *is* that aspect which is known as "natural inclination" although it does not exist distinctly. As an aspect of the act, it is something more than a sheer relation, but as simply an aspect, it is not itself the act.

At any rate, we proceed to the other aspect of elicited act. Elicited acts are also distinguished from imperated acts. This distinction regards the diverse ways in which an act is related to a given power. Thomas offers this definition: "That act is properly said to be elicited which proceeds immediately from that power, as 'to understand' proceeds from the intellect."[11] By contrast, that act is "imperated" by some power X which proceeds immediately not from X but from some other power Y. The definition can be made even more precise with respect to the relation of an act to a habit. Accordingly, that act is elicited by some power and habit T (Q) which proceeds immediately from that power and habit T (Q).[12] Contrarily, that act is imperated by some power and habit R (Q) which proceeds immediately either from some other power S or from the same power but by a different habit R (W).

A sheep's desire for food is elicited by its sensitive appetite because it proceeds immediately therefrom. The sheep's motion towards the food by way of its legs is imperated by its sensitive appetite because this motion proceeds only mediately from the appetite but immediately from its motive power. The distinction between appetitive and motive powers is clearer than the distinctions between various habits of one power. Still, a distinction can also be drawn in the latter case. By the habit of justice within me, I can command an act of righteous indignation, rooted in fortitude, against a criminal use of authority. Similarly, by an act of charity, whereby one loves God above all things as Friend, one can command oneself to make an act of hope. In this monograph, we employ this distinction between elicited and imperated acts with regard to the will's commanding other powers to their acts and with regard to one species of love commanding the act of another species of love. Human acts are thus moral acts because they are under the control of the will, which either elicits or imperates them.[13]

---

[11] *Sent.* 2.25.1.3. See also *Sent.* 3.27.2.4, qla. 3. We should not confuse this sense of "command" or "imperation" with the act of reason ordaining to an end.

[12] See *Sent.* 3.27.2.4, ad 3 and *ST* 2-2.3.1, ad 3.

[13] See *Sent.* 3.23.1.4, qla 2 and *ST* 1-2.6.4.

The Order of the Passions: Thomas's Mature Position

Thomas calls the acts or movements of the appetitive faculty "passions." For him, love is the most primordial appetitive movement, or passion, on which all others depend as on a foundation.[14] This claim Thomas establishes as follows.

Thomas identifies three principles of division. First, the object of some passions is good, and the object of others is evil. Second, the object of some is simple or absolute, and the object of others includes an added note of difficulty and ardor, either of attainment or of avoidance. Third, the presence or absence of the object also diversifies all but two passions. These principles cut through the passions differently; together, they help one determine the order and nature of the passions.

First, according to the diversity of good and evil, there is an exhaustive division of the passions. The passions whose object is the good, whether absolute or with the added note of ardor, are love, desire, delight (or joy), hope, and despair. The passions whose object is the evil, whether absolute or with the added note of ardor, are hatred, avoidance (or dislike), sadness, daring, fear, and anger. These are the eleven passions.

Second, according to the diversity of object as absolute or as having the added note of ardor, there is an exhaustive division of the passions. The concupiscible passions regard the good or evil taken simply or absolutely. Those that regard the good taken simply are love, desire, and delight, whereas those that regard the evil taken simply are hatred, avoidance, and sadness. The irascible passions regard an object as having the added note of being arduous either to attain or to avoid; thus there are the following irascible passions: hope, despair, daring, fear, and anger.[15] This added note of ardor calls into play another principle of division, that of approach or withdrawal.[16] Thus, some irascible passions approach the arduousness in the good or the evil, whereas others withdraw from it. Hope approaches the arduous good, and daring approaches the arduous evil. Despair withdraws from the arduous good, and fear withdraws from the arduous evil. What about anger? Anger regards the evil that is not only arduous to avoid but also present and attacking. This note of "presence" brings us to the third principle of division.

---

[14] For an account of the various sources at play in Aquinas's treatment of the passions, from the *Sent.* to the *ST*, see Mark D. Jordan, "Aquinas's Construction of a Moral Account of the Passions," *Freiburger Zeitschrift für Philosophie und Theologie* 33 (1986): 71–97.

[15] See *ST* 1-2.23.1.

[16] See *ST* 1-2.23.2.

Third, the presence or absence of the object diversifies nine of the passions. When the object is absent, certain passions are called into play. Such passions constitute appetitive dynamisms towards or away from the object, for one is either moving towards the absent good or (further) away from the absent evil. (Presence and absence regard not just proximity but actual or imminent sensitive contact, whether vision or tactile, etc.) The passions regarding an absent good or evil are desire, avoidance, hope, despair, fear, and daring. These passions, above all, have the note of *motion* (the act of the potential, as such) in their character. The passions regarding a present good or evil are delight, sadness, and anger. Only two passions are not specified by the presence or absence of the object; these are love and hatred. The reason, as we shall see, is that love and hatred are foundational to the entire dynamism of any cognizant living thing towards its end (love) and away from its contrary (hatred).

With these principles of division in mind, Thomas unfolds the diversity and order of the passions. As we would expect, Thomas distinguishes two kinds of order, that of intention and that of execution. Clearly, each thing seeks ultimately the attainment of its good. The passion that arises in the attainment of the good is delight. Thus, in the order of intention, delight is first. The present good does not have the note of ardor in attainment; thus, all the passions, concupiscible or irascible, have an implicit order to their ultimate rest in delight. Similarly, in the case of unavoidable evil, sadness constitutes a certain appetitive finality, whereas anger does not.

As for the order of execution or development, love is the first of all the passions. Evil is a privation of good; it is because good is loved that evil is hated. Thus, all of the passions regarding an evil object are premised upon love and desire for the good.[17] Further, all of the irascible passions regard an object as having an added note of difficulty in attainment or avoidance. Any object which happens to be difficult to attain or avoid is a target of any passion first because it is good or evil for some cognizant being. Thus, in the order of development, all the irascible passions have their foundations in the concupiscible passions of love, desire, hatred, and avoidance. Which of these passions is prior? The question can be simplified when we turn simply to love and desire, since their object is prior to that of hatred and avoidance.

Which is prior, love or desire? In his mature thought, Thomas approaches the question by analogy with motion. In any motion, the end is last in execution while first in intention. The end is first in intention

---

[17] See *ST* 1-2.25.2.

because it is a fitting end. It is fitting because the thing tending to the end has "an aptitude or proportion to that end, for nothing tends to a disproportionate end."[18] This proportion to the end is the basis or foundation of the movement towards the end, which terminates in attainment of the end. Thus, there are three "stages" of movement: proportion, tending, and attainment or rest. Desire pertains to the second stage, because desire itself does not make one appetitively apt for attaining the end; rather, desire presupposes an appetitive aptitude for attaining the end. The foundation itself is that appetitive aptitude. Thomas concludes that love is prior to desire: "this very aptitude or proportion of the appetite to good is love, which is complacency in good."[19] Thomas frequently uses this expression "complacency (*complacentia*)."[20] The term has no available common English equivalent.[21] Following the standard translations, I render *complacentia* as "complacency" in the sense of early twentieth century usage, meaning the state of being pleased with something.[22] The Latin adds the note of "very pleasing." Contemporary colloquial usage is, admittedly, another story. Desire and delight thus follow love. Desire arises if the loved good is absent, and delight arises if the loved good is present. Thus, "the motion towards the good is desire or concupiscence, and rest in the good is joy or delight."[23] Since love founds both desire and delight, love regards its object whether it is present or absent.[24] Similarly, hatred founds avoidance and sadness.

Thomas's analysis of the relationship of love, desire, and delight can be set in relief by his discussion of three kinds of union connected with these passions: union of similitude (substantial union in the case of self-love), union of affection, and union of possession.[25] Thomas writes,

---

[18] *ST* 1-2.25.2.
[19] *ST* 1-2.25.2.
[20] See *Sent.* 1.10.1.3; *ST* 1-25.2; *ST* 1-2.26.1; *ST* 1-2.26.2; *ST* 1-2.27.1; and *ST* 1-2.28.2.
[21] William Mattison conveys Thomas's insight with the word "aptitude-ization." It is difficult to convey Thomas's thought, but this word targets the idea. William Mattison III: "Movements of Love: A Thomistic Perspective on *Agape* & *Eros*," *Journal of Moral Theology* 1 (2012): 35.
[22] "The fact or state of being pleased with oneself or others." *New Standard Dictionary of the English Language*, vol. 1, ed. Isaac K. Funk (New York: Funk & Wagnalls Company, 1940), 542. The sense of laziness or indifference is not implied in this use of the term.
[23] *ST* 1-2.25.2 (my translation).
[24] See *ST* 1.20.1.
[25] Mark Drost rightly shows the dependence of both desire and delight on love. Unfortunately, he proceeds to argue that for Thomas one can simply love or "appreciate" good without desiring or delighting in that good: "A consequence of Aquinas's thesis is the

Union has a threefold relation to love. There is a union which causes love; and this is substantial union, as regards the love with which one loves oneself; while as regards the love wherewith one loves other things, it is the union of likeness, as stated above. There is also a union which is essentially love itself. This union is according to a bond of affection, and is likened to substantial union, inasmuch as the lover stands to the object of his love, as to himself, if it be love of friendship; as to something belonging to himself, if it be love of concupiscence. Again there is a union, which is the effect of love. This is real union, which the lover seeks with the object of his love.[26]

Of these three unions, love is the second, the union of affection. Love depends on the first union, and impels, through desire, towards the third union, in which it rests, by delight.[27] The union of similitude is the fittingness or compatibility of one thing for another. We may think of this fittingness as an objective or "ontological" fact. For example, food both nourishing and tasty for some animal is good for it. The cognitive judgment that precedes love looks to this union of similitude or to its opposite. Still, the insight and judgment determining suitability, or the lack thereof, does not constitute the appetitive aptitude to the suitable thing. So, love is not constituted by union of similitude. Union of similitude and cognitive recognition thereof are necessary conditions for love.

In irrational animals the movement from union of similitude to union of affection (love) is caused by an instinctive judgment of the estimative power concerning what is sensed as either beneficial or harmful to the animal as a whole. In rational beings, sensitive love is caused by a cogitative judgment. By the affective union that is love, the lover is moved by the loved good as by an end or final cause. In the lover, love is the propor-

---

ontological possibility of loving something without taking delight in it or desiring it." Mark P. Drost, "In the Realm of the Senses: Love, Delight, etc.," *The Thomist* 59 (1995): 48.

Drost suggests that whereas "typically" either desire or delight does follow love, it is possible that neither do: It is possible that the lover, rather than delighting in possession of the loved, "can also be complacent in the mere vision of the beloved" (58). The argument to be developed in this monograph will show that Drost's claim cannot be sustained as a legitimate reading of Thomas.

[26] *ST* 1-2.28.1, ad 2. See also *DDN* 4.9, pars. 401–02.
[27] See *ST* 1-2.28.1.

tionate motive principle.²⁸ Thus, one embraces the end before being really united with it. In short, love is directed toward an object that is had or not had, though love's aim is "having," that is, union of possession. Thomas did not always perceive this remarkably lucid distinction and ordering of the passions. This development of doctrine has intrinsic historical interest and may help explain other elements of his developing thought on the problem of love.

Thomas's Early Teaching on the Order of the Passions

Very early in his career, Thomas entertained a different account of the order of love and desire. In some passages of his commentary on the *Sentences*, Thomas refers to desire as the first movement of the appetite, equating it with imperfect love, while defining perfect love as regarding only an attained good.²⁹ In such passages, he often cites what he took to be a saying from St. Augustine: "Desire is of something not possessed, but love is of something possessed."³⁰ Thus understood, desire is prior to love.

---

²⁸ See *SCG* 4.19, par. 4.

²⁹ I would like to thank *The Thomist* for permission to borrow heavily in this section from my article on this topic. See Christopher J. Malloy, "Thomas on the Order of Love and Desire: A Development of Doctrine," *The Thomist* 71 (2007): 65–87.

³⁰ *Sent.* 2.1.2.1. Mandonnet refers the reader to Augustine's Commentary on the Psalms 118.8.4 (PL 37, 1521). See Thomas Aquinas, *Scriptum super libros Sententiarum*, vol. 2, ed. R. P. Mandonnet (Paris: Lethielleux, 1929), 46. I have not been able to locate this saying of Augustine anywhere. In any case, the text to which Mandonnet refers does not contain the saying. It does, however, contain a discussion of the difference between "concupiscere" and "desiderare." The former is a broader category, though often used regarding goods already had. The latter is of that which is absent. See Augustine, *Ennarationes in Psalmos*, in Corpus Christianorum, Series Latina, vol. 40 (1956), 1688: 48–52. If anything, this citation only contradicts what Aquinas attributes to Augustine, were we to liken "*concupiscere*" to "*amare*," since to the former pertain both "*quae habentur*" and "*quae non habentur*."

Perhaps Thomas has in mind a homily of Gregory the Great on Matt 4:18–20. Gregory writes, "Certainly we both possess with love things we have, and we seek by desire the things we do not have." Gregory the Great, *Homiliae in euangelia*, Bk 1, hom. 5, par. 2, in Corpus Christianorum, Series Latina, vol. 141 (1999), 34: 20. In his *Catena*, Thomas cites the sentences immediately preceding and following this one but shies away from this sentence itself, perhaps reverently. Thomas Aquinas, *Catena aureae, In Matt*, chap. 4, lect. 7; in English, vol. I, part I (Albany, 1995), 136–37. In a work of doubtful authorship, attributed to Augustine, there appears a passage closer to Thomas's mature opinion, yet still ambiguous. See *De substantia dilectionis*, I, chap. 2; PL 40, 845; see also, *De substantia*, chap. 4; *PL* 40, 846.

Two noteworthy scholars comment on this ordering of desire and love in the *Sent.*, L.-B. Gillon and H.-D. Simonin.[31] Gillon notices that the "Augustinian" saying in the *Sent.*—"love is of what is already possessed"—contrasts with Thomas's later teachings. Touching upon the difficulty implicit in this saying, Gillon attempts to resolve it by claiming that Thomas speaks only of perfect love as "already having" its object. Gillon adds that perfect love is the same specific passion as imperfect love, differing from the latter only by reason of the possession of the good.[32] Gillon's reading enjoys support in the *Sent.*, for therein (as we shall see) Thomas sometimes conflates desire and imperfect love. Still, the conflation of imperfect love with desire obscures the priority of love as principle of desire.

H.-D. Simonin also observes the inverted order in the *Sent.* He, too, attributes the apparent generational priority of desire to the conflation of imperfect love and desire. Closely following Thomas's *ex professo* treatment of the issue in the *Sent.* (*Sent.* 3.27.1.3), Simonin hesitates to conclude that Thomas took a definitive position about the order of the passions in the *Sent.*[33] He grants that Thomas's placement of desire before love (because of the conflation of desire and imperfect love) is unambiguous with respect to things intended in light of the end (*ea quae sunt ad finem*). As shall become evident below, I concur with this reading of *Sent.* 3.27.1.3, ad 3. Simonin adds, further, that the textual evidence is inconclusive as to whether Thomas also thought that the end is desired before it is loved.[34] I find the evidence conclusive that Thomas places desire of the end before love of the end.

Sent. 2.1.2.1
The following text raises a question about whether God acts for an end:

> It must be known, therefore, that to act in this way [i.e., for an end] is twofold: either on account of a desire for the end or on account of a love for the end. For desire is of something not had, but love is of something that is had, as Augustine says. Thus, it is fitting for every creature to act on account of a desire for the end because for every creature the good that it does not have of

---

[31] See L.-B. Gillon, "Genèse de la théorie thomiste de l'amour," *Revue thomiste* 46 (1946): 322–29 and H.-D. Simonin, "Autour de la solution thomiste du problème de l'amour," *Archives d'histoire doctrinale et littéraire du moyen âge* 6 (1931): 174–274.
[32] See Gillon, 322 ff.
[33] See Simonin, "Autour," 184.
[34] See Simonin, "Autour," 183.

itself is acquired from another. But it belongs to God—to whose goodness nothing can be added—to act on account of love for the end.[35]

This argument presupposes that love is of something that is possessed while desire is of something that is not possessed.[36] Since God alone has or is the goodness that is the end of His action, He alone always acts on account of love for the ultimate end. No creature can act out of love for the ultimate good until it somehow "has" that good. For creatures, therefore, desire of the end precedes love of the end in the order of generation. If desire for the end precedes love for the end, then desire precedes love *simpliciter*. So, this passage conclusively implies a generational priority of desire.

Sent. 3.26.1.3
The most notable instance of Thomas's struggle can be discerned through comparison of two drafts of *Sent.* 3.26.1.3. This article treats hope, broaching discussion of the order of the passions. An initial draft reads:

> The first concupiscible passion, therefore, caused by the apprehension of a good not yet had, is desire; the second passion, to be sure, caused by the apprehension of an evil not yet had, is unnamed, but it may be called flight or avoidance; now the third passion, caused by the apprehension of the good that is had, is love, to which is contrasted the fourth passion, hate. The fifth passion, in truth, which is caused by the present appetible itself, is delight or joy. The sixth, to be sure, is its contrary, which is pain or sadness.[37]

---

[35] *Sent.* 2.1.2.1.
[36] On the other hand, it may be that here love regards giving whereas desire regards receiving.
[37] "*Passio ergo (+prima concupiscibilis+) causata ex apprehensione boni nondum habiti est [-concupiscentia vel] desiderium; passio vero (+secunda+) causata ex apprehensione mali nondum habiti innominata est, dicatur autem fuga vel vitatio; passio vero tertia causata ex apprehensione boni habiti est amor, cui contrariatur quarta quae est odium; passio vero quinta causata ex [-apprehensione] ipso appetibili praesente est delectatio vel gaudium; [-passio] sexta vero est contraria, quae est dolor vel tristitia.*" P.-M. Gils, "Textes inédits de S. Thomas: Les premières rédactions du *Scriptum super Tertio Sententiarum*," *Revue des sciences philosophiques et théologiques* 46 (1962), 460.

    Gils utilizes a critical apparatus in his citations of Thomas's manuscripts. Gils expressly adopts this apparatus from the Leonine critical edition. The apparatus reflects additions, corrections and deletions from Thomas's own hand. Words that Thomas crossed out appear within brackets and are preceded by a single "minus" sign. For in-

This draft unambiguously depicts desire as preceding love in the order of generation; similarly, the draft presents avoidance as preceding hate. In fact, Thomas added the words "first concupiscible" to this draft, between the lines of the text. Curiously, this text presumes a distinction between a good as "had" and a good as "present." Just what is that distinction? Could "having" be conceived simply as the "union of affection" arising from definitive choice of the good, an appetitive stance more committed and confirmed than a restless search to identify some object of love?[38] A more promising suggestion might be gleaned from advertence to an editorial change Thomas makes to this first draft.[39] Here, he links love with the "apprehension of the had good" and delight or joy with the "present appetible itself." Apprehension of the good causes love, but the present good itself causes delight.

At any rate, in the final draft Thomas simply scraps the above enumeration of the passions. He offers an analysis bearing greater resemblance to his mature thought:

> Love implies a relation of the concupiscible power to good, and hate, to evil, for love makes the beloved connatural and as though one with the lover, while hate does the contrary. And since this relation is perfected by the presence of the object, therefore love, according to its perfect nature, is of something had, as Augustine says. . . . But the motion of the concupiscible power towards good is called desire.[40]

This final draft offers an interpretation of the Augustinian dictum that can be harmonized with Thomas's later teaching. Note also that hatred is given priority with regard to evil as object. In his mature works, Thomas

---

stance, if Thomas crossed out the word "primum" the text would read as follows: "[-primum] autem." Sometimes, Thomas added words to his original draft. These additions appear between lines of the manuscript.

Thomas's additions are found within parentheses, bounded by two "plus" signs. Such additions appear as follows: "(+primum+) autem." Our translations, in the text of the dissertation, reflect Thomas's final redaction *of the cited draft* in order to read more smoothly. For Gils's explanation of the apparatus, see P.-M. Gils, "Textes inédits de S. Thomas: Les premières rédactions du *Scriptum super Tertio Sententiarum*," *Revue des sciences philosophiques et théologiques* 45 (1961): 204n14.

[38] To emphasize love as "having," in this manner, might seem Augustinian.
[39] We are still dealing with the first draft, considering the marginal changes Thomas makes.
[40] *Sent.* 3.26.1.3.

offers his own dictum in lieu of Augustine's: "Love regards the good in general, whether that good is possessed or not possessed."[41] Further, despite the editorial changes from the first to the final draft in this passage, Thomas continues to struggle elsewhere in the *Sent.*

Sent. 3.26.2.3.2
In this passage, as Simonin and Gillon note, Thomas conflates imperfect love and desire:

> Desire and love differ in this: that love implies a certain fitness and connaturality of the lover towards the beloved. Now this fitness is perfected when the beloved is in some way had or possessed by the lover. Desire, however, implies a motion towards the lovable thing itself that is not yet had. Thus, the motion of the appetite begins in desire and terminates in perfect love. So desire is a certain inchoate beginning of love and, as it were, a kind of imperfect love.
>
> But since the first way in which a thing is had is according as it is in potency (for that which is in the faculty of the one possessing it, is considered as something already had), the first thing that leads to love is the faculty of having that which is desired. Therefore, love of a distant object, which is not actually possessed, presupposes hope. But hope is only for that which is good, and the first motion of the appetite to the good is desire. Hence, hope presupposes desire and comes between love and desire.[42]

Before analyzing this text, I would simply note that herein "presence" (the opposite of "absence") and "having" are identified. Thomas appears, then, to have countenanced the difficulty implied in the unedited first draft of *Sent.* 3.26.1.3.

---

[41] *ST* 1.20.1 (my translation). Not surprisingly, Thomas's Roman lecture on the *Sentences* also bears his mature teaching: "Among all the affections, love is the first and more common than the rest. It is first because no affection proceeds except from love.... It is more common because desire is only for something absent, and joy is for something already had, while love is not only for something already had but also for something to be had." Thomas Aquinas, *Lectura romana in primum Sententiarum Petri Lombardi*, d. 1, q. 1, art. 1 (my translation). Thomas cites Augustine as placing love first for these two reasons.

[42] *Sent.* 3.26.2.3.2.

This text bears some marks of Thomas's immature position: desire is an imperfect love; it is the first motion of the appetite towards the good; and perfect love requires possession of the desired good. Desire and imperfect love are conflated. This text also bears a mark of the mature position, for it mentions "love of a distant object." An object cannot be possessed if it is distant. Still, the full statement reads, "love of a distant object, which is not actually possessed, *presupposes hope*" (emphasis mine), and Thomas's constant position is that hope presupposes desire. So, Thomas here presents hope as following desire yet preceding (perfect) love: "The act of faith precedes desire, because every act of the affective part presupposes an act of the cognitive part; now, desire precedes hope, but hope precedes love."[43]

Thomas's responses to two objects corroborate this reading. One objection is that hope cannot be unformed, for example, cannot exist without charity towards God: hope tends towards God, but the faith that tends towards God must be formed faith. Thomas responds: "It must be said that formed faith tends toward God out of love, but unformed faith is not from love but from desire."[44] Once again, desire is prior. Another objection seems to point to the priority of love, citing another Augustinian dictum, one in harmony with Thomas's mature formulation: "Every affection comes from love."[45] As the objector notes, this saying implies that desire follows love. Thomas responds, "It must be said that love is there taken in a wide sense for imperfect love, which is desire, the first motion of the appetitive power."[46] Once again, Thomas here conflates imperfect love and desire.

Sent. 3.27.1.1
The name "appetite" first signifies outward orientation to a good not identical with the creature's essence (recall *Sent.* 2.1.2.1). Similarly, the word "desire" connotes unrest because it signifies a tendency towards a good distinct from and not possessed by the one desiring. Love, however, does not imply this unrest or this tendency. Rather, love implies union with

---

[43] *Sent.* 3.26.2.3.2.
[44] *Sent.* 3.26.2.3.2, ad 2.
[45] *Sent.* 3.26.2.3.2, obj. 3. Moos attributes this saying to *De civitate Dei*, Book XIV, chap. 9 (although Moos's first reference to this text is a typo [chapter 19]). The saying is not found in Augustine's text in so many words; however, the thrust of the saying is clearly evident. See Corpus Christianorum, Series Latina, vol. 48 (1955), 425–30. The more relevant chapter, cited by the Fathers of the English Dominican Province in their translation of the *Summa*, is XIV, chap. 7.
[46] *Sent.* 3.26.2.3.2, ad 3.

the good. Now, all creatures begin in states of unfulfillment and strive towards fulfillment. Consequently, when the creature begins to have an appetitive movement, it cannot but desire. Desire always occurs in a creature that begins to have any appetitive movement; further, the signs of desire are more immediately evident.[47] These observations may explain Thomas's identification of desire with imperfect love and his failure to infer a distinct love foundational to both desire and delight. Another explanation may be that in the *Sent.* Thomas does not consistently and simultaneously distinguish three unions with the good—union of similitude, union of affection, and union of possession.

Chiefly, Thomas does not distinguish—precisely when it matters to his analysis of the order of the passions—between the union of affection and the union of possession.[48] This inadvertence leads Thomas to assert the priority of desire. If union of affection is not distinct from union of possession, then the desire that precedes union must also precede the love that presupposes union. Aquinas presents the matter in this way:

> Now every passive power is perfected according as it is informed by the form of its active power. In this its motion reaches its end and rests, as the intellect, before it is formed by the form of the intelligible thing, searches and wavers. This inquiry, when the intellect has been informed, ceases and the intellect is fixed upon its object. Thus, the intellect is said to inhere firmly in that thing.
>
> Similarly, when the affection or appetite is thoroughly imbued with the form of the good that is its object, it takes complacency in that thing and adheres to it as though fixed in it. And then, it is said to love that thing. Therefore, love is nothing other than a

---

[47] Desire for self-preservation is presupposed to avoidance of an evil that threatens life.

[48] Scholars will surely point to passages in which Thomas explicitly distinguishes union of affection from union of possession: e.g., *Sent.* 3.27.1.3, ad 2. On this basis, he distinguishes love and delight. The accurate analyses in these passages, however, lack inferences about the relationship between desire and love. However, those passages that treat of this latter relationship tend to conflate love and delight. Compare, for instance the definition of delight in *Sent.* 3.27.1.2, ad 3 with that of love in *Sent.* 3.27.1.1, ad 2.

For a more explicit conflation see *Sent.* 4.49.1.1.4: "It must be said that as motion is related to the end in natural things, so (in volitional matters) is the appetite for both the end and for the means related to the attainment of the end. Therefore, as when a natural thing attains to the end, its motion ceases, so too when the will has what it seeks, its appetite desists and is converted into love or delight."

certain transformation of the affection into the beloved thing.[49]

According to this passage, love begins when the appetite is thoroughly *informed by* or united with the object of its affection.

We might evaluate this conception of love in two ways. First, Michael Sherwin argues that Aquinas changes his definition of love. Early in his career, he defines the act of love much as he defines the act of intellect, by way of the notion of "information." As the intellect achieves the goal of its operation when "informed" by the intelligible content of the known, so the will achieves the goal of its operation when "informed" by the known good. This early definition, Sherwin indicates, is later replaced by a definition of love in terms of the "complacency" in the good, the foundational appetitive orientation to the good. For Sherwin, given the earlier definition of love as "information," Aquinas cannot but describe love as the final passion, conflating it with joy. Why? The process of information begins with the potency to be informed and ends with "being informed."[50] If love is the will's "being informed" by the known good, then love must be the final passion. However, if love is the final passion, it cannot be adequately distinguished from delight.

Sherwin's observation of change is largely accurate, and his argument about the order of passions is somewhat compelling. With regard to this monograph's interest, Sherwin's observation may partially account for Aquinas's immature ordering of the passions in the *Sent*. Nevertheless, Sherwin's account does not suffice. First, the date Sherwin identifies as the point of transition is too late to account for Aquinas early development concerning the order of the passions. Sherwin recognizes that Aquinas continues to understand love as "information of the appetite by the known good" in the *DV*. Sherwin indicates the *Prima secundae* as the first text defining love as "complacency."[51] However, the mature view of the order of the passions appears considerably earlier, certainly by the *DDN*.[52] Not without minor ambiguity,[53] the mature view is present even in the *DV*.[54] Further, in *Sent*. 3.27.1.1 Aquinas speaks of perfect love not only as

---

[49] *Sent*. 3.27.1.1.
[50] See Michael Sherwin, *By Knowledge & By Love: Charity and Knowledge in the Moral Theology of St. Thomas Aquinas* (Notre Dame: University of Notre Dame Press, 2005), 64–81.
[51] See Sherwin, *By Knowledge*, 70ff.
[52] See *DDN* 4.9, pars. 401–2 and *SCG* 1.91.
[53] See *DV* 23.1, ad 8.
[54] See *DV* 26.4.

"transformation" but also as "complacency." Moreover, as I have already shown, signs of the mature view begin to surface even in the *Sent.*, which shows development from its first draft to its final edition. Finally, Aquinas defines love in terms of "information" in a late work, *DS*: "In the animal appetite, the first thing is a certain information of the appetite itself by the good; and this is love, which unites the beloved to the lover."[55] The reader will also note that in this text Aquinas combines the mature order of the passions with a notion of love as uniting the beloved to the lover. However, he immediately notes that desire emerges if the loved good is distant from the lover; so, he does not in this text think of love's "union" as real union. In conclusion, if the immature definition of love partly explains Aquinas's immature ordering of the passions, other factors must also be at play, and these may be somewhat separable from the former.

So, second, another element may be considered as well. From the viewpoint of Aquinas's mature insight, the union that Aquinas identifies with (perfect) love in *Sent.* 3.27.1.1 would be not that of affection but rather that of possession. In this text, love is not simply an affective stance underlying either desire or delight, but rather rest in the possessed good. Hence, the description of love given here merges with Thomas's mature view of delight; consequently, desire appears as the first motion of the appetite or as imperfect love. In short, Thomas's description here of the union of love bears some resemblance to his later description of union of possession.[56]

The conflation of the union of love and the union of possession appears again in a response to an objection. The following objection is raised: Dionysius's saying that love is a "unitive power," for example, a force driv-

---

[55] *DS* 3.

[56] A difficulty would seem to arise for this account of love even at this stage in Aquinas's career. The "thorough information" conducive to or constitutive of rest is predicated of the appetitive power and not of the cognitive power. On the other hand, as early as the *Sent.*, Thomas argues that the act of the appetite cannot be the final end *quo* or attainment of the end that is God. The appetite can rest only if God is attained but its act is not that attainment itself. God is first attained by the cognitive act of vision (see *Sent.* 4.49.1.1.2). In short, the first object of the appetite cannot be an act of appetite. What kind of rest, then, can Aquinas have in mind when he defines love in terms of rest?

Perhaps Thomas here takes this "rest" to be the firm commitment to a determinate goal of life, allowing one to focus one's energies in hope. Such rest would differ significantly from the restless search to identify a real goal, a restlessness bordering on despair. (Such would resemble Thomas's suggestion that something may be had in two ways, perfectly or imperfectly. We have an end imperfectly when we have it only in intention. See *ST* 1-2.11.4.) Or perhaps he is thinking that the will's being "thoroughly informed" by the known good occurs through the attainment of the good by some other power.

ing towards union, appears to conflict with Augustine's dictum that love is of what is already had: "Augustine says that love is of something that is already had. But that which is already had is in a certain way united. Therefore, love is not a unitive power but something following union."[57]

The Angelic Doctor offers two ways of reconciling Dionysius with Augustine:

> To the second it must be said that love is said to be of something had, as the formed thing has its form. Desire precedes this formation, tending towards it, as reason precedes understanding or science. Therefore, desire is said to be of something not had. Thus is love called a unitive power formally, since it is the union itself or bond or transformation by which the one loving is transformed into the beloved and in a certain way changed into it.
>
> Or it must be said that the quieting of the affection in something, which love implies, is not able to exist except on account of the fitness of one for the other. This fitness is indeed according as one thing participates in that which belongs to another. So in a way the one loving has the beloved. Therefore, the conjunction that is implied in the word "to have" (*habere*) is the conjunction of one thing to another and precedes the union of the object to the affection. This latter union is love.[58]

The response is divided into two because there are two possible (even complementary) explanations for love as both following union and being "unitive," for example, driving towards union. The first response deals with Dionysius's saying. Rather than reading Dionysius's term "unitive" as signifying a quest for union, Thomas interprets it as signifying the essence of union itself. Love is "unitive" in the sense of a formal cause: its very nature is the appetitive "transformation" of the lover into the beloved. In terms of his later distinction of three unions, Thomas here defines love as the second of the three unions. In this text, he does not simultaneously distinguish union of affection from union of possession. Since desire precedes possession, with which love is linked, love is not generationally prior to desire.

The second response treats Augustine's saying that love follows union.

---

[57] *Sent.* 3.27.1.1, obj. 2.
[58] *Sent.* 3.27.1.1, ad 2.

Aquinas here distinguishes two types of union: that of similitude (or proportion) and that of affection. Love is of something "already had" in that there must already be a union of similitude between some good and the lover. Love is of what is "already had" by way of similitude. This explanation has the merit of distinguishing two unions, that of similitude and that of affection. Neglected here is real union; rather, Thomas describes love as the rest (*quietatio*) of the appetite, thereby obscuring the distinction between love and delight, which is rest in the real presence of the beloved. At the end of his response, he labels love the "termination (*terminatio*)" of the appetitive motion.[59] Further, the place of desire is not treated. In light of all the above considerations, the reader is still led to believe that desire precedes love, which is of something "already had."

Early Signs of His Mature Teaching on the Order of the Passions

The foregoing analysis shows Aquinas ascribing a generational priority to desire. There are, to be sure, several early texts in which Thomas's mature teaching begins to surface. First, as already noted, the final draft of *Sent.* 3.26.1.3 is to some degree amenable to Thomas's mature teaching. At the very least, Thomas scrapped an initial draft in which he clearly taught the priority of desire.

Second, in treating of charity, Thomas contends that love—a broad term—includes desire: "Love includes desire for the beloved, by which the presence of the beloved is desired."[60] If love includes desire for the presence of the beloved, it would appear to come before desire in the order of generation, for it also remains without desire in the presence of the beloved. Still, even with this the text might be read differently. Thomas is arguing that charity (a supernatural love) is a friendship with God. It is love for God but includes other notes. One of these notes is desire for the presence of the beloved. Anyone who loves another with true friendship also desires to communicate with that person. Here, there are two distinguishable though inseparable *rationes* of love: that of friendship and that of concupiscence. Further, Thomas concludes this reflection with a statement that has the mark of his immature thought: "But love, above the four items previously mentioned, adds something, namely, a rest of the appetite in the thing loved, without which [rest] any of the aforesaid items is able to

---

[59] *Sent.* 3.27.1.2.
[60] *Sent.* 3.27.2.1.

exist."⁶¹ This text, then, bears the marks of the immature and the mature positions.

Third, and most importantly, we have Thomas's *ex professo* treatment in *Sent.* 3.27.1.3. Here, Thomas asks whether love is the first and most principal passion. He answers in the affirmative, citing the second Augustinian saying noted previously: "Every affection comes from love." Love is prior to the other passions because love "names the termination of the affection by the fact that it is informed by its object."⁶² Just as the intellect begins from an understanding of principles, which it grasps without discursive movement, so the appetite begins from this "information" by the apprehended good. Thus, "every motion proceeds affectively from the rest and completion [*terminatione*] of love."⁶³ Here, there may be a clue to resolving the tension in Thomas's *Sent.* Thomas rarely, if ever, predicates motion (*motus*) of love (*amor*) in the *Sent.* Therein, love designates quiet, termination, information, and rest. Desire, by contrast, designates a motion towards an object. In some sense, desire truly is the first *motion* of the appetite, if by motion we mean the act of the potential as such. The principle of tending (love) is not defined in terms of potency, but the tending (desire) is. Still, motion has a broader sense, and in his later works, Thomas describes love as a motion in a broad sense.⁶⁴ Love is a motion in the sense of operation or second act; it is the appetite's actually being proportioned to some apprehended good. It is not necessarily a motion in the sense of potency for the absent.⁶⁵

More importantly, Aquinas does not emphasize love's *terminative* character in later works. To describe love in such a way would risk conflating love with delight itself. Perhaps Thomas's emphasis in the *Sent.* on love's terminative character reflects an existential approach to a "decision to be made," whereby one considers the wayfarer's struggle to identify a true good to seek. Vacillating among various apparent goods and not yet committed wholeheartedly to one, the wayfarer is "restless" and full of desire to identify one goal. Thus read, love would involve a "full affective acceptance" of this good as a true good to pursue here and now.

---

⁶¹ *Sent.* 3.27.2.1.
⁶² *Sent.* 3.27.1.3.
⁶³ *Sent.* 3.27.1.3.
⁶⁴ See *ST* 1-2.4.3. See also, *DDN* 4.11, par. 449 and *ST* 1-2.28.4. For Thomas's rationale for the use of the term motion, see *DA* 3.15, par. 831 and *ST* 2-2.179.1, ad 3. Cf., Drost, 54–55.
⁶⁵ See *ST* 1-2.26.2, ad 3. Drost is accurate on this point. The appetite's being informed *is* its actualization in second act; hence, such *is* operation.

In any case, in his *ex professo* treatment in the *Sent.*, Thomas indeed maintains the generational priority of love, implying that desire is an effect of love that arises because of the absence of the beloved. Still, Thomas's analysis here differs noticeably from those of later works. Thomas raises the following objection: "Motion precedes the end. But love is the determination of the appetitive motion, as is evident from what is said above. Therefore, love follows desire, which implies the motion itself of the appetite."[66] The very objection expresses concisely Thomas's immature position. Thomas responds by recalling the comparison of intellect and will. Both intellect and will have circular movements. The intellect begins by understanding some principles naturally, reasons to a grasp of conclusions, and comes to rest by relating those conclusions back to the principles that it understands with natural certitude. Comparing this to love, Thomas writes:

> Similarly, too, the affection, out of love for the end (which love is a kind of principle), proceeds by desire towards those things that are for the end—things that it accepts as in some way containing the end in themselves. Through love it rests in them, and therefore, desire follows love of the end although it precedes love of those things that are for the end. Love is also a more vehement affection than desire insofar as it signifies the end and formation of the affection by the appetible thing, towards which (thing) desire moves.[67]

Two important features of this response differ from Thomas's presentation in the *ST*, wherein he states unequivocally: "Desire for anything always presupposes love for that thing." As taught in the *ST*, desire *never* precedes love, except with respect to a change of objects, where one thing is loved on account of desire for another: "But desire for one thing may arouse love for some different thing: as one who desires wealth loves, on account of this, the man from whom he receives wealth."[68] By contrast, in the *Sent.*, Thomas admits that desire for those things that are for the end precedes love for those same things. This admission is consonant with his insistence in the *Sent.* that love is of something already had, but it contrasts with his mature teaching.

---

[66] *Sent.* 3.27.1.3, obj. 1.
[67] *Sent.* 3.27.1.3, ad 1.
[68] See *ST* 1-2.27.4, ad 2 (my translation).

Second, in the *Sent.*, love of the end is prior to desire for those things that are for the end. The priority of love depends upon a change of objects, whereas the priority of desire is determined with regard to the same object. This article in the *Sent.*, however, does not explicitly state that love of the end precedes desire for the end. Simonin, it will be recalled, accurately noted this difficulty. Yet, did Thomas uphold love of the end as prior to desire for the end? For want of evidence, Simonin was reluctant to make any pronouncement. Perhaps his is the wisest route. I join him in not pronouncing either way with regard to this text; however, I would draw attention to two items partially suggestive of a negative answer.

First, and most importantly, in an already-cited passage (*Sent.* 2.1.2.1), Thomas declares that God alone always acts out of love for the end. Creatures not yet beatified act out of desire for the end, since desire is of something not had. The implication is that desire of the end precedes love of the end. Second, even in this *ex professo* article, Thomas's response to the fifth and last objection reverts to the priority of desire. The fifth objection contends that because, as Dionysius teaches, all things act on account of peace, love has less effective power (is less principal) than peace. The response bespeaks Thomas's belief that desire is generationally prior to love: "Peace is not distinguished from love, but is something belonging to it—for it denotes a kind of rest of the appetite. But love denotes, further, a transformation and a certain conversion of the appetite itself into the beloved. Therefore, peace stands between desire and love."[69] Because love adds additional notes to the appetitive rest implied in peace, peace stands between restless desire and restful love. Thus, desire precedes both peace and love. In the very article in which Thomas argues for the principal role of love, he still includes statements indicative of the generational priority of desire.

Conclusion

For Thomas, love is the most primordial of all appetitive movements. Love, the appetitive complacency in an apprehended good, underlies desire and delight. Hence, as Sherwin contends, Aquinas's mature thesis is that love is "primarily the principle (not the terminus) of the agent's action."[70] The analysis of love in this chapter focuses on love in the sensitive appetite. This analysis is applicable analogically to rational love, or dilection, and to graced love, or charity.

---

[69] *Sent.* 3.27.1.3, ad 5.
[70] Sherwin, *By Knowledge*, 71.

CHAPTER 2

Rational Love

In Itself, Natural Dilection as Root of Choice, and Love's Twofold Structure

IN THE PRECEDING CHAPTER, I studied love in general, especially as its essence and structure are realized in the sensitive appetite. Here, I treat rational love, or dilection, itself. I then examine natural dilection as the root of election and also the scope of free choice. Finally, I will treat the twofold structure of the act of dilection.

RATIONAL LOVE OR DILECTION

As Thomas observes, "[s]ome inclination follows every form."[1] Following the natural form, for example, the substantial form, there is a natural inclination, but there is a higher form of inclination following apprehended forms. The sensitive appetite is the power for inclination following the forms apprehended by the senses, and love is the foundational act of this appetite. Now, just as there is a proper power of inclination following the forms in sense cognition, so there is a proper power of inclination following the forms in intellectual or rational cognition. The appetitive power following intellectual cognition is the rational appetite or the will, and its foundational act is dilection or rational love.

There are two characteristic notes by which to distinguish sensitive and rational loves. One can distinguish them causally on the basis of the distinct apprehensions upon which they are based. One can also distinguish them with respect to freedom or its absence.

---

[1] *ST* 1.80.1.

Distinction Based on Kinds of Apprehension

Rational and sensitive loves are distinguished causally by the modes of apprehension they follow. The argument can be stated summarily and then unpacked. Appetite is a passive power. Passive powers are distinguished by the active powers that move them, and the active power of appetite is apprehension. Diverse modes of apprehension distinguish the cognitive power essentially. Thus, distinct modes of apprehension cause essentially distinct kinds of love. Whereas there is a sensitive mode of apprehension, there is also a rational mode of apprehension. Thus, whereas there is sensitive appetite, there is also rational appetite or will.

This tight summary can be unpacked. The appetite is a passive power in the sense that the apprehended good is the end that draws it or to which it is drawn. The appetite's object is the apprehended good. For Thomas, the causality of the apprehended good on the appetite, rather than the converse, is self-evident: something is good not because it is loved and desired; rather, it is loved and desired because it is good. Ice cream, for instance, is not good or attractive because one desires it.[2] Rather, one desires it because it is good. With regard to goods naturally harmonious with a given power or organism, this point is evident. The animal naturally shrinks from too bright a light but strains to hear the whispered promise of prey. Of course, some goods require sufficient disposition to appreciate. Bad habits can make what is naturally repugnant seem attractive. Still, at the end of the day, no ideology can forever mask the hunger for the truly good that lies deep in the heart. There is rest only in true goods.

Since the appetite is a passive power, appetitive powers are distinguished by a proper difference of moving powers.[3] Now, the intellect and the sense powers are properly distinct. The sense powers of themselves target only the accidents of individual corporeal objects. The common sense combines these to some extent, allowing for an instinctive judgment concerning an external corporeal object as a whole. Such judgments can concern how such objects affect the good of the animal as a whole: the lamb sees not just furry and grey, but a wolf, coming. The inclination following sense apprehension can be only towards or away from individual corporeal objects as here-and-now attractive or repulsive. This attraction or repul-

---

[2] On the level of second nature, good acts can cultivate good attractions, and evil acts can cultivate unnatural attractions. Such attractions are nothing short of vice. For example, it is naturally revolting to look at pornographic material. The first encounter of disgust is an indication of this. However, perverse actions can lead to devastating addictions.

[3] See *ST* 1.80.2.

sion is a passion regarding what is good or evil for the animal as a whole.

The intellect contains the perfections of natural appetite but in a higher way, and it also transcends these perfections. The higher way is evident in that the intellect searches explicitly for the essence underlying the accidents; it searches for causes of effects; it infers; it examines and verifies; its object is truth as such; and it can recognize things under the general character of the good. Consequently, the appetite that follows intellectual cognition inclines to things under the general character of the good. It can also explicitly target a thing as a whole, as a good subsisting in itself, and not simply as harmful or helpful in virtue of this or that of its characteristics. Above all, the intellect can appreciate the goodness of shareable or common goods.[4] Insofar as the senses target only the individual sensible thing, the appetite to which they give rise targets goods less shareable and more proper to the individual. Hence, this particular animal is drawn by what is pleasant for it. The Author of nature, however, draws the animal to pleasure so as to order it to fecundity and the good of the species. Since man is endowed with reason, he can follow the order of the divine intention and is not ruled by a drive simply for particular finite sensitive goods. Right reason follows not simply the order of animal appetite but that of the divine intention.[5] Of course, some animal mothers care for their offspring even at the cost of life. Still, such mothers protect the good of another particular animal. The mother does not directly protect the shareable good.

Our concern is the difference of appetites in the human being. Of course, although we distinguish the sensitive appetite and the rational appetite, we must continually remember that these are powers of a human being. Similarly, the intellect and the will are operative powers of a human being. In all our analyses, we must return to this basic point. The temptation to reify or hypostatize powers should be resisted, while the precision of analysis should be retained. A more precise expression would be this: One human being acts by way of these powers. Since the powers are powers of one substance, some can have an influence upon others. One can, for example, cultivate a sensitive love of certain cheeses or stretches or routines.

Distinction Based on Freedom

Another note of distinction between sensitive and rational loves is the

---

[4] See *De spiritualibus creaturis*, 8, ad 5.
[5] See *ST* 1-2.4.2, ad 2.

freedom proper to rational love. As Aquinas observes, the Latin word *dilectio* connotes the voluntary character of rational appetite: "*Dilectio* implies, in addition to love, a choice (*electionem*) made beforehand, as the very word denotes; and therefore *dilectio* is not in the concupiscible power, but only in the will, and only in the rational nature."[6] Freedom is proper to the rational appetite but absent from the sensitive appetite.

Geiger remarks that early in his career Thomas seems to have stressed this mark of freedom, while he later stressed the causal difference in distinct modes of apprehension. This difference plays out in diverse treatments Thomas gives to the following objection: There is only one appetite because there is only one object of the appetite, the good. Since powers are distinguished by their acts, and acts by their objects, a common object ought to imply a single power. Thomas's early reply in *DV* identifies the distinguishing mark in freedom:

> The will is not distinguished from sense appetite directly on the basis of the apprehension which it follows but on that of determining one's inclination for oneself or having it determined by another. These two sorts of inclination require different kinds of powers. And such a diversity further demands a difference in the apprehensions, as appears from what has been said. Hence the distinction of the appetitive powers is more or less resultantly based upon the distinction of the apprehensive, not principally.[7]

It seems that here the essential distinction between rational appetite and sensitive appetite is that only the former involves the freedom of self-determination. Difference in apprehension is not the determining factor but the necessary condition: intellectual operation is required for the will to determine its own inclination. So, it seems that Thomas early in his career holds that the intellectual appetite is distinguished from the sensitive appetite primarily because of the freedom by which the former tends towards its object. In the *ST*, however, Thomas replies differently:

---

[6] *ST* 1-2.26.3.

[7] *DV* 22.4, ad 1. Unless otherwise specified, the English is taken from Thomas Aquinas, *Truth*, trans. Robert W. Schmidt, SJ, 3 vols. (Chicago: Henry Regnery Company, 1954). See Geiger, *Le Problème*, 46. For another early text along these lines, see *Sent.* 1.41.1.2, sc 1.

> [I]t is not accidental to the thing desired to be apprehended by the sense or the intellect; on the contrary, this belongs to it by its nature; for the appetible does not move the appetite except as it is apprehended. Wherefore differences in the thing apprehended are of themselves differences of the appetible. And so the appetitive powers are distinct according to the distinction of the things apprehended, as their proper objects.[8]

This latter response strikes at the root cause of the difference, since the very object of appetite is an *apprehended* good:

> [G]ood is not the object of the appetite, except as apprehended. And therefore love demands some apprehension of the good that is loved. For this reason the Philosopher (*Ethic.* ix. 5, 12) says that bodily sight is the beginning of sensitive love: and in like manner the contemplation of spiritual beauty or goodness is the beginning of spiritual love. Accordingly, knowledge is the cause of love for the same reason as good is, which can be loved only if known.[9]

Perhaps the apparent difference between these two responses should not be overemphasized. After all, Thomas refers to the mark of freedom as distinguishing the rational appetite throughout his career.[10] Conversely, the early Thomas does not state that all volitional acts are freely chosen. Rather, he recognizes that the rational appetite has a natural inclination that is not freely chosen but instilled by the Author of nature.[11]

At any rate, the above two ways of distinguishing the appetites are interrelated. The universality of the intellectual power correlates with the will's transcendence over particular goods. As by the intellect one conceives the notion of house as such and can thus entertain a variety of architectural designs, so one is not necessarily inclined to one particular design but can consider a variety of them and select one.[12] Ultimately, freedom rests on the apprehensive capacity to transcend knowledge of the particular goodness of things so as to reach knowledge of things *as* good. Freedom rests on the capacity to conceive of the good as such.[13] In light of the appre-

---

[8] *ST* 1.80.2, ad 1.
[9] *ST* 1-2.27.2.
[10] See *DDN* 4.9, par. 402; *ST* 1-2.26.3; and *In Ioan.* 21.3, par. 2622.
[11] See *DV* 22.5.
[12] See *DM* 6.
[13] See David Gallagher, "Thomas Aquinas on the Will as Rational Appetite," *Journal of*

hension of the good as such, one can seek or love things under this light. Thus, one can judge in the concrete that this particular good instantiates the lovable good better than that particular good, or vice versa. The reason is that the intellect grasps each of the particular goods as particular, as falling under or beneath the general character of the good as such.

Of course, many dispositions may incline one to judge goods this way or that. Such dispositions include bodily conditions, past judgments, opportune circumstances, habits, upbringing, etc. Still, there remains a fundamental condition for liberty of judgment with regard to particular goods. The following account in the *SCG* illustrates the interdependence of Thomas's two ways of distinguishing sensitive and rational appetite:

> Certain things lack liberty of judgment, either because they have no judgment at all, as plants and stones, or because they have a judgment determined by nature to one thing, as do irrational animals; the sheep, by natural estimation, judges the wolf to be harmful to it, and in consequence of this judgment flees from the wolf; and so it is in other cases. Hence, so far as matters of action are concerned, whatever things possess judgment that is not determined to one thing by nature are of necessity endowed with freedom of choice. And such are all intellectual beings. For the intellect apprehends not only this or that good, but good itself, as common to all things. Now, the intellect, through the form apprehended, moves the will; and in all things mover and moved must be proportionate to one another. It follows that the will of an intellectual substance will not be determined by nature to anything except the good as common to all things. So it is possible for the will to be inclined toward anything whatever that is presented to it under the aspect of good, there being no natural determination to the contrary to prevent it. Therefore, all intellectual beings have a free will, resulting from the judgment of the intellect. And this means that they have freedom of choice, which is defined as *the free judgment of reason*.[14]

So, freely chosen complacency of the appetite in a concrete good depends on the intellect's capacity to grasp things *as* good, as falling under the character of the good. Of course, there is more to be said about freedom.

---

the *History of Philosophy* 29 (1991): 559–84.

[14] *SCG* 2.49.6.

As indicated in the above passage, the will does have a necessary appetite for the good as such. As he often puts it, the will has a natural love of beatitude as the root of freely chosen loves.

Natural Dilection for Beatitude as Root of Free Choice

Aquinas acknowledges what seems evident to reflective experience: humans choose among various goods in order to achieve the end(s) they seek. For instance, a hungry man chooses to eat a hamburger rather than a bratwurst; he fries rather than microwaves leftover potatoes. There is, Thomas ultimately submits, a root appetitive cause of all choices, namely, a non-elected love of beatitude. Though non-elected, love of beatitude is not an extrinsic or compulsory force but a natural inclination, an inclination rooted in an interior principle. Thomas argues to or exhibits the existence of this necessary or non-elected inclination to beatitude in various related ways.

First, Thomas contends that all created agents act for an end. He finds the evidence to be the determinate relationship between agent and action.[15] Not just any action comes from any agent; rather, an agent of a certain kind undertakes a certain kind of action. For each agent, there is a proper kind of action. For example, heat heats, and cold cools. Whether the action itself or some external result is the "product," every agent tends towards its determinate action or "effect." Were this not the case, were an agent indifferent to all effects, it would not incline to any one action and thus nothing would happen. Since things do happen, agents are ordered to their determinate actions or effects.[16] Precisely this determinate action or its proper effect, Aquinas infers, is the agent's end. Thus, every created agent, including man, acts for an end. Now, the reason anything tends to an end is that the end is fitting (*conveniens*) for it. Since what is fitting for a thing is its good, the reason anything tends to an end is that the end is its good.[17] Moreover, a thing tends not just to anything fitting but to its perfect and crowning good[18] and strives for this, as for completion, in striving for anything short of it.[19] Now, the perfect and crowning good of a rational

---

[15] See *SCG* 3.2.2. See also, *ST* 1-2.1.2.
[16] See *SCG* 3.2.8.
[17] See *SCG* 3.3.2.
[18] See *ST* 1-2.1.5.
[19] See *ST* 1-2.1.6.

creature is called happiness or beatitude. Hence, man is determinately ordered to happiness as his last end. Since choice regards contingent matters, all choice is rooted in this determinate order to happiness.

In a second way, Thomas argues for a natural love of the end, or beatitude, from the character of distinctively human actions. Humans are distinguished from other animals in that they have dominion over their actions. Hence, a properly human action is one over which the agent has control. Now, a man has control over his actions by his powers of intellect and will: "Those actions are properly called human which proceed from a deliberate will." A power brings about its act, however, "in accordance with the nature of its object." Now, the "object of the will is the end and the good."[20] Hence, every action over which a man has control is "on account of the end."[21] To have control over any action, the will must also have this order to its end; the will must love the end. So, in addition to those actions over which a man has control, there is something over which he does not have control (or election), namely, non-elected dilection of the end.

In another way, Thomas argues from the primordial character of nature. Each thing has an essence, which is its nature. Proper to every nature is an inclination. This inclination is found in diverse ways, proper to each kind of nature. Proper to intellectual things, then, is an appetitive inclination that is natural and intellectual. Such is the natural appetite of the will.[22] We encountered this contention in the previous chapter, when we treated the dictum that some inclination follows every form. Since the will is a kind of form, an operative power, a proper inclination attends it. Of course, the will also has freely chosen inclinations or loves. Since nature is primordial in each thing, natural dilection must be prior to elected dilection.[23] A sign of this priority is that natural dilection is invariant and regards the good in general, whereas elected loves are contingent and regard various objects.

In yet another way, Thomas argues from the nature of choice. The two foregoing ways also draw on this approach, as this approach in turn draws on them. The approach from the nature of choice in some ways solidifies the matter. All choice involves election of one option among one or more others. The one who chooses prefers one option to the others. Why the preference? This question directs us towards a crucial element in choice.

---

[20] *ST* 1-2.1.1
[21] *ST* 1-2.1.1 (my translation).
[22] See *ST* 1.60.1.
[23] See *ST* 1.60.2.

Preference is determined with respect to an *end* already desired.[24] The one choosing judges that one option promises fulfillment of the desired end better than the others. Two elements come to light. We can discern a cognitive element, since judgment is an intellectual act, itself requiring deliberation, also an intellectual act. There is also a volitional element, yet this element regards not the end but the "means" to the end.[25]

Actually, the word "means" does not quite capture Thomas's phrase, which is *ea quae sunt ad finem*. The phrase is better translated as "those things that are *for* the end." The English word "means" connotes a utilitarian lack of intrinsic appeal in the object chosen, which is "*only* a means" to what one really wants. Bitter medicine, for example, is *only* chosen in view of its utility in procuring health. The phrase *ea quae sunt ad finem* is broader in scope, simply indicating things that are desired with respect to an end already loved or desired. Such things may be attractive in themselves or they may be merely useful means to something in itself desirable. Crucially, however, every choice presupposes love of an end. Hence, no object of choice is, as such, an end.[26]

Obviously, however, the love of some ends can be chosen. Say that (A) and (B) are options for me in light of my love of (Y). It may be that I have chosen the love of (Y). Of course, if I chose the love of (Y) instead of the love of (X), I would have done so with respect to a love for some other end (Q). For instance, the desired end that is presupposed to the choice between sushi and steak can itself be chosen. I chose to go out to eat rather than to stay home to eat, and this choice serves as an end with respect to the options regarding restaurants. Again, this end (Q) can itself be an object of choice, but only on the basis of yet another presupposed loved end (R). My choice to go out rather than to stay home can be based on another chosen love, my choice to eat rather than to study, yet I would have chosen to eat on the basis of some other presupposed end, such as using my time most expediently. The series of ends and means under consideration is clearly a causal series ordered *per se*.[27] In every case of choice, an already actual love of some end is the cause rendering choice among options possible. In light of the love of the end, certain things have a note of desirability and thus constitute options. Further, the loved end is a principle for discern-

---

[24] See *ST* 1-2.13.3 and *ST* 1.82.1, ad 3.
[25] See *ST* 1.83.3.
[26] Were we to integrate the current investigation with other relevant precisions in Aquinas's work, we would study intention and choice. Intention generates love of the end and choice generates love of the means. See Sherwin, *By Knowledge*, 91.
[27] See *ST* 1-2.1.4.

ment, providing criteria for judgment of preference among the options.[28]

Thomas's next move is to note the impossibility of an infinite regress in this causal series. Every act of choice presupposes an already determined love of some end. That is to say, every act of choice is *caused* by (in terms at least of a cause *sine qua non*) this already determined love of some end. If this already determined love is itself determined by a choice, it too is caused by some other already determined love. Now, it is impossible that this series goes on infinitely, for if it did, no love could take place. If every love were itself the object of choice, every love would be caused. Thus, there would be an infinite regress of caused causes, each of which requires a proximate proportional cause. I say "proximate proportional cause" because I am indicating a cause *immanent* within the one choosing and not one that is itself transcendent.[29] Now, if the regress of a *per se* causal series went on indefinitely in the upward direction, the will could never begin to move freely towards any object, since the end is the cause of free choice.[30] Thus, no choice could ever be made. In fact, however, human experience indicates that free choices are indeed made. Therefore, there must be a love not caused by choice, that is, not chosen. The one choosing must love some end without having chosen that love. Such love of the end must be causally prior to all choice. It must be an appetitive inclination rooted in the very nature of the will. Further, as the ultimate appetitive cause in light of which particular goods are taken to be fitting goods, it must be love of the ultimate end.[31] Such is what Thomas means by a natural inclination to the final end.[32] For Thomas, and arguably for the voice of history, such an end is beatitude.

The notion of the practical syllogism also provides another way of considering this issue. Election, Aquinas contends, is "as a conclusion in a practical (*operabilium*) syllogism, whereas the end is as principle in practical matters."[33] Thus, with respect to any act of choice, the end is as a cause or starting point in the order of intention. Now, in theoretical syllogisms, some propositions that form premises in arguments can themselves be demonstrated by other arguments on the basis of yet other premises. How-

---

[28] See *ST* 1-2.13; and *ST* 1-2.14. I would note especially *ST* 1-2.14.2, ad 1.
[29] See *ST* 1-2.9.4, ad 1.
[30] Again, see *ST* 1-2.1.4.
[31] Here, I mean "ultimate" in such a way as to prescind from the thorny questions concerned with nature and grace. Here, "ultimate" only means final; it does not necessarily mean perfect, as though perfect in every order.
[32] See esp. *ST* 1-2.1.4; *ST* 1-2.8; 1-2.10; and *ST* 1-2.13.
[33] *ST* 1-2.13.3 (my translation).

ever, the process of demonstration must have its ultimate roots, namely, the first indemonstrable principles. The case is similar with practical syllogisms. Clearly, some things that are ends with regard to one choice, and hence principles of a given practical syllogism, can be themselves objects of choice in another respect, namely, in light of another end serving as a starting point. However, the process of practical reasoning cannot go on indefinitely in the upward direction. If it did, no conclusion would be reached. Since practical conclusions are reached, there must be an end that "in no way is an object of choice."[34] That is, if actual choices take place, there must be actual non-elected love of the ultimate end.

Finally, Thomas's global sketch of these matters is expressed with his analogy between the will's relationships to the end and to *ea quae sunt ad finem* and the intellect's relationships to principles and conclusions. The analogy highlights the primordial or foundational role of the love of beatitude in human action. As the intellect's action is based on natural understanding of principles, the primary indemonstrable principles, so the will's action is based on natural love of beatitude:

> For the intellect knows principles naturally; and from such knowledge in man comes the knowledge of conclusions, which are known by him not naturally, but by discovery, or by teaching. In like manner, the end acts in the will in the same way as the principle does in the intellect. . . . Consequently the will tends naturally to its last end; for every man naturally wills [beatitude]: and all other desires are caused by this natural desire; since whatever a man wills he wills on account of the end. Therefore the love of that good, which a man naturally wills as an end, is his natural love; but the love derived from this, which is of something loved for the end's sake, is the love of choice.[35]

In short, the love of beatitude is the proximate font and root of all volitional operations.

All freedom is embedded in this fundamental drive towards the ultimate end. For any given choice that a man makes, the foundational appetitive reason is love of happiness:

---

[34] *ST* 1-2.13.3. See also *ST* 1.82.1.
[35] *ST* 1.60.2, corp. References abound: see also *Sent.* 2.25.1.5, ad 4; *DV* 23.4; *DP* 1.5 and 2.3, ad 6; *SCG* 3.26.10 and 109.6–7; *ST* 1.82.1–2; *ST* 1.94.1; *ST* 1-2.1.6; *ST* 1-2.10.1–2; *ST* 1-2.13.3; *DM* 6; and *DM* 16.5.

> Now among the objects of appetite the end is the principle and foundation of [those things that are for the end], because the latter, being for the sake of the end, are not desired except by reason of the end. Accordingly, what the will necessarily wills, determined to it by a natural inclination, is the last end, happiness, and whatever is included in it: to be, knowledge of truth, and the like.[36]

Choice rests on an ineradicable, non-elected love of beatitude. Clearly, Thomas considers the love of beatitude to be not only good but also necessary and foundational:

> [N]either is natural necessity repugnant to the will. Indeed, more than this, for as the intellect of necessity adheres to the first principles, the will must of necessity adhere to the last end, which is happiness: since the end is in practical matters what the principle is in speculative matters. For what befits a thing naturally and immovably must be the root and principle of all else appertaining thereto, since the nature of a thing is the first in everything, and every movement arises from something immovable.[37]

This point bears foundational relevance for our inquiry. Thomas does not juxtapose to this love of beatitude a "disinterested" love of the good, as though positing two separate and equally primordial appetites. Much less does he oppose natural love of beatitude to disinterested love of the good.

Thomas's account of the root of free choice in the love of happiness has raised a persistent question. If freedom is rooted in an ineradicable love of happiness, what is the scope of freedom? Theories of love as disinterested correlate with views of free choice as having greater scope. For his part, Thomas is commonly understood to have developed his appreciation of the scope of free choice. To his mature view of the scope of freedom we now turn.

The Scope of Freedom

Thomas's best treatments of free choice occur in his mature works, *DM*,

---

[36] *DV* 22.5.
[37] *ST* 1.82.1.

q. 6, and *Prima secundae*.[38] He distinguishes two considerations regarding how powers are moved. We can consider how a power is moved with respect to its object and how it is moved with respect to its subject. He calls the former the "specification" of the act and the latter the "exercise" or performance of the act. A power is moved to its "exercise" by what causes the act or movement in a manner comparable to efficient causality. Now, efficient causes act for an end. So, the first source of movement, even with regard to the exercise of an act, comes from the end, which falls under the good.

Turning to the powers of the soul, Thomas observes that the will is the source of the *exercise* of these powers, since the object of the will is the good inclusive of the final end. Conversely, the intellect is the source of their *specification*, since the object of the will, whether the means or the end, is the *understood* good. The will moves the soul to some particular act, say, to think about some matter, on account of its already willing the end that the particular act either instantiates or leads towards. Since the will cannot will the end unless it understands it, the intellect has a certain priority over the will as setting its ultimate target. Further, the means cannot be chosen unless known. Thus, the intellect is also involved in the determination of particular targets. What in these matters is a matter of free choice?

First, there is wide room for freedom regarding the specification of the act. Only that object which is good "universally and from every point of view," without any drawback, can specify the act to be one of love, not hate.[39] Only in cases such as this does the intellect, in presenting the object, necessarily determine the will with regard to the specification of its act. Any object that is good but not good in every respect can be either loved or hated. There are few objects that can be presented as good in every respect and without drawback. Even life can become burdensome insofar as it occasions great illness or pain. The only object that determines the will even in terms of specification is beatitude.[40]

Second, there is even wider scope for freedom concerning the "exercise" of the act. Even in the face of an object good in every respect and without drawback, the pilgrim is free to act or not to act concerning it. This latter freedom is the freedom of "exercise." A pilgrim, who by definition does not have immediate union with God, has freedom of exercise, to

---

[38] See, e.g., *ST* 1-2.10.2.
[39] *ST* 1-2.10.2.
[40] See *DM* 6; *ST* 1.82.1; and *ST* 1-2.10.2.

act or not to act, in the face of any object he considers.[41]

Illustrations will help clarify the freedom of specification and the freedom of exercise. If one were able to portray some way of life that in its every particular aspect is good without burden or detriment, then this way of life could be an object of only love.[42] One could not "hate" such an object or choose its contrary. In the case of such an object, the intellect necessarily specifies the act of the will as one of love. However, one need not "exercise" any act of will towards it. One can choose not to consider it or to think of something else. Thus, the intellect does not bring about an act of will as efficient cause in this case; the will is the cause of its own act. *A fortiori*, the will has freedom of exercise with regard to any other object. Moreover, the will has freedom of specification with regard to any other object. Some objects can be understood to have drawbacks. One can hate such objects. If, for instance, a hamburger at a popular greasy spoon is good to the taste but bad for health, one can choose to "hate" it on account of its threat to one's well-being. Similarly, even a good lacking in some particular can be hated if it is an obstacle to the attainment of that which it lacks. An immature teenager can on occasion be repulsed by her good friend, since, in the company of her friend, she cannot approach the boy in whom she is currently interested. As it seems, the converse can be said about evil objects. If there were an object understood to be evil in every particular, and in no way a means towards the good, it could only be hated. Eternal damnation comes to mind. With regard to such an object, the intellect specifies the act of the will. Any "evil" object that is understood to be good in some respect can be loved. For instance, adultery is evil, but one can perversely love it as a way of pleasure or revenge. Suffering is contrary

---

[41] The temporary phenomenon of rapture, *even if* it truly has God for its immediate object, is not a *state* of union with God and is thus not considered here.

[42] It remains a serious question whether such an object is conceivable. In my judgment, Aquinas's argument is hypothetical: were such an object to be considered, it could only be loved. After all, the "what" of the object is somewhat of a construct at any rate. It is a proposal. Now, the labor of description and proposing involves the will. Hence, there is an effort involved even in identifying the object.

Is it not possible that one might think of some drawback for the object? For instance, such an object seems difficult to attain, and a sinful pleasure that is really attainable, though ignoble, may seem more attractive, and such a pleasure is certainly incompatible with the object so described. Further, the very status of being "good in every conceivable particular" calls for further consideration. Is it "good" in appearance? Thus, someone enslaved to a passion might, perhaps, consider a drug trip to be "good in every conceivable way." At any rate, Aquinas's judgment certainly involves at least the hypothetical statement.

to the natural appetite, for the bodily appetite as such shrinks from it, but it can be understood as a means towards good and so loved in this regard. Athletes, for example, embrace at least some of the pain they experience in training and performance.

As we can see, Thomas's principles, as developed in his most mature period, allow wide room for freedom. With regard to specification of its act, the will is free concerning any object not understood to be both good in every respect and also without drawback. With regard to exercise of the act, the will of a pilgrim is free concerning any object at all. These are the two primary and essential aspects Aquinas identifies concerning the scope of freedom of choice, the specification and the exercise of the act. Still, Thomas does not neglect to mention other significant factors that color and limit choice. These include subjective dispositions, habits, circumstances, etc. Such factors have significant roles to play in a full treatment of human freedom. Although for want of space I only mention these in passing, an account of freedom in moral theology cannot neglect them. This monograph, however, treats a focused topic in theological anthropology and so must bypass these considerations.[43]

Finally, however, we should not forget that for Thomas all election presupposes love of the end, so that, ultimately, a natural or innate, non-elected love of the end is the necessary causal support for every choice. From the forgoing arguments, we have seen that freedom of specification requires this natural love. In addition, the freedom of exercise also presupposes this non-elected love of the end, for "the cause of movement acts for the sake of an end. And so we conclude that the first source of movement as to the performance of an act comes from the end."[44] Since even the freedom of exercise rests on love of the end, this non-elected love is the foundation even of the choice to love as the ultimate end the good proposed by the intellect as the candidate most apt to meet the *ratio* of the intellectual appetite's range. Even if such a concrete good is also good in every particular and in no way burdensome, one can still choose not to have an act of the will concerning it. Since it is electable, such a good is among *ea quae sunt ad finem*; nevertheless, it is *sui generis* in this category. It is not a useful "means," but rather the concrete good that one considers to be that wherein the end naturally loved is instantiated or realized. Is the choice not to love such a perfect good likewise made only on the founda-

---

[43] Note also that some conditions are themselves rooted in prior acts of freedom: bad habits come from bad free choices.

[44] *DM* 6.

tion of natural dilection for beatitude? If not to act constitutes an option for choice, it would seem not to be simply non-action. If it is not simply non-action, then not to act would seem to be chosen in light of natural dilection for beatitude.

Perhaps we should reach for further precision regarding this non-elected love of the end. Insofar as this love is constant and invariant, it seems to name not an act but the *relation* of the power of the will to its object, the good in universal. The will is not always in act even though it always has the good in universal as its object. However, I have suggested that this relation really obtains in the order of things as a feature of any act of the will insofar as it is ordered to the good in universal.

At any rate, a question arises. If the will is not always in act, how does it change from potency to act? Sometimes, the will moves itself to act. However, it cannot both move and be moved in the same respect. Rather, actually willing some end, the will moves itself to choose among *ea quae sunt ad finem*: actually willing to eat out, one deliberates about and chooses to go for sushi. Now, if the will is not always actually willing that specific end presupposed to this particular choice, it must be moved to will that specific end. Again, sometimes the will moves itself to will one end rather than another. Still, every choice is preceded by deliberation. Although one may choose to deliberate, the very choice to deliberate about means itself requires a prior will of a higher end. This process cannot go on forever, since then one would never begin to will to deliberate. Since one does begin to will to deliberate, "[i]t is necessary to affirm that will proceeds to its first motion from the instigation of an external mover, as Aristotle concludes somewhere in *Eudemian Ethics*."[45]

This external mover of the will can be none other than God. One reason for this conclusion is that the motion of the will is that of an intrinsic principle. Thus, as are all natural motions, the motion of the will is opposed to violent motion, the principle of which is from without. The only agent that can move another thing according to motion natural to the moved thing is the very cause of the moved thing's nature or substance: in generating something, the cause bestows on it the very principles of its motion. Now, whereas one animal generates another, the human soul with its intellectual powers cannot be generated at all; it is simply created *ex nihilo* by God. Thus, the immediate author of the will is God. So, only God can be the external efficient cause of the movement of the will. A second reason for this claim is specific to the character of the will, the object of which

---

[45] *ST* 1-2.9.4. See also *DM* 6 and Sherwin, *By Knowledge*, 53–62.

is the universal good. No agent that is a particular good is competent to direct any power to such an object or "give [it] a universal inclination."[46] Thus, the only agent competent to direct the will to its object, to give it stably an orientation to the universal good, is the infinite, uncreated good that is God.

If we put the foregoing elements together, the following portrait emerges. Our will is moved from potency to act, to some volitional movement the object of which is targeted under the aspect of the good as such, by divine efficient causality. That the object of this volitional act is targeted under the aspect of the good as such, that the good as such is the formal object of the will, is in the sole competence of God so orienting the will. In one sense, this orientation is simply a relation; in this manner, the orientation is just the very object of the power of the will. In another sense, this orientation is a real structural ingredient in the actual movement; in this sense, the orientation is the tendency of the will to target what it targets *only* under the aspect of the good. The material object of the (pilgrim's) will is not that very aspect, but some item falling under that aspect. *That* the will (a) targets what it targets *under* the aspect of the good as such and (b) is in act from having been in potency are both due to the causality of God the First Mover.

From these considerations, Michael Sherwin concludes, further, that the primal motion of the will is not caused by the intellect but by God and that, conversely, the primal motion of the intellect is not caused by the will but by God.[47] I would qualify this remark: The object of the will is always that of the intellect. Thus, the will cannot target what it does not know in any way. The object one takes to be ultimate is an object that one in some way knows; even the object of the first act of the will is understood by the intellect. The universal reach of the will, an appetitive power, arises from the universal reach of the cognitive power of the intellect. This qualification is not a denial that the first act of the will—as it regards (a) and (b) above—does not fall under the directing power (*ordinatione*) of the intellect. The intellect shows the will its object but does not move it in this first act.[48] The aspect of volitional action that regards the material object chosen, something among *ea quae sunt ad finem*, falls under the directing power of the intellect. That the will targets such an object only under the

---

[46] *ST* 1-2.9.6.
[47] See Sherwin, *By Knowledge*, 57ff.
[48] Similarly, the virtue of faith shows the object but does not moderate the will's tendency to God (see *ST* 1-2.66.6, ad 1, and Sherwin, *By Knowledge*, 161).

aspect of the good, which aspect in this light stretches beyond the chosen good, depends upon the universal reach of the intellect which enables one to consider the chosen good in various aspects, whether rightly or wrongly. Since the intellect can so approach the object, the will remains free with respect to it, both in terms of specification and in terms of exercise, provided it is set in act by God as First Mover.

Before I conclude this treatment of choice, one further comment is in order. The natural, non-elected love of the end regards the general notion of the ultimate end or happiness and is common to all rational agents: "Everyone seeks for his perfection to be fulfilled."[49] However, as is obvious, different men judge differently regarding what actual or apparent goods constitute that perfection. Thus, Aquinas distinguishes the general character of the ultimate end from that in which this or that man finds, or thinks he finds, this end. Whereas there is no choice regarding the appetite for the ultimate end in its general notion, that is, happiness in general, there is choice regarding that in which one thinks to find this happiness. If some choose honor and others choose pleasure, still others choose God.

We should immediately address a difficulty. If all choice regards *ea quae sunt ad finem*, is God among *ea quae sunt ad finem*? Is Thomas implying that the pilgrim who chooses to love God orders God to some higher, more generic end? Of course, God is beyond all genera, and so cannot be ordered to anything else. Further, to attempt to order God to a higher end would be disordered. The difficulty can be resolved by recalling a distinction noted above. Among *ea quae sunt ad finem* there is a highest thing (or set of things), namely, that which one takes to be the realization of the end naturally loved. Chosen as that wherein the end is to be realized, this highest thing serves as the explicit end with respect to which other things may be *ea quae sunt ad finem*. So, the earthly pilgrim's choice of God is a choice of that which manifests or instantiates the end he seeks, rather than of that which is a means to the end he seeks. The pilgrim labors in faith, but the blessed recognize the identity of God with that which they were seeking on earth.[50] Indeed, the end or happiness "in general" is simply an aspect of possible objects and not itself an object.

So far, we have treated dilection in general. This love admits a distinction in the very structure of its act. This distinction is critical to an evaluation of the relationship between love of the Divine Other and the love of happiness.

---

[49] *ST* 1-2.1.7 (my translation).
[50] See *ST* 1-2.5.8.

Twofold Structure of Dilection: Love of Friendship and Love of Concupiscence

Thomas borrows a distinction, variously understood in the tradition, in order to articulate the structure of the act of dilection. He wields the distinction in his own ways, coming to a mature position over time, although admittedly he continues to employ the distinction in extended ways. We will here treat his mature, explicit use of the distinction, the rationale for this use, and acknowledge his continued variations in uses of the distinction.

The Distinction Itself

The proper place to discover Thomas's most precise rendering of the distinction of loves is the mature article in which he explicitly raises the question of their distinction, *ST* 1-2.26.4.[51] He writes,

> As the Philosopher says in *Rhetoric* 2, "To love is to will good to someone." Thus, the motion of love tends to two things: firstly, to the good that one wills to someone, whether to oneself or to another; secondly, to the person for whom one wills the good. Towards that good, therefore, which one wills for another there is love of concupiscence. But towards that for whom someone wills the good there is love of friendship.[52]

A movement, or act, of love tends to two objects: the person loved and the perfecting good of that person. Note that Thomas is describing *one* movement or act of love. This movement targets two goods. Insofar as it targets a person, Thomas calls it "love of friendship" whether it is for oneself or for another. Insofar as it targets a perfecting good, Thomas calls it "love of concupiscence," whatever the perfecting good may be (virtue, pleasure, etc.). Read in this fashion, the distinction has superior explanatory power.[53] For this reason, this is the employment I shall make of the distinc-

---

[51] See the excellent treatment by David Gallagher, "Desire for Beatitude and Love of Friendship in Thomas Aquinas," *Mediaeval Studies* 58 (1996): 1–45. Also see 26–29 of David Gallagher, "Thomas Aquinas on Self-Love as the Basis for Love of Others," *Acta philosophica* 8 (1999): 23–44. Gallagher, however, does not seem to address the difficulties treated in Chapter Eight of this volume.

[52] *ST* 1-2.26.4 (my translation).

[53] See Mansini, "*Duplex Amor* and the Structure of Love in Aquinas," in *Thomistica*, ed. E. Manning, Recherches de théologie ancienne et médiévale, Supplementa, vol. 1 (Leuven: Peeters, 1995), 189.

tion. This decision will enable closer attention "to the things," rendering agreement and disagreement in interpretations and in systematic positions easier. Of course, disagreement may involve objection to this very decision. I submit that articulation of any disagreement, including one about this decision, can take crisper form precisely because of this rendering of the distinction. In the end, not interpretative disagreements but "the real things" count the most.

I shall argue that my decision is in harmony with Thomas's mature *ex professo* treatment of the distinction. Still, textual and historical matters are quite complicated. Diverse readings of the distinction arise no doubt because of these matters. Various readings of the distinction at variance from mine can be noted. Here, I will briefly note four of these, evaluating each from the standard adopted above. This evaluation, then, does not concern readings of Aquinas according to this or that stage of development; rather, it regards the aptitude of such readings for a mature Thomistic analysis of the problem of love.

First, some read the distinction simply as indicative of the directional tendency of love vis-à-vis the lover.[54] But this reading is misleading. As Thomas explicitly states in his *ex professo* treatment, love of concupiscence can target not only one's own perfecting good but also another's. When one loves another, one wills his perfecting good by love of concupiscence.

---

[54] See, for instance, Rousselot, 92 and Peter Oesterreich, "Thomas von Aquins Lehre von der Liebe als menschlicher Grundleidenschaft," *Theologie und Philosophie* 66 (1991): 91–92. In a certain respect, traces of this are found in Simonin, "Autor" 263, and, to some extent, in Gillon, "Genèse," 324–26.

Even the fine analysis of Benezet Bujo bears some of these marks. He defends the goodness of *amor concupiscentiae*. Benezet Bujo, *Die Begründung des Sittlichen: Zur Frage des Eudämonismus bei Thomas von Aquin*, no. 33, Veröffentlichungen des Grabmann-Institutes zur Erforschung der mittelalterlichen Theologie und Philosophie, ed. Michael Schmaus, Werner Dettloff, and Richard Heinzmann (Paderborn: Ferdinand Schöningh, 1984), 156ff. Then, he remarks that *amor concupiscentiae* is "not unconditionally negative" (*Die Begründung*, 157). This may simply be an infelicity of expression. Bujo is keen to the fact that although the proper act of charity consists "more" in loving than in being loved, yet "to be loved" is something pertinent to charity (see *Die Begründung*, 168).

Mattison contends that other-directedness is an ingredient in the most precise way in which Thomas wields the distinction (see "Movements," 37–39). The other ingredient, according to Mattison, is that in love of friendship, the good is possessed (see "Movements," 40). Here, Mattison is following Mansini, whose textual study is important and keen. My approach is to follow Thomas's more foundational judgments in order to explicate his various expressions. In my opinion, his most precise *and* widely applicable judgment concerning the distinction is the one I have just laid out.

Conversely, love of friendship is not defined by directional tendency away from the lover and towards another. Instead, love of friendship simply names the aspect of love as targeting a person, whether oneself or another. Aquinas ascribes love of concupiscence even to God's love of the created order, insofar as it targets goods ordered to the good of man, whom of all His material creatures God chiefly loves:

> God does not love irrational creatures with the love of friendship but as it were with the love of [concupiscence], in so far as He orders them to rational creatures, and even to Himself. Yet this is not because He stands in need of them; but only on account of His goodness, and of the services they render to us. *For we can desire a thing for others as well as for ourselves.*[55]

God has love of concupiscence for non-rational creatures. It is not that God's love is complex, but the goods that His love targets are many and ordered.

Second, some hold that love of concupiscence is desire and thus regards only an absent good. To the contrary, love of concupiscence, since it is love, may be for a present good in which one rests. Granted, the isolated word "concupiscence" has etymological roots in and connotations of desire. However, "love of concupiscence" is a phrase not reducible to "concupiscence" as desire; instead, it indicates one aspect of the structure of an act of love, and the object of love can be present or absent. Although a word might at first be used to signify one thing, through mature reflection it can come to be used to signify something else. Similarly, the word "appetite" is first employed in the context of need, but it later signifies the affective power and even the will.

Third, some suggest that love of concupiscence is only or primarily for ephemeral or base goods.[56] To the contrary, one with virtuous self-love will

---

[55] *ST* 1.20.2, ad 3 (emphasis mine).
[56] See E. Schockenhoff, *Bonum hominis: Die anthropologischen und theologischen Grundlagen der Tugendethik des Thomas von Aquin* (Mainz: Matthias-Grünewald-Verlag, 1987), 498 and 501; Gillon, 324–26; Bujo, 153; and James McEvoy, "Amitié, attirance et amour chez S. Thomas d'Aquin," *Revue Philosophique de Louvain* 91 (1993): 391–92. A marvelous piece potentially corrective of such views is *De perf.* 13. This work was finished around 1270 (Torrell, 347). Aquinas does state that the word "love" is said almost "abusively" when it regards objects to be used for temporary benefits, such as wine, food, etc. Still, to the person whom we love, we will virtues, happiness, etc. Such "things" are indeed loved not by *amor amicitiae* but by *amor concupiscentiae*, and these are of great

love the goods of health and virtue in proper order. Yet, neither of these is his very essence or substance. So, in a mature employment of the phrase, love of concupiscence can designate love of the good that perfects another. The very love of charity is lovable in the way that defines the love of concupiscence and its object: "Something is loved by friendship in two ways. In one way, as the friend himself for whom we have friendship and to whom we will good things. In another way, as the good thing that we will for the friend. And in this way charity is loved by charity."[57] Charity is loved as the perfecting good of a friend, but the love of the perfecting good of a friend is love of concupiscence. Thus, charity, queen of the virtues, is loved by a love of concupiscence as defined in Thomas's *ex professo* treatment.

Fourth, some seem to regard love of friendship and love of concupiscence as two separable acts.[58] Indeed, some of the above readings are premised on such a separation.[59] For Thomas, however, "an act of love always tends to two goods."[60] He makes this claim with good reason. Why would one will some good for oneself unless one loved oneself? We do not rightly or sanely love our perfection as though dedicating ourselves *to* a non-subsistent perfection. We love our perfection as our having come to fruition.[61] Again, why would one will a good for another unless one loved the other? Clearly, love of concupiscence for another's perfecting good rests on love of friendship. Conversely, how could we say we love another if we did not will his good? One cannot love an already happy friend unless one rejoices in his perfection for his sake. Since all joy is rooted in love, which is an act of will, one indeed wills one's friend's good.[62] Thus, love of friendship

---

interest to us and to our friends.

[57] *ST* 2-2.25.2.
[58] See, for instance, Schockenhoff's misleading translation of *ST* 1-2.26.4 in *Bonum hominis*, 493. Schockenhoff elsewhere recognizes the unity of the two aspects of love: see *Bonum hominis*, 494.
[59] Others lead to this possible separation. See Mattison, "Movements," 40.
[60] See *ST* 1.20.1, ad 3. See Sherwin, *By Knowledge*, 75.
[61] This thesis is also well defended in a profound article on the topic, which I approved for peer review publication in *Res Philosophica* but have not yet seen in print, then entitled, "The Good that We Will: Thomas Aquinas and the Problem of Love."
[62] If we contend that love of concupiscence is for the absent good, then possession of the good should bring about a cessation of love of concupiscence (see Mattison, "Movements," 42). However, if there is no love of concupiscence, then there can be no resultant joy. Nor can joy for one's own possession of the good emerge from love of friendship for oneself, *if* such love is always other-directed. Thomas, however, affirms that the beatified rejoice (*ST* 1.2–4.1). In light of these problems, I suggest that we distinguish the terms in their precise meanings from the etymology associated with their initially

requires love of concupiscence.

It will be observed that "to will" has connotations of (a) targeting a perfecting but non-subsistent good[63] which (b) is as yet absent but possible of attainment.[64] The observation correctly identifies the etymology and even the use of the term. The term "to will" does not simply point out its referent, an act of will; it also carries the connotations of targeting a non-subsistent, absent good. Since these connotations are alien to some of the connotations in the term "to love," we do not say, "I will you" to our beloved. Notwithstanding, "to will good to someone" is a primary manifestation of the act of love.[65] Further, an act of love is an act of the will.[66] Since one can love another, that to which the term "object of the will" refers need not be non-subsisting and need not be absent.

Before turning to the rationale of the distinction, I would note some elements of this distinction's applicability in the complexity of life. There may be a *per se* ordered series of goods loved in one act of love of concupiscence (which itself is always referred to the love of friendship for the one for whom one wills such goods). For example, one may love a man on account of his money, and his money on account of wine, and wine on account of the delights of the palate. The chief good willed here, the end in this order, is one's own sensible delight. A nobler example is this: one may love a book for the counsel it provides, the counsel for the sake of virtue, and the virtue for the sake of fellowship with another. An inhering good is at stake in both the noble love and the base love, for both delight and virtue are "inhering" perfections. Each is loved by love of concupiscence.

The Rationale for the Distinction

What is the rationale for Thomas's mature use of this distinction? The very character of genuine love for a created person, never identical with his flour-

---

proper employment. Intellectual developments reconfigure the meanings of terms and hence call for reassessment of their proper and improper significations. "The light that lightens every mind" becomes a proper analogy.

[63] See Jordan Olver, "*Bonum Nostrum*: Thomas Aquinas and Love of Others for Their Own Sake," *Review of Metaphysics* 70 (2017): 692. I suggest that Olver is correct about the way the term is used. In fact, Thomists do not find it appropriate to say, "I will you." Love of friendship is, however, an act of will always coupled with love of concupiscence, at least as it regards pilgrims and is found in pilgrims.

[64] See Mattison, "Movements," 41ff.

[65] See *ST* 2-2.25.2, ad 1.

[66] *Diligere est quoddam velle. DC* 1.

ishing, requires it. Analogically, the distinction will have a role both with respect to our love of God and with respect to our understanding of God's love for us and for Himself. The distinction has its most proper seat in the rational love for another person. However, as reason is the perfection of nature, it is useful to consider the distinction at the level of nature itself.[67]

Recall that animal passions regard the relation of an object to the animal as a whole. Grass is good for the lamb on the whole. Evident in this attraction are both a love of the animal's self and a love of the particular good as ordered to the animal. While the animal does not rationally deliberate about the relation of the good or evil to itself, it does size up this relation by its "estimative power." A bird picks appropriately sized sticks; the weaker Texas Spiny Lizard surrenders a pushup challenge when faced with a stronger Spiny. Seeking the good for oneself is premised on love of self.

There is, also, instinctive love of another. Mother bears labor for their cubs, and the female pelican pours out her blood for her starving young. In these latter cases, the individual animal seeks the good of her particular offspring, thereby serving the good of the species. Thus, even in the irrational appetite, the elements of the rationale for a distinction can be found. Further, as Jordan Olver points out, Aquinas contends that even non-cognitive fire has a twofold tendency, that towards its own good and that towards the good of the fire it produces. In virtue of the former, it inclines upward; in virtue of the latter, it produces fire in adjacent wood.[68] So, the distinction applies in an extended sense even at the level of inanimate nature.

The act of rational love best justifies this distinction. It is not just that some of our acts of dilection have this twofold structure; every act of dilection has it:

> An act of love always tends towards two things; to the good that one wills, and to the person for whom one wills it: since to love a person is to wish that person good. Hence, inasmuch as [someone loves himself, he wills his own good. Thus, as far as it is possible, he seeks to unite that good to himself].[69]

This structural duality in the act of love is fundamentally necessary for any pilgrim's love of an intellectual creature. Why? No intellectual crea-

---

[67] See Olver, "*Bonum*," 678ff.
[68] *Quod.* 1.4.3. See Olver's astute reading of the distinction at Olver, "*Bonum*," 681–83.
[69] *ST* 1.20.1, ad 3.

ture is its own virtue or beatitude. However, life is not truly lovable for one who has no virtue or beatitude, at least in potency. If we truly love our friend, we will his good, since "to love is to will good to someone."

Love targets the good, the full character of which is the perfect. Now, insofar as anything has substantial existence, it is *in a way* good, because it exists in first act. However, being good *simply* or having perfection in the truest sense implies flourishing or existence in second act. No creature exists in second act simply by virtue of being in first act. Hence, no creature is simply good just because it exists.[70] One can already be called good by one's essence insofar as (a) substantial existence itself is good and (b) one's order to one's end, included in one's substantial existence, is good.[71] Still, this is only relative goodness. "Good" properly speaking involves perfection, which in creatures requires the composition of first act reduced to second act. For rational beings capable of immanent spiritual operations—which perfect the agent while "remaining within" the agent and which put these beings in touch with the Good and the True—the composition rendering them perfect is that of first act (existence in their substantial nature) as reduced to second act (the operations by which they attain their ends). In particular, man attains his perfection by attaining the highest act possible, and that act is, according to Aquinas, an act of the speculative intellect understanding the most perfect object, God. Divine contemplation, therefore, is man's ultimate perfection. Under the concrete providence of God, the ultimate end is supernatural or beatifying union with God.

True love wills the perfect good of the beloved. Given the composite character of each created being, especially that of substance and perfection, true love of a created friend must have a twofold character: one (a) loves a friend (b) *that* he may be perfect. That is, one who loves another wills (b) the perfect good (a) to his friend. There are two goods involved here: a person who exists and the operation by which that person attains his end. Rather, there is a complex good that is willed: (a) the friend (b) as having attained his good. The love by which one loves another targets both goods in the precise order indicated: willing that (a) the friend (b) have his perfecting good.[72]

As a result, true love of another cannot simply be a "response to the

---

[70] See *ST* 1.5.1, ad 1. See Jean-Hervé Nicolas, "Amour de soi, amour de Dieu, amour des autres," *Revue thomiste* 56 (1956): 8.
[71] See *SCG* 3.20, par. 5, and Nicolas, 7.
[72] For Thomas's rich discussion of modes of being and modes of love, see *DDN* 4.10, pars. 427–29. Again, I refer the reader to the fine article, hopefully to be found published in a worthy journal, entitled, "The Good that We Will."

goodness and value of a person," if by this one means the rational substance as such.⁷³ Love that simply wills "the good of existence" for the beloved is not adequately love, unless we read "existence" analogously, as inclusive of operative flourishing.⁷⁴ True, the foundational good of anything is its substance-in-act. Hence, the good I "first" will to a friend is that he "be and live."⁷⁵ This good is "first" in a primordial way, as that without which flourishing cannot be. However, it cannot be first in an isolated sense, since the following is true for each of the damned: "It would have been better for that man if he had not been born" (Matt 26:24, RSV). In short, one does not adequately love a created rational being who does not will him to attain his perfection, his finality.⁷⁶

In the age of philosophical personalism, it may seem unbecoming to deny that "simple regard" constitutes the essence of love. Three points are in order here. First, as we have indicated, everyone wants to be fulfilled. Hence, insofar as one wants to be loved, one wants the lover to will this fulfillment. When I am vicious or in pain, a mere "regard" for me does not suffice, unless it has an eye to my well-being. Second, dependent persons want to be in communion with others. This communion will be realized only through interactions that actualize an interpersonal nexus.⁷⁷ Hence, if I will a truly personal good to a neighbor, I must undertake, together with him, activities of interaction that constitute our relational fulfill-

---

73 From the otherwise excellent work of Sherwin, *By Knowledge*, 93. Sherwin rightly stresses the primacy of the person loved. Yet, love is not sheer appreciation of the substantial being of the beloved. Love has an eye to the beloved's well-being. It is not "well-being" that is ultimately loved; it is the beloved being well. So, love has an eye to the happiness of the beloved, for only in willing my beloved happiness can I be said to love him truly. The metaphysical underpinnings of the structure of love are as follows. "Good" adds to "being," not really but notionally, the note of perfection and desirability. One is said "to be" absolutely in accordance with one's substantial existence; one is said "to be" relatively (*secundum quid*) in accordance with the attainment of some perfection.

Conversely, one is said "to be good" relatively in accordance with one's substantial existence (first act); and one is said "to be good" absolutely in accordance with one's attainment of some perfection. See *ST* 1.5.1 and *DM* 1.5. Another thoughtful scholar, Daniel Shields, suggests that whereas the principal act of love of friendship is "to will good to someone," the essence of the love is union of affection. The suggestion seems premised on a reading of the distinction of love of friendship and love of concupiscence as a distinction of two acts. I hold that this is not the essence of the distinction. See Shields, "Will," 114, n. 5 and Shields, "Ultimate Ends," 597.
74 By contrast, see Sherwin, *By Knowledge*, 93ff.
75 See Sherwin, *By Knowledge*, 156, citing *ST* 2-2.25.7.
76 See Nicolas, 24.
77 See Nicolas, 10.

ment. Third, the preceding two points take on their dramatic seriousness when one considers the final outcomes of created persons, salvation and damnation. These outcomes are hardly neutral; they are radically opposed. Sinners should be loved insofar as they are men "capable of beatitude." However, insofar as they are sinners laden with fault, they should be hated as enemies of God. This hate is ordered to their conversion, of course, insofar as such conversion is possible.[78] The damned, however, are no longer capable of beatitude but forever committed to wickedness.[79] Hence, insofar as they are sinners, there is nothing left but to hate them as enemies of God. God Himself loves the damned only in a certain respect.[80] This hatred is far from the malice that delights in punishment for its own sake. Rather, this hatred is rooted in love of justice and right, whereby one wills that the evil of fault be countered by righteous punishment, even eternally.[81] In short, God's friend does not have perfect love for any whom he knows to be damned; he loves such only in a certain respect (*secundum quid*).[82] This "limit" case reveals the operative structure of love for created persons, operative before the end of the ages. Loving my neighbor properly, for Aquinas, requires that I will his good (love of concupiscence) for his own sake (love of friendship).

Clearly, the distinction is applicable with regard to love of created persons for created persons. Is this the limit of its applicability? Can its use be extended? Indeed it can, and with great analytical benefit for our study of the problem of love.[83] First, we can apply this distinction to our love for God.[84] When we love God, we will His good, by a love of concupiscence, for Him, whom we love with love of friendship. Understandably, one might counter that God *is* His own goodness. Thus, in our love of God, is not the distinction between love of friendship and love of concupiscence irrelevant? The objection bears on an important truth: the simplicity of God. Still, human love is a human act. We love according to our mode of loving, rooted in our mode of knowing. It is connatural for us to love in

---

[78] See *ST* 2-2.25.6.
[79] See *DC* 8, ad 9.
[80] See *Sent.* 3.32.1.2.
[81] See *ST* 2-2.25.6, ad 3.
[82] See *ST* 2-2.25.11 and also *Sent.* 3.28.1.5. On the topic, see Bujo, 178ff and 186.
[83] Nicolas agrees in principle with this claim (see Nicolas, 28).
[84] Shields inclines to reject the application for understandable reasons. See Shields, "Will," 129, n. 58. My argument has to do with the human modality of love, especially in its pilgrim state and as targeting pilgrims. In its heavenly state and as targeting God, perhaps the distinction melts into identity.

this twofold respect. Hence, we love God in this twofold way, even though we correctly judge that He is not distinct from His attainment of goodness but is His own perfection. We find an analogy to this situation in our use of divine names. We attribute several pure perfections to God, signifying them non-synonymously, though judging them to target the one simple essence of God.[85] Were we, on account of divine simplicity, to use but one name for God, we would not so much exalt Him in praise as render our own appreciation of Him impoverished, for not one of our concepts can bear all the weight of even the limited praise we are able to render Him.[86] We must praise Him with many names, as with timbrel and harp. So, too, we must love Him in our manner of loving, rejoicing that He is His own Perfection. This side of the grave, we cannot escape this situation. Perhaps beatific charity tells another story, the words of which we must find in the signs still legible this side of death.

I offer the following additional defense of the foregoing contention. Aquinas finds no objection in speaking of *God* as having a twofold love of Himself. He writes:

> An act of love always tends to two things, namely, to the good that one wills for someone and to the one for whom he wills the good. For this is properly what it means to love someone: to will good to him. Wherefore, when someone loves himself, he wills himself good and thus seeks to be united with this good insofar as it is possible. For this reason is love called a *unitive force* even in God, but without composition, for the good that he wills for himself is not other than himself, who is good by his essence.[87]

If Thomas can speak of God loving Himself with a twofold love, all the more does he justify speaking of man as loving God in this way. "[A]n act of love *always* tends to two things." We are not dealing with two distinct acts but with one complex act targeting two goods.[88]

Of course, when it comes to the holy person loving simply, the twofold dimension of this love becomes simplified, dissolves into one: a pure love of God.[89] Perhaps it is this deeper vision that is contemplated by those who

---

[85] See *ST* 1.13.3–4 and 12. A pure perfection is a concept the definition of which includes no imperfection.
[86] Thus, Moses Maimonides gives us a terribly impoverished theology of God.
[87] *ST* 1.20.1, ad 3 (my translation).
[88] On the unity of the act, discernible as twofold by intelligence, see Nicolas, 24.
[89] See Nicolas, 28.

speak of a "simple regard" for another. Still, if we would for a moment distinguish in order, returning to the real, to unite, it will be useful to retain the distinction in discussing precisely what kind of love we are dealing with, to whom it is directed, and for what good.

Reasons for Divergent Readings of the Distinction

If the distinction so read has such great explanatory power, why has it so often been missed, neglected, or simply treated as one possible reading of Aquinas's thought? In fact, there are numerous grounds for divergent readings.

First, in light of their usage in Christian tradition, the isolated terms "friendship" and "concupiscence" evoke certain evaluative judgments spontaneously. The former calls to mind something virtuous, and the latter, something vicious. Catholic tradition uses the term "concupiscence" to signify acts of the not-so-spiritual sensitive appetite. Moreover, the tradition even uses the term to signify the disordered inclinations of fallen man, anterior to choice.

Second, close reading of Thomas's texts is a reason. Indeed, this is quite a good reason for divergent readings, and no quibble can be made against it. My defense of my option has to do with a judgment that the way Thomas renders it in his mature *ex professo* treatment yields a great and dexterous analytical tool for addressing the problem of love. In his corpus, however, Thomas not seldomly uses the terms in isolation from one another, making the loves appear separable.[90] However, a careful reading of Aquinas should not consist simply in collations of seemingly overt meanings. Insofar as the historical question is the object, Aquinas's mind and judgment, at this stage or that, to be sure, should be of primary concern. Further, it is not impossible in many cases to assert that, at some given stage of development, Thomas would entirely concur with a more precise expression than he gives in a given text. An isolated mention of "love of friendship" might tempt one to think, mistakenly, that Aquinas in that passage judges such love able to exist without love of concupiscence for the proper good of the beloved. Similarly, an isolated use of "love of concupiscence" may seem to obscure its necessary dependence upon love of friendship, for when it is so employed, it almost invariably *happens* to refer to oneself. In cases such as these, we can follow Thomas's judgment as he looks at *things*, adverting to

---

[90] See, for instance, *ST* 1-2.28.3 and 4. Most notably, there is *In Ioan.* 15.4, par. 2036. Of course, earlier in his career this is more pointed. See esp. *Sent.* 2.3.4.

the unstated qualification that love of concupiscence belongs inseparably to love of friendship, whether for oneself or for another. In short, we may ascribe a justifiable economy to Thomas's expressions.[91]

Third, Thomas's predecessors read the distinction as indicative of love's direction. William of Auxerre, apparently among the early users of the distinction, considered love of concupiscence to be self-regarding, albeit not immoral.[92] For St. Albert the Great, Thomas's master, "friendship tends towards another; whereas, concupiscence, which is natural love, always tends towards the proper good of the subject."[93] Albert denied that, properly speaking, there is love of friendship for oneself: "Similarly, it was not well said that someone may love himself with a love of friendship, since friendship is a relation requiring a diversity between the lover and the beloved."[94] A. Stévaux comments, "Until St. Thomas, friendship was conceived especially as a disinterested benevolence, as the desire to please another and to obtain his good. St. Albert failed to see how to reconcile this disinterested friendship with the tendency to possess God."[95] Other contemporaries considered the desire to possess God to be a love of concupiscence that sinfully orders God to the creature.

Fourth, St. Thomas explicitly embraces divergent uses of the distinc-

---

[91] The discussions of *amor concupiscentiae* in *ST* 1-2.28.3 and 4 presuppose *amor amicitiae* for self. Thomas at times indicates that love of wine is rooted in love of self (see *ST* 1-2.77.4, ad 3) and explicitly refers to love of self (see *Sent.* 3.29.3 and *ST* 1.60.5). Conversely, Thomas implicitly includes in *amor amicitiae* for a friend an *amor concupiscentiae* for the friend's good. Richard Egenter points out a number of the difficulties with the terminology and Thomas's use of it. Richard Egenter, *Gottesfreundschaft: Die Lehre von der Gottesfreundschaft in der Scholastik und Mystik des 12. und 13. Jahrhunderts* (Augsburg: Dr. Benno Filser Verlag, 1928), 19–21.

Egenter contends that the act of love should be defined solely as the *"complacentia"* in the beloved that is worked by the (natural or freely chosen) transformation of the appetite. Love of friendship and love of concupiscence follow upon this *complacentia* (*Gottesfreundschaft*, 21). I prefer to characterize the differentiation of loves as two aspects of the one love that is the *complacentia* regarding the beloved.

[92] See Guy Mansini, *"Duplex Amor,"* 138–51.

[93] H.-D. Simonin, "La doctrine de l'amour naturel de Dieu d'après le Bienheureux Albert le Grand," *Revue thomiste* 36 (1931): 363. See Albert the Great, *Commentarii in III Sententiarum*, vol. 28, *Opera omnia* (Paris: Ludovicum Vivès, 1894), 3.27.1.1, ad 3, p. 509.

[94] Albert the Great, *Commentarii in Sent.*, 3.28.1.2, in *Commentarii*,537. See also Schockenhoff, *Bonum Hominis*, 492n67.

[95] A. Stévaux, "La doctrine de la charité dans les Commentaires des Sentences de saint Albert, de saint Bonaventure et de saint Thomas," *Ephemerides theologicae Lovanienses* 24 (1948): 81.

tion in various texts.⁹⁶ In *Sent.*, Book 2, he distinguishes the two as though they are distinct and separable acts: "These two," Thomas writes, "if we consider them diligently, differ according as two acts of the will, namely, to tend towards (*appetere*) which is of something not possessed and to love, which is of something had, as Augustine claims." Note also that in this citation he links concupiscence with desire and love of friendship with love of that which is already united with the lover, in accordance with his immature reading of love. Further, Thomas reads the distinction directionally: "There is a love of concupiscence by which someone desires to covet that which is good for himself in a certain way." This love turns back towards the lover. In contrast, "there is a love of friendship whereby someone loves something in another, or a similitude of that which he has within himself, willing the good of him with whom he has a similitude."⁹⁷ This text witnesses Thomas subscribing to three positions that diverge from his later *ex professo* wielding of the distinction.

In rough drafts for Book 3 of the *Sent.*, Thomas bases the distinction upon the directional tendency of love. An early draft of *Sent.* 3.27.2.1, corp., states:

> Now love sometimes is terminated at the lover himself, and other things that are outside himself he turns toward himself, . . . as with those things that he is said to love on account of delight or profit. Therefore, he does not properly love these things, but himself, actually desiring these things for himself. Because of this,

---

⁹⁶ Mansini contends that early in his career, Aquinas followed the lead of the tradition (see Mansini, "*Duplex Amor*," 151–59). Stévaux, pp. 81ff, maintains that Thomas renders this distinction in two different ways in the *Sent.* In the first way, the loves are conceived as two distinct acts, each of which treats its object differently. Love of concupiscence treats its object as a means to some further end and love of friendship treats its object as an end in itself. Since one and the same object ought not to be treated as both means and end, a lover cannot love the same object with both loves.

So, love of concupiscence for God subordinates God to a creature since the good perceived in God is referred to the good of some other being. In a second way, however, the loves are still seen as two distinct acts with two different directions. But they are no longer seen as incompatible ways of treating the same object. Love of concupiscence refers to the lover's desire to have his beloved present. Since the nature of friendship naturally includes this desire, love of concupiscence is not incompatible with love of friendship. In fact, genuine friendship implies this desire. As regards Thomas's use of the distinction in the *Sent.*, Stévaux's analysis is astute. Chapter Five shall return to this point about the nature of friendship implying desire for the friend's presence.

⁹⁷ *Sent.* 2.3.4. For a discussion of this, see Mansini, "*Duplex Amor*," 151–59.

such love is called concupiscence for those things."⁹⁸

According to this reading, it is not possible to refer love of concupiscence to the perfecting good one wills for another person. An early draft of *Sent.* 3.29.1.4 contains a similar description: "The consideration of reward pertains to the love by which someone desires a good for himself and turns it toward himself—love of concupiscence."⁹⁹ Worthy of note is that these manuscripts contain corrections atop each page upon which the previous two citations are found. Twice, Thomas notes: "to be corrected: regarding this, that there can be concupiscence also towards another."¹⁰⁰ Thomas shows his genius in progressing beyond the traditional usage of the terms to forge his own meaning in order to interpret human love more accurately. Still, the *Sent.* does not explicitly maintain the inseparability of the two loves in every act of love.¹⁰¹

Fifth, sometimes Thomas describes love of concupiscence as targeting useful and pleasurable goods.¹⁰² Thus, it might seem that one would not have love of concupiscence for virtue and true happiness. Love of concupiscence would be only for temporary goods.

Sixth, even in later works Thomas falls into earlier usages. Cases abound. Two interesting ones can be noted. In treating mutual indwelling as an effect of love, Thomas presents a subtle analysis that is not quite clear. At any rate, he seems to link "love of concupiscence" with a desire to be with the beloved or with his goods. There is no connotation of vicious friendship. At the same time, he seems to state that we will good things

---

⁹⁸ P.-M. Gils, "Textes inédits de S. Thomas: Les premières rédactions du *Scriptum super Tertio Sententiarum*," *Revue des sciences philosophiques et théologiques* 46 (1962): 612.
⁹⁹ Gils, 614.
¹⁰⁰ Gils, 613. Gils contends, in n. 134, that the phrase "*de hoc quod*" is Thomas's characteristic seal, as evident from other manuscripts. See also Gils, 615.
¹⁰¹ Love of concupiscence is, at best, described as "included" in friendship. See *Sent.* 3.28.1 and 2. Mansini holds, on the contrary, that *Sent.* 3.29.3 introduces the terminal, non-terminal nature of the distinction of loves. He concludes that this makes it "possible to conceive of them, not as taking place in two distinct acts, but in one act of concupiscently loving X for the sake of Y loved terminally as a friend: the love of concupiscence is included in the love of friendship, as the texts from distinction 28 had it." Mansini, "*Duplex Amor*," 163; see also 159–63. It should be noted that distinction 29 does provide the possibility to conceive the two loves in one act, but Thomas does not explicitly express it this way.
¹⁰² Bujo lists numerous texts in which he perceives *amor concupiscentiae* to target the useful or pleasurable good, rather than the honorable good (see Bujo, 154n88).

for our friend *by* love of friendship.[103] By the standard developed two questions earlier, these locutions are imprecise. More importantly, they can be rendered more precise by recourse to that earlier treatment in *ST* 1-2.26.

In another case, Thomas seems to base the distinction upon the possession or non-possession of the object of love. The analysis occurs in an inquiry about the causes of love. Thomas affirms that likeness is a cause of love, but he distinguishes two types of likeness, potential and actual. He writes,

> Likeness, properly speaking, is a cause of love. But it must be observed that likeness between things is twofold. One kind of likeness arises from each thing having the same [thing in act]: for example, two things possessing the quality of whiteness are said to be alike. Another kind of likeness arises from one thing having potentially and by way of inclination, [that] which the other has actually: thus we may say that a heavy body existing outside its proper place is like another heavy body that exists in its proper place: or again, according as potentiality bears a resemblance to its act; since act is contained, in a manner, in the potentiality itself.
>
> Accordingly, the first kind of likeness causes love of friendship or [benevolence]. For the very fact that two men are alike, having, as it were, one form, makes them to be, in a manner, one in that form: thus two men are one thing in the species of humanity, and two white men are one thing in whiteness. Hence, the affections of one tend to the other, as being one with him; and he wishes good to him as to himself. But the second kind of likeness causes love of concupiscence, or friendship founded on usefulness or pleasure: because whatever is in potentiality, as such, has the desire for its act; and it takes pleasure in its realization, if it be a sentient and cognitive being.[104]

Recognition of potential likeness gives rise to desire to seek actual likeness. A lover having actual likeness with another acquiesces in the good of the other.

Has the Augustinian dictum—love, properly speaking, is of that which is already had—implicitly crept in again? Does this article, *ST*

---

[103] See *ST* 1-2.28.2.
[104] *ST* 1-2.27.3.

1-2.27.3, relegate love of concupiscence to merely self-regarding love? Some scholars read the article in this way, suggesting that pure love of others, which they call love of friendship, is possible only when the lover already has the object of his love.[105] I argue to the contrary. First, above all evidence to the contrary, there is Thomas's most direct and precise treatment of the distinction only a few articles earlier, in *ST* 1-2.26.4.[106] Second, there is a significant difference between *Sent.* 2.3.4 and *ST* 1-2.27.3. In the former, Thomas opines that desire precedes love because love itself is possible only when the beloved is possessed. Accordingly, when early in his career Thomas distinguishes love of concupiscence and love of friendship as two separable acts, he treats them as desire and love, respectively. What he there terms desire, or love of concupiscence, he restricts to self-directed appetite. The treatment in the *Summa*, however, is embedded in a context in which Thomas consistently holds that love precedes desire in the genetic order.[107] There can be love for an object, whether that object is actually possessed or not possessed. If in *ST* 1-2.27.3 Thomas limits love of friendship only to those objects that are already possessed, this would, to my knowledge, constitute one of the only two late exceptions to his mature teaching.[108] Careful inspection shows that in *ST* 1-2.27.3 he does not refer the distinction of loves to the possession or non-possession of the beloved object itself. Rather, he here refers this distinction to the actual or potential similitude to that which forms the basis of some given love for some given person. So, the beloved person can be loved whether or not he is really present to the lover.[109] However, the type of love that can at that moment be actualized depends upon whether or not the attractive good in the beloved is at that moment only potentially or already actually possessed by the lover. If a poor man loves a rich man on the basis of the wealth the latter possesses, the poor man's love for the rich man can be only love of concupiscence, based upon love of friendship for himself. Even if the wealthy man is present, the poor man can love him-as-wealthy only by love of concupiscence. However, if a virtuous man loves another virtu-

---

[105] See Bujo, *Die Begründung*, 156.
[106] A summary of this article appears at the beginning of this chapter, and a detailed analysis follows below.
[107] See *ST* 1-2.25.2.
[108] The other exception regards charity and will be treated in Chapter Four.
[109] Real presence or real union with the beloved good (*unio realis*) is distinct from any merely notional presence or presence of similitude. Real presence consists in the actual possession of the beloved good through the apprehensive powers. Because "possession" of a person has negative connotations, we use the term real presence.

ous man for his virtue, a love of friendship is possible, whether or not the friend is really present to the lover.[110] Crucially, this love of friendship is inseparable from the love of concupiscence for the friend's own virtue (and health and life, etc.). And this love of concupiscence for the friend's virtue remains, even when the friend already has virtue. In short, it does not seem that the Augustinian dictum has returned.

One final note about *ST* 1-2.27.3 in anticipation of Chapter Four. Some consider this text to promote the idea of a disinterested love of others that does not regard love of self. As I read the text, it supports the notion that love of self is a necessary basis for love of others. As one wills good to oneself, so one wills good to others. If one loves but does not have a good that another person has, then the love one has for the other person *with regard to this good* consists in love of concupiscence for one's own perfecting good. One may simultaneously love him with love of friendship as well. For instance, one may hope for a tennis racket or a drink from a friend whom one already loves with love of friendship. When, however, one loves another for his own sake, this love is still rooted in self-love, for one loves the other *as* one loves oneself. That is, the lover takes the other person as one with himself and thus wills him to enjoy the good that he himself also has. So, that actual possession of similitude seems requisite for love of another only reaffirms the genetic priority of self-love over love of neighbor. In short, the cause of love is not "objective good" simply speaking, but the good for which one has a similitude or aptitude.

Finally, to distinguish the loves on the basis of the presence or absence of the beloved does not help one to analyze the problem of pilgrim man's love for God. First, both Thomas and his critics admit that it is possible, with the help of grace, for pilgrim man to love God for His own sake. Since such a man does not yet enjoy God's beatifying presence, he still has the divine beatitude only in potency. Nevertheless, he is capable of a genuine love of friendship for God. Second and more importantly, even though a man already enjoys or possesses some good, he still loves that good with love of concupiscence. A healthy man, for instance, still loves health by love of concupiscence. Stable health may mask the love's presence or allow it to remain only as a habit, but the love's constant presence is the basis upon which desire stirs in the event of illness. The presence or absence of the beloved to the lover, then, is not the primary criterion by which to

---

[110] Of course, the friendship depends upon and tends toward some interaction. But the interaction, which the lover wishes by a love of concupiscence for himself, does not need always to be present.

determine the relationship between love of God and love of self.

Conclusion

To distinguish the love of friendship and the love of concupiscence in the precise sense laid out above yields great explanatory power for a study of the problem of love. All created persons have a substance that is not their fruition. Truly to love such a person is not simply to will that they exist, but to will that they flourish. Thus, the love of a created person by its nature has a dual structure of the person himself *as* flourishing. The dual structure of this love is discernible in a creature's love of God because the mode of human loving follows the mode of human knowing, and we know the Simple God in a complex manner. Aquinas does not shrink from applying this dual structure of love even to God's love as we understand it.

The distinction of love of friendship and love of concupiscence helps one express the ultimate object of some act of love, self or other. It also helps one identify the kind of love rendered, since according to the diverse kinds of love there are diverse kinds of goods. More precisely, since true love of another includes all the relevant licit goods, true love of another regards all such goods in proper order: beatitude, virtues, health, the means of living well, etc. Primordially, the very existence of the friend is always a foundational object. However, existence-as-substance is not for its own sake but for the sake of existence-in-the-state-of-fruition. Love of non-subsistent objects is not evil but an ingredient to true love of created persons. The question is, what goods and in what order? So, the problem of love requires comparison between love of friendship for oneself and love of friendship for God. Correct assessment of this relationship requires, in turn, accurate understanding of love of friendship and love of concupiscence as two inseparable aspects of every act of love. Before turning to this question in Chapter Four, we must now turn to the twofold character of beatitude and the love thereof.

CHAPTER 3

Twofold Beatitude and the Love Thereof

IN HIS TREATMENT OF MAN'S LAST END, Thomas draws upon an Aristotelian distinction regarding the end: the good object to be attained and the attainment of that object. God, of course, is the good object. Spiritual operation—knowing and loving—is the attainment of God. In this chapter, I first treat the twofold end and then examine how this end is loved.

THE TWOFOLD END

Object and Attainment

As is obvious, man is not his own end but tends towards his end. For Aquinas, man tends towards his perfecting and crowning good, which is happiness.[1] The poverty of man makes it obvious that this crowning good is not a product to be produced by human action but an existing good to be attained by some operation.[2] What is that good, and what is that operation?

Aquinas's famous analysis in Question 2 of the *Prima secundae* involves an inductive examination of existing goods as possible candidates for the object of happiness. The first six articles argue, in Augustinian fashion, against the judgment of the world: neither money, nor food, nor honor, nor glory, nor power, nor health, nor pleasure is man's last end. The seventh and eight articles argue positively that nothing but God can be man's last end as object. The human soul itself cannot be the last end, since it begins in potentiality or poverty. Neither can any power or habit or act of the soul be the last end as object, since "man's appetite, otherwise the will, is for the universal good." However, "any good inherent to the soul is

---

[1] See *ST* 1-2.1.5, 8.
[2] See *SCG* 3.18.

a participated good."³ Indeed, since the object of the will is the universal good, nothing but God can be man's last end, since the universal good "is to be found, not in any creature, but in God alone.... Therefore God alone constitutes man's happiness."⁴

Nevertheless, in a certain way, all creatures are ordered to God as to an end.⁵ We must identify how, precisely, man is to attain God. Simply by existing, man is not happy and thus has not yet attained God. Some created change must take place in man for him to attain God.⁶ Aquinas argues that this change must be an operation of man. An operation is a "second act," the further actualization of a being through one of its powers. An operation is a being's dynamic actualization in relation to something else; the operation either produces or attains something else. As an actualization of the thing, an ultimate operation is the thing's flourishing. Man's flourishing or happiness, then, is the operation whereby he attains God. It is the end by which (*finis quo*) man attains God as object (*finis cuius*).⁷ But what is this operation?

Attainment as Act of Intellect

Clearly, the operation that attains God cannot be in the sensitive part of man. The powers of sense regard only corporeal objects, but God is not a body.⁸ Of course, in the consummated heavenly life itself, man will certainly have acts of sensation because he will have a glorified body. However, such acts cannot attain God Himself and so none of these can be the very operation that is happiness itself. Only the spiritual powers of man can attain God.

This brings us to the fundamental question. Do we attain God as beatitude through an operation of the intellect or an operation of the will? Aquinas offers a classic argument against the thesis that the formal attainment of beatitude is an act of the will. Three primordial movements of the will parallel the three primordial passions: love, desire, and delight (or joy). Love regards the good whether present or absent. Hence, love cannot be the attainment of the good. Desire arises in the absence of the loved good; hence, neither can desire be the attainment of the good. Delight

---

³ *ST* 1-2.2.7.
⁴ *ST* 1-2.2.8.
⁵ See *SCG* 3.17–18 and *ST* 1-2.1.8.
⁶ See *ST* 1-2.3.1.
⁷ See *ST* 1-2.1.8.
⁸ See *ST* 1-2.3.3.

arises in the presence of the loved good and thus presupposes this presence or attainment of the good. To illustrate his contention, Thomas draws on love of sensible goods:

> This is evidently the case in regard to sensible ends. For if the acquisition of money were through an act of the will, the covetous man would have it from the very moment that he wished for it. But at that moment it is far from him; and he attains it, by grasping it in his hand, or in some like manner; and then he delights in the money got. And so it is with an intelligible end. For at first we desire to attain an intelligible end; we attain it, through its being made present to us by an act of the intellect; and then the delighted will rests in the end when attained.[9]

If none of the primordial movements of the will can be the attainment of beatitude, no movement of the will can be attainment of beatitude. Formal happiness must be an operation of the intellect.

If happiness is an operation of the intellect, is it an act of the intellect as speculative or as practical? As the ultimate end, beatitude cannot be an act of the practical intellect. An act of the practical intellect, or an act of the intellect as practical, is ordered to some other action or some product. God, however, cannot be produced by human action. Further, what is ordered to some other action is not the ultimate end; so, the knowledge of God, insofar as it constitutes the ultimate operation, cannot be ordered to some further human action.[10] Hence, it is by an operation of the speculative intellect considering truth for its own sake that man attains the existing God.

Notwithstanding the primacy of the intellect in attainment of the end, the will's acts are crucial. Volitional acts are necessary for the journey towards attainment of beatitude, and they play a major role in what one might call the blessed life in general.[11] Beatitude, or happiness, is twofold,

---

[9] *ST* 1-2.3.4. See also *SCG* 3.26, par. 8 and *Quodl.* 8.9.1.
[10] See *ST* 1-2.3.5 and *SCG* 3.18.
[11] When Thomas speaks of the beatific vision, he declares it to consist in an act of the intellect, which is simply consummated by the will. He has been criticized for this, yet there are two important considerations to make in regard to his position on the intellectual nature of the vision. First, he includes in heavenly life much more than the beatific vision itself, even though this is central. For instance, heavenly life also consists in acts of love and joy. Secondly, his teaching on beatitude should be taken in light of his

God and the act of the intellect by which one somehow attains God, which attainment is prepared by and flowers in volitional acts: "So, therefore, the essence of happiness consists in an act of the intellect: but the delight that results from happiness pertains to the will. In this sense Augustine says (*Conf.* x. 23) that happiness is joy in truth, because to wit, joy itself is the consummation of happiness."[12]

EXCURSUS ON THE QUESTION OF DESIRE FOR THE SUPERNATURAL END

As many are aware, lively debate concerning the natural desire for the beatific vision has recently been reignited.[13] Diverse judgments concerning

---

teaching on charity, which, he says, is perfected in heaven.

Recently, Joseph Stenberg defends what he calls a "combined account": "Aquinas does not fall into the vision-alone camp, but rather . . . defends an intellectualist version of the combined account. . . . I mean to say that he holds that heavenly happiness consists both in the vision of God *and* delight in God, but—unlike some who think that happiness consists in this combination—he unequivocally affirms that the vision is more important than the delight" (Joseph Stenberg, "Aquinas on the Relationship between the Vision and Delight in Perfect Happiness," *American Catholic Philosophical Quarterly* 90 [2016]: 667). I agree with Stenberg that heavenly life itself is richer than an intellectual act. It consists also in volitional acts, in bodily acts, in friendships, etc.

[12] *ST* 1-2.3.4.

[13] The work that recently sparked renewed discussion of this issue is Lawrence Feingold, *The Natural Desire*. For some recent literature in English since Feingold's work, see Serge-Thomas Bonino, ed., *Surnaturel: A Controversy at the Heart of Twentieth-Century Thomistic Thought*, trans. Robert Williams and rev. Matthew Levering (Ave Maria, FL: Sapientia Press, 2009); David Braine, "The Debate between Henri de Lubac and His Critics," *Nova et Vetera* 6 (2008): 543–89; Yilun Cai, "*Desiderium naturale vivendi Deum* in Robert Bellarmine's Commentary on *Summa theologiae*," *Gregorianum* 95 (2014): 511–34; Christopher Cullen, "The Natural Desire for God and Pure Nature: A Debate Renewed," *American Catholic Philosophical Quarterly* 86 (2012): 705–30; Connor Cunningham, "*Natura Pura*, the Invention of the Anti-Christ: A Week with No Sabbath," *Communio* 37 (2010): 243–54 ; David Grumett, "De Lubac, Grace, and the Pure Nature Debate," *Modern Theology* 31 (2015):123–46; Nicholas Healy, "Henri de Lubac on Nature and Grace: A Note on Some Recent Contributions to the Debate," *Communio* 35 (2008): 535–64; Reinhard Hütter, "Aquinas on the Natural Desire for the Vision of God: A Relecture of *Summa contra Gentiles* III, c. 25 *après* Henri de Lubac," *The Thomist* 73 (2009): 523–91; Steven A. Long, *Natura Pura*: On the Recovery of Nature in the Doctrine of Grace (New York: Fordham University Press, 2010); Christopher J. Malloy, "De Lubac on Natural Desire: Difficulties and Antitheses," *Nova et Vetera* 9 (2011): 567–624; Malloy, "Rahner's Supernatural Existential: What *is* It?" *Freiburger Zeitschrift für Philosophie und Theologie* 63 (2016): 402–21; Ryan McAnnally-Linz, "Extrinsic Grace and *Eccentric Existence*," *Modern*

this difficult topic are significant for but not dispositive of the interpretative claims I am advancing in this monograph.[14] As I shall argue below, there are various ways in which the one ultimate end, supernatural union with God, is loved. The relations among these loves and their relations with the love of God for His own sake constitute the subject of inquiry in the present monograph. Diverse positions on the matter of the natural desire are not necessarily correlated with diverse interpretations of Aquinas on these relations. At any rate, a brief word on my current position on the issue, apart from Thomas's own texts, is in order.

God orders things wisely. Thus, He intends that His creatures attain their proper ends. While each thing has its proper end, only rational things (angels and men) are capable of appreciating the end as an end, as constituting a meaningful existence. Thus, only rational things that fail to attain the end can be said to have a meaningless existence—meaningless, that is, for them. In the order of providence, their existence exhibits God's patience and justice. Now, because God orders things wisely, there must correspond to human nature considered as such a natural end that is (a) naturally attainable and (b) meaningful or sufficiently finalizing. Only thus is a man, *qua* man, meaningfully made; only thus is he wisely made. Such an end cannot be the beatific vision, which requires grace for its attainment. If one were to suppose, on the other hand, that the only end that could bring sufficient meaning to man, considered as such, were the vision of God, the following dilemma would arise. Grace would be either owed or not owed. If it were not owed, rational creatures would be *per se*, apart from sin, unable to attain their ends. Thus, their existence would be essentially meaningless and causative of despair; they would be made unwisely, made to no end, unless rescued from this meaninglessness by unowed grace. This position portrays God as arbitrary and whimsical, and it portrays nature as essentially miserable and even wretched. On at least

---

Theology 31 (2015): 178–94; Guy Mansini, "The Abiding Theological Significance of Henri de Lubac's *Surnaturel*," *The Thomist* 73 (2009): 593–619; John Milbank, *The Suspended Middle: Henri de Lubac and the Debate Concerning the Supernatural* (Grand Rapids, MI: Eerdmans, 2005); Bernard Mulcahy, *Aquinas's Notion of Pure Nature and the Christian Integralism of Henri de Lubac: Not Everything is Grace* (New York: Peter Lang, 2011); Edward T. Oakes, "Nature and Grace," chap. in *A Theology of Grace in Six Controversies* (Grand Rapids: Eerdmans, 2016), 1–46; Oakes, "The Surnaturel Controversy: A Survey and a Response," *Nova et Vetera* 9 (2011): 625–56; and Andrew Dean Swafford, *Nature and Grace: A New Approach to Thomistic Ressourcement* (Eugene, OR: Pickwick Publications, 2014).

[14] See, for instance, Shields, "Will," 115n9.

these counts, it is unacceptable. On the other hand, if grace were owed, it would no longer be grace. This position is heretical. Since neither horn of this dilemma is acceptable, it must be the case that there corresponds to human nature considered as such a natural end as above described.

There are, of course, a number of well-known texts in Aquinas's corpus that at first sight suggest the supposition that entails the dilemma. Nevertheless, a reasonable argument against reading them in this way can be made. First, the dilemma just presented rests on Thomas's own principles concerning God's wisdom and justice. These lead me to judge that Thomas would reject the thesis that there is an innate, unconditional desire for beatific vision. Second, the same set of principles indicates positively that there corresponds to human nature as such a natural end. Further, Thomas presumes this correspondence as causally relevant in our actual world in his postulation of Limbo.[15] Third, there are, as Steven Long puts it, "*two* sets of texts" in Thomas's works. One set explicitly affirms a natural end corresponding to human nature as such and thus contradicts the supposition.[16] Fourth, there are alternative exegetical options consonant with Thomas's principles for almost every text of Aquinas that appears to promote the notion of an innate desire for beatific vision. By contrast, no such options are available for the "second set" of texts so importantly rediscovered this century by Lawrence Feingold. A fifth reason anticipates the treatment of charity to come. Thomas contends that charity is not a virtue of man *qua* man.[17] Rather, it is a virtue of man *qua* deified. The reason? Virtue is the good disposition of a nature. Thus, virtue has reference to nature. Sailing is not the virtue of a worm, while burrowing in dirt is. Dribbling is not the virtue of a whale. If the end T of some habit X surpasses the end to which a given thing Q is naturally ordered by its essence, then Q's essence must be further actualized or elevated so as to be proportioned to T before X can be a virtue for Q. Now, charity is a love properly divine and is thus not a virtue of man as man but of deified man. For this reason, Thomas insists that charity is not the deepest habit of sanctifying grace but a habit abiding in the will. The deep habit of sanctifying grace abides in the soul.[18]

---

[15] See *DM* 5.3.

[16] Steven Long, "On the Loss, and the Recovery, of Nature as a Theonomic Principle: Reflections on the Nature/Grace Controversy," *Nova et Vetera* 5 (2007): 137. The second set of texts includes the following: *ST* 1.62; *ST* 1-2.62; *ST* 1-2.110.3; *ST* 1-2.114.2; *ST* 2-2.4.7; *DM* 5; and *Super II Ad Corinth*., chap. 5, lect. 2, pars. 160f. The principles at stake are more important and lead to the claims made in the second set.

[17] See *ST* 1-2.110.3 and *DC* 2 ad 15.

[18] See *ST* 1-2.110.3–4.

Of course, through the knowledge of God attainable by nature, the desire to know God's essence spontaneously arises. Since it arises, it is elicited. Since it arises spontaneously, it is natural.[19] Thus, there is a natural elicited desire for knowledge of God's essence. Such a desire can in fact be fulfilled only by the beatific vision, which is a supernatural act. However, the formal object of said desire is God *as* source and end of creation. This formal object is not identifiable with God as supernatural friend. With this latter formality, man by his natural principles can have no contact. Further, the study of God as source and end, a contemplation that would constitute man's crowning good in the order of integral nature, is a freely chosen activity. As such, the desire thereof is moderated by what one judges concretely possible and prudent. Thus, the elicited natural desire for knowledge of God would be justly moderated by a virtuous person.[20]

Except for some remarks in the treatment of faith, the present monograph does not have space for further comment on this matter. Whereas a significant correction of my thesis on nature and grace would touch some claims in the present study, it would not undercut the edifice.

Love of the Twofold End

How the Twofold End Is Loved

How is this twofold end loved? Before all else, we should note that, for Thomas, "We love each thing that we love insofar as it is our good (*bonum nostrum*)."[21] The ultimate end, the vision of God, is indeed our good. Hence, it is lovable. Regarding its lovability, we should consider both the object attained and the attainment. First, let us consider the vision itself of God. How does the natural love of beatitude, as touched by grace of course, target the vision?[22] Vision is a human operation; as such, it inheres

---

[19] These twin contentions form a major theme in Feingold's *The Natural Desire to See God*.
[20] See *DM* 5.3.
[21] *DDN* 4.9, par. 406. See also *Sent.* 3.29.5 and 6; *SCG* 1.91, par. 4; *In Ioan.* 15.4; *ST* 1-2. 8.1; *DM* 16.2. There is a natural appetite for one's own good: *ST* 1-2.47.1. The end, towards which an agent tends, must be fitting (*conveniens*) for the agent (*SCG* 3.3). The begetter tends to beget the begotten on account of the similarity the begotten will have to the begetter (see *ST* 1.44.4, ad 2, and Bujo, 147–49).
[22] In raising this question, we need not find ourselves on one side of the nature-grace dispute concerning the natural desire. Our question regards the division of this love/desire into love of friendship and love of concupiscence. When a man is touched by grace, this natural desire is able to target the vision of God as an appetible good.

in the lover as his ultimate perfection *quo*. Vision is the operation by which (*quo*) he attains the loved object (*finis cuius*). This act of attainment can be called "created beatitude."[23] Clearly, a man loves this good for himself. So, he loves the vision as he loves all inhering perfections, with a love of concupiscence.

Second, we may consider God Himself as object of vision. God is both the object and the gratuitous source of this vision, which is beyond the natural capacity of created intellects. Now, according to Aquinas, the distinction between God as beatifying object and the vision or attainment of God does not indicate two distinct ends. The vision and God as object of vision comprise *one* final end. Thomas implies this in an article on the act of fruition in the last end. He writes, "The end is said in two ways. In one way, it is the thing itself; in another way, it is the attainment of the thing. To be sure, these are not two ends but one end, considered both in itself and as applied to another."[24] It has already been established that the vision itself is loved with a love of concupiscence. Therefore, *as* the object of vision, God is also loved with love of concupiscence.[25]

Objections and Replies

A number of objections can be raised. First, one can object to my reading of the just-cited passage, indicating that the passage regards *fruition*, not vision, since it continues as follows: "Therefore, God is the ultimate end as the ultimate thing sought, but fruition as the attainment of this ultimate end."[26] Now, fruition is an act of the appetitive power. As one might object, the passage regards the appetitive act and thus does not directly state that there is one end, God and the *vision* of God. Hence, the passage does not express the reading I suggest.

To the contrary, there are three arguments in favor of my reading. First, Aquinas is here using the word "fruition" somewhat loosely to stand for attainment (*adeptio*) of the object. This is clearly the case in the reply to the objection, wherein we find the phrase "fruition as the attainment."[27]

---

[23] See *ST* 1-2.3.1.
[24] *ST* 1-2.11.3, ad 3 (my translation).
[25] See *ST* 2-2.26.3, ad 3, and T.-M. Hamonic, "Dieu peut-il être légitimement convoité?," *Revue thomiste* 92 (1992): 239–66.
[26] See *ST* 1-2.11.3, ad 3 (my translation).
[27] Stenberg reads *ST* 1-2.11.3 and *ST* 1-2.5.2 as indicating that happiness itself consists partially in delight because such passages state that the one who delights more is happier. I would argue that, for Aquinas, the cause of greater delight in the order of being

We know from Thomas's own argumentation, however, that the end is formally attained not by the appetitive power but by the intellectual power. Thomas expresses, in the first article, the relationship between fruition and attainment. The objector argues that fruition is an act of the intellect since it implies delight and since, on the level of sensation, delight occurs in the acts of sensitive cognition. Thomas replies that one and the same ultimate end for man relates to two powers, the intellect and the will:

> Therefore, the vision itself of God, insofar as it is vision, is an act of the intellect. Insofar as it is a good and an end, it is an object of the will, and in this way it is the fruition of him. Thus, the intellect attains this end as the agent power, whereas the will does so as the power moving towards the end and enjoying the end already attained.[28]

This article treats the distinction between attainment and delight explicitly, grounding delight in attainment. The third article treats the distinction between the ultimate object that is the end and the attainment of the end. The third article rests on the achievement of the first article. Thus, in this third article, Thomas uses "fruition" to stand for attainment, which primarily and first is an intellectual operation. Such use is by no means anomalous in Aquinas.[29]

The passage continues: "Thus, as God is not one end and the fruition of God another end, so it is the same reason (*ratio*) for fruition by which we enjoy God and by which we enjoy the divine fruition. It is the same reason (*ratio*) concerning created beatitude, which consists in fruition."[30] If perhaps one disputes the preceding argument, here Aquinas explicitly calls created *beatitude* "fruition." This is obviously a loose use of the term "fruition" as standing for an intellectual operation. Third, Aquinas here speaks of our enjoying our divine fruition. Now, speaking precisely, one does not enjoy the enjoyment but the attainment, whether one's own attainment or another's attainment. So, there is no reason to speak of "enjoying (*fruimur*) fruition (*fruitio*)" unless the second use of the word "fruition" is taken loosely, for intellectual *attainment* of the end. Fourth, in stating that there

---

is greater happiness, which is an intellectual act. The cause of greater happiness in the order of moving is greater love. Thus, I do not find these passages to suggest what Stenberg finds in them. See Stenberg, "Vision," 671.

[28] *ST* 1-2.11.1, ad 1 (my translation).
[29] See, for instance, *SCG* 4.54, par. 5.
[30] *ST* 1-2.11.3, ad 3.

is one reason for enjoying God Himself and the attainment of God, Aquinas implies that the end itself, though twofold, is one. Hence, the very love by which one loves the vision is the love by which one loves the object of vision, namely, the love of concupiscence.

Another objection is that the twofold end admits further consideration. God is not simply the object of beatitude as *finis cuius* but more precisely the end *to which* or *to whom* (*finis cui*) we will the good. Now, an end *to whom* we will the good is the friend, loved by love of friendship. So, this objection would contend that the twofold end consists, on the one hand, in the *finis quo* or attainment, which we love with a love of concupiscence for ourselves. It consists, on the other hand, in the *finis cuius*, which is more precisely a *finis cui*, for whom we will the good by love of friendship.[31] I am thinking of the position of Santiago Ramírez, a profound thinker.[32] We find the following central, twofold thesis in his dense work. First, one loves created beatitude (attainment of God) with a love of concupiscence, ordered to oneself whom one loves with love of friendship. Second, one loves uncreated beatitude (God Himself) with love of friendship, ordering oneself to God by the love of concupiscence with which one loves oneself on account of God. In this portrait, the self (as spiritual) is as it were a medium between the act of created beatitude and the divine persons of uncreated beatitude.[33] More recently, Daniel Shields has suggested a similar line of thought:

> Aquinas holds not to common but to what I call "subordinated eudaimonism." According to Aquinas, one's own happiness, which it is impossible not to will, is a legitimate and directive end of virtuous moral action, but it is at the same time a *penultimate*

---

[31] Nicolas raises this as a question at Nicolas, 21.

[32] Adequate treatment of the work of Santiago Ramírez would require a monograph, something obviously not possible in this treatment here.

[33] See Santiago Ramírez, *De hominis beatitudine: In I–II "Summae theologiae" divi Thomae commentaria (QQ. I-V)*, ed. Victor Rodríguez, in vol. 3, pt. 2, *Edición de las obras completas de Santiago Ramírez* (Madrid: Instituto de filosofia "Luis Vives," 1972), 299–303. Ramírez distinguishes beatitude as either objective (uncreated object) or formal (created attainment). Formal or subjective beatitude is loved by a love of concupiscence, all other created goods being ordered to it (including grace and charity). As such, it is ordered to the person for whom it is loved; hence, formal beatitude is loved as the good one wills for oneself, loved by a love of friendship. Hence, I am the *finem cui* in this order. Ramírez is expounding upon Thomas's response to the second objection in *ST* 1-2.2.7. The objection contends that since beatitude is what is most loved for oneself, then one loves oneself more than beatitude. But what one wills for oneself (by a love of concupiscence) is a good of the soul. Therefore, beatitude consists in something created.

end for the virtuous individual, *subordinated* to God, the truly ultimate end.³⁴

According to Shields, happiness is a penultimate end, or an end in a certain respect, loved with a love of concupiscence. God Himself is the supreme end, loved with love of friendship.³⁵

This objection has some merit. Aquinas not only allows for a love of God above all things and for His own sake, but also stresses this love. Still, the following considerations pose difficulties for this line of thought, without necessarily refuting Ramírez's and Shields's concerns. One cannot but

---

Thomas's response is that there is a false comparison here between two loves.

What is loved by love of concupiscence cannot be compared (as being more or less loved) to what is loved by love of friendship. Ramírez comments that formal beatitude is loved as the greatest "thing" loved by love of concupiscence, but the self is not loved as the greatest person loved by love of friendship. Yet, formal beatitude is willed *for* the self. One cannot appeal to the saying "*propter quod unumquodque tale, et illud magis*" because, as Thomas argues (*ST* 1.87.2, ad 3), the axiom applies only to things of one order. It is better to say, simply, that one loves oneself with a more perfect kind of love (a love of friendship) than one loves formal beatitude. Since God, on the other hand, is perfect subsisting being, the ultimate good, and "of" the genus "person," He is the most lovable according to the love of friendship "and not, explicitly, in the love of concupiscence."

Ramírez then shows that the basis for the proper comparison is the relation between love of self and love of God. Each is a love of friendship. In the state of integral nature we would love God, objective beatitude, more than self. In the state of grace, we love God, objective supernatural beatitude, more than self. "[Objective] beatitude ... is loved by man absolutely, much more than the soul or self, in all ways, for a man loves himself on account of this [objective beatitude], as on account of the primary ultimate end *cuius gratia et cui*" (Ramírez, *De hominis beatitudine*, 301). Given this ultimate love of God for His own sake, given this ordering of oneself to God, therefore, one loves oneself as a kind of "thing" belonging to God. Indeed, one loves oneself by, as it were, a kind of love of concupiscence grounded in love of friendship for God: one wills oneself as conducive to the glory of God. The self forms a medium between objective and subjective beatitude: one wills subjective beatitude for oneself but oneself for God (see Ramírez, 303).

Again, in his treatment of charity, Ramírez argues as follows. Certainly, when one is speaking of charity and its acts, it must be the case that the formal object of charity, that for the reason of which (*finis cuius gratia*) we are loving, is God; further, God must be the ultimate person whom we love in charity, referring our entire selves to Him as to the end. Although we have a love of concupiscence for God grounded in our love of friendship for ourselves, yet if we are upright we order this love to the love of God for His own sake (i.e., to charity). See Ramírez, *De caritate: In II–II Summae theologiae Divi Thomae Expositio*, ed. Victor Rodríguez, in vol. 12, *Edición de las obras completas de Santiago Ramírez* (Salamanca: Editorial San Esteban, 1999), q. 27, art. 3, no. 844–46.

³⁴ See Shields, "Will," 115.
³⁵ See Shields, "Ultimate Ends," 583–84.

concur with these thinkers that the virtuous person loves God above all things, more intensely than oneself and for His own sake. The same person also seeks his own perfection. I would nonetheless suggest that in the love of self, the love of concupiscence for one's happiness is not simply a love of a subjective *act* isolated from its object; rather, the love of the act includes God in its scope, God loved as object of the act. Along my line of thought, it must be added that one ought further to order oneself to God as to the end *cui*. If Ramírez and Shields agree with this point, perhaps there is no disagreement.[36] I offer the following arguments in defense of the claim that God, as target of vision, is loved with a love of concupiscence.

First, in an early text Aquinas explicitly teaches this. A significant passage from the *Sent.* broaches the distinction between love of friendship and love of concupiscence in a sufficiently mature formulation:

> There are two ways in which something is lovable. One thing is loved by way of benevolence, when we will someone's good for his own sake. In this way we love friends, even if we should gain nothing from them. Another thing is loved by the love of concupiscence. This is either the good that is in us or that from which some good comes to us. In this way we love delight or the wine inasmuch as it brings delight.[37]

Aquinas then applies this distinction to how created beatitude is loved:

> Now, whatever is loved by the love of concupiscence cannot be the ultimate thing loved, since it is referred to the good of another, the good of the one, that is, for whom it is desired. But that which is loved by a love of friendship can be the ultimate thing loved. Therefore, the created beatitude which is in us is not loved except by the love of concupiscence. So we refer the love of it to ourselves. Consequently, we refer it to God, since we also ought to refer ourselves to God. Thus, created beatitude cannot be the ultimate thing loved.[38]

---

[36] Olver offers another thoughtful analysis of this matter. In editing my manuscript for publication, I noted that he recently makes this very contention against Shields. See Olver, "*Bonum*," 669 and 693.
[37] *Sent.* 4.49.1.2.1, ad 3.
[38] *Sent.* 4.49.1.2.1, ad 3.

Created beatitude is loved by a love of concupiscence, not by a love of friendship, for it is not a person but rather a person's state or act of perfection. Hence, we always love created beatitude with reference to the person it perfects, since we love the person *that* he may achieve his good. Created beatitude is the ultimate good we will for the one we love; so, in self-love, it is the ultimate perfection we will for ourselves:

> [Created beatitude] is, however, the ultimate thing desired (*concupitum*) because it is the greatest good that comes to us from our union to God. For this reason, it is said to be sought or desired on account of itself. For in both ways it includes something ultimate in those things that are loved by a love of concupiscence.[39]

So far, so clear. In what follows, Thomas shows that, at least at this stage of his career, he finds the object of created beatitude, for example, uncreated beatitude, to be loved with the same love with which created beatitude is loved: "For although God is desired (*concupiscatur*), it is the same to desire God and to desire the greatest of goods that come to us from God, just as it is the same to desire wine and the effect wine has on us, namely, delight."[40] A man loves God as his beatitude for himself because he loves himself with a love of friendship and his beatitude with a love of concupiscence. Hence, in the love of beatitude, God is not the *finis cui* although He is the *finis cui* of a higher love.

Second, I find Thomas to hold this doctrine later in his career as well. For example, in *SCG* 3.18, he writes,

> The effect must tend toward the end in the same way that the agent works for the end. Now, God, Who is the first agent of all things, does not act in such a way that something is attained by His action, but in such a way that something is enriched by His action. For He is not in potency to the possibility of obtaining something; rather He is in perfect act simply, and as a result He is a source of enrichment. So, things are not ordered to God as to an end *for which* (*cui*) something may be obtained, but rather so that they may attain Himself from Himself, according to their measure, since He is their end.[41]

---

[39] *Sent.* 4.49.1.2.1, ad 3.
[40] *Sent.* 4.49.1.2.1, ad 3.
[41] *SCG* 3.18, par. 5. The English is taken from Thomas Aquinas, *Summa Contra Gentiles,*

An end for which (*cui*) is an end to whom one wills good, as in the friend loved by love of friendship. Here, Aquinas is arguing that the order of a creature to its end is not the order of something to an end for which (*cui*). Thus, as ordered to beatitude, creatures are ordered to the object of beatitude as an end which (*finis cuius*) is to be attained but not an end for which (*cui*) good is willed. Again, we find the same contention in the *Prima pars*: "Natural love is said to be of the end itself, not however of the end to which (*cui*) someone wills good. Rather, it is of the good that someone wishes for himself and, as a consequence, to others insofar as they are one with him."[42] The love of beatitude is this natural love of the end. God as object of this natural love is loved with a love of concupiscence. We find a similar approach in the *Prima secundae*. In *ST* 1-2.3.1, Thomas refers to the twofold distinction of the ultimate end, the *finis cuius* and the *finis quo*. With regard to the *former*, he writes, "In one way [the end is] the thing itself which we desire to attain."[43] Note that it is the *finis cuius* that we *desire to attain* (*quam cupimus adipisci*). Now, that which we desire to attain is that which we love by a love of concupiscence. Indeed, the entire treatise on beatitude is a treatise on the human search for the ultimate end, and this ultimate end is not two ends but one.[44] Again, in *DS* 3, ad 4, Aquinas speaks of the "love of oneself by which someone seeks the divine good." In the response to the ninth objection, he writes, "The divine good, as it is loved on its own account is the object of charity, but as it is loved so as to be obtained, it is the object of hope."[45]

In addition to the foregoing textual observations, we should consider speculative arguments in response to the objection. So, third, for Thomas, a natural love of beatitude, which remains even in the damned who despair,[46] is the basis for the theological virtue of hope, whereby we lean

---

Book Three: Providence (Part I), trans. Vernon J. Bourke (New York: Doubleday and Company, Inc., 1956).

[42] *ST* 1.60.4, ad 3.

[43] *ST* 1-2.3.1.

[44] See *ST* 1-2.11.3, ad 3. Thomas cites, in this question, Augustine's statement "to enjoy something is to love to inhere in it on account of itself (*frui est amore inhaerere alicui rei propter seipsam*)." *ST* 1-2.11.1, sc. See Augustine, *De Doctrina* I, chap. 4 and *De Trin*. X, chap. 10. When using the term precisely, Aquinas understands "*frui*" as an act of the will. However, the precise meaning of "*frui*" should not distract our attention from the import of this passage, for the question at stake in the objection regards the "having" of the ultimate end. The question thus pertains to the relation of the lover to his end and not to the lover willing God to have His own good.

[45] *DS* 3, ad 9.

[46] See *ST* 1.60.4, ad 3.

on God in order to obtain for ourselves some good we seek by love of concupiscence. Hope builds on this natural love of beatitude, whereas charity builds on the natural love of God for His own sake. Hope reaches out to God so as to gain something from Him.[47] Hence, the love on which hope is based is a love of concupiscence for one's good: "Hope presupposes love of that which one hopes to attain for himself."[48] Charity, by contrast, reaches out to God as one loved for His own sake.[49] Nevertheless, the natural love of beatitude is distinct from the love of God for His own sake and remains distinct from such love.[50]

Fourth, if the love of beatitude, as it targets its object, were identified with the love of God for His own sake, then love of beatitude would be a love of friendship for the uncreated beatitude. What, then, would love of created beatitude be? It would be a love of concupiscence based upon love of friendship for oneself. Suddenly, it sounds as though there would be two distinct ends. Shields argues in this direction.[51] How, then, would these ends be related? As I read him, Aquinas distinguishes the end as being "twofold" but not as being two ends.[52]

Fifth, to separate the love of created beatitude, as a love of concupiscence based upon self-love, from the love of uncreated beatitude would entail the following difficulty, related to the preceding one. Created beatitude is not an object-less reality in man. The very act is "intentional,"

---

[47] God is the target of hope as desired object. See *ST* 1-2.67.4, ad 3. Of course, He is also the target as the source of strength.

[48] *ST* 1-2.66.6, ad 2 (my translation).

[49] See *DS* 3, especially ad 9. See also *ST* 2-2.17, arts. 6 and 8.

[50] Ramírez argues to the contrary in his *La esencia de la caridad*, trans. Victor Rodríguez (Madrid: Biblioteca de teologos españoles, 1978), 313–20. Ramírez argues that only in its unformed state is the love of hope based upon a love of concupiscence rooted in self-love. Once it is formed, he contends, that love upon which hope is based becomes simply the love of friendship for the divine good, necessarily connected to which is a love of concupiscence for the attainment of that good, vision. This latter love of concupiscence, he argues, is the secondary act of charity that is not self-directed even though it does concern that which pertains to one's welfare. Ramírez seems to be proposing a love of charity that does away with self-love.

For Aquinas, however, grace does not destroy but perfects nature. I would argue that charity gives *another* foundation for hope but does not supplant the natural foundation. The natural foundation of hope is the love of beatitude. Of course, hope cannot arise without the twofold grace of faith, making one aware of God in light of a new formality, i.e., supernatural beatitude, and the proper grace of hope itself, strengthening the will to lean on God so as to overcome great obstacles.

[51] See Shields, "Will," 115ff.

[52] See *ST* 1-2.1.8; *ST* 1-2.2.7; and *ST* 1-2.3.1.

that is, it consists in intellection or vision *of* an object. Now, an intentional operation cannot be described without reference to the objected intended. Created beatitude is just the created pole of the twofold end; it is the *vision* of God. Hence, in the love of beatitude, the love targets both operation and object under one formal aspect of love. Therefore, contrary to the aforesaid objection, love of beatitude is a love of concupiscence based upon love of self. In the love of beatitude, God is thus loved for oneself by a love of concupiscence.

Of course, God Himself is the same material object of both love of beatitude and love of God for His own sake. The difference between the two loves, then, lies in their formal *rationes*. That is, the difference lies in the formal aspect under which the one material object, God, is loved in each case. In the case of love of beatitude, God is loved as the object by the attainment of which man achieves perfection. In the case of love of God for His own sake, God is loved on account of His own goodness, wherein man's good is most truly found. To the love of others for their own sake, especially the Other that is God, we now turn.

CHAPTER 4

Dilection for Others

THE PRECEDING CHAPTER LEAVES US WITH A PROBLEM, the problem of love. According to my reading of Thomas, the beatitude one wills for oneself by a love of concupiscence is a single end distinguishable into the *finis cuius* and the *finis quo*. But, as Chapter Two argues, this love is the natural love of the end that constitutes an ineradicable root of all free choice. We are naturally confronted with a difficult question: on Thomas's principles, can a man love God above all things and for His own sake?

Anders Nygren, famous Lutheran critic of the Catholic approach generally, answers in the negative, reducing the relevant principles in Aquinas to two: (1) everything in Christianity can be traced back to love, and (2) everything in love can be traced back to self-love. The idea that there is no other love than self-love is already included at the point where Thomas's doctrine of love begins, inasmuch as he asserts that man can only love that which denotes a good for himself (*bonum suum*).[1] If Nygren is correct, Aquinas would clearly represent a eudaimonism unto the contempt of God.

The concern Nygren raises is hardly new. If Scotus does not directly address Aquinas's work on this topic, his thought touches Thomas's principles and contains a divergent thesis important to consider when reckoning with Thomas's opinions. Scotus posits that the will has two fundamental tendencies or inclinations, the affection for the fitting and pleasing (*affectio commodi*) and the affection for what is right in itself (*affectio iustitiae*). As Scotus sees it, the former sums up the inclination to happiness; it is the orientation to one's own ultimate perfection. The latter is the inclination to will what is right in itself, to love God simply because He is God. This distinction of fundamental tendencies is one way in which Scotus ac-

---

[1] Nygren, 643–44.

counts for free choice.² Short of the distinction, he contends, choice would not be properly ethical (right or wrong) but only eudaimonistic (merely instrumental to happiness). Scotus writes,

> According to the *affectio commodi*, one cannot will anything except under the aspect of its being directed to the self. And this [the limitation of love to self-love] would be the case if there were simply the intellectual appetite following on intellectual cognition, without liberty, as the sensitive appetite follows upon sensitive cognition.³

For Scotus, choice regards power for opposites. The distinction of the two

---

2 Among experts on Scotus, there is some disagreement. Allan Wolter argues that Scotus offers two grounds for freedom. Even with respect to the *affectio commodi*, Wolter argues, Scotus holds that we are free to act or not to act. John Duns Scotus, *Duns Scotus on the Will and Morality*, trans. Allan B. Wolter, OFM, ed. William A. Frank (Washington, DC: The Catholic University of America Press, 1997), 39. That is, we can elicit acts on the basis of this desire or not.

Thomas Osborne argues that this reading (supported by Marilyn McCord Adams and John Boler as well) is erroneous. Osborne claims that Scotus holds that without the second *affectio* one would not be free. Osborne cites in support Sukjae Lee, "Scotus on the Will: The Rational Power and the Dual Affections," *Vivarium* 37 (1998): 40–54. See also, Thomas Williams, "The Libertarian Foundations of Scotus's Moral Philosophy," *The Thomist* 62 (1998): 198f. See *Ord.* 2, d. 39, q. 2, n. 5. Tobias Hoffmann initially (perhaps due to imprecision of expression) appears to side with Wolter. Tobias Hoffmann, "The Distinction between Nature and Will in Duns Scotus," *Archives d'Histoire doctrinale et littéraire du Moyen Age* 66 (1999): 209.

For a bibliography on the issue, see *Archives d'Histoire*, 209n114. Hoffmann also relates that "[a]ccording to Scotus, the affection for justice would be inconceivable if the will were a natural active principle rather than a free active principle" (*Archives d'Histoire*, 210). Yet, Hoffmann goes on to state that Scotus identifies the *affectio iustitiae* with the very freedom of the will itself (*Archives d'Histoire*, 210ff, citing *Ord.* II, d. 6, q. 2, n. 8.). Moreover, he claims, were one to lack the *affectio iustitiae*, one would have no moderating inclination; one would pursue one's own beatitude above all and to the extreme. See Hoffmann, 211, and *Ord.* II, d. 6, q. 2, n. 8.

In sum, perhaps we may say that for Scotus, each of these inclinations indicates a relation of the will to its object, one *qua* intellectual appetite and the other *qua* free. Indeed, one way to cut off the first reading is this. We may ask "to what end" would we elicit an act freely that we would not order to happiness? Would it be to any good end, an end good in itself and apart from its being perfective of me? Thus, whatever "freedom" the will might be said to have without having an *affectio iustitiae*, such freedom would be merely calculative of the way to happiness.

3 Scotus, *Ord.* III, d. 26, q. 1, n. 17, in *Opera omnia*, vol. 15 (Vivès, 1894), 340b–341a (my translation).

affections, he holds, provides for opposites conducive to real freedom of choice. Given these two affections, man is free either to pursue his own happiness unto the neglect of God or to pursue the love of God for His own sake.

Were the will not endowed with *affectio iustitiae*, man would not be free to love God more than himself. Without this affection, one would only will, maximally, one's maximal perfection.[4] Any variation in this pursuit of one's own good (one's perfection) would be reduced to a calculus of prudence ordered to maximal self-perfection. Hence, one would not truly be free to moderate this desire and to love another person, even God, for His own sake.[5] Since merit requires freedom to elicit an act as one's own, Scotus also holds that merit presupposes this distinction of affections.[6] This is not necessarily to say that, for Scotus, a man thus unable to love God more than himself would sin. One cannot sin in those things that one cannot but do.

Critics of Thomas, as early as Scotus and as recent as last century, read him as reducing the human will to the appetite for one's own good. As Hans Reiner reads him, for instance, Thomas holds that "*all* men strive after their own beatitude as their *own* last *end*."[7] Unlike today's post-Kantian enthusiasts for "disinterested love," however, Scotus is not allergic to the *affectio commodi*. For him, this affection is good and natural. Indeed, if man had not this affection, God would not for him have the perfect

---

[4] See Scotus, *Ord.* IV, d. 49, q. 5, in *Opera omnia*, vol. 21 (Vivès, 1894), 173a, and Hoffmann, "The Distinction," 209–12.

[5] Scotus reiterates his thesis that the *affectio iustitiae* is the freedom whereby the will is the will. The will also has affection for what is fitting. According to these two affections, there are two acts of the will that regard the good in two ways, as delectable (*delectabile*) and as good in itself (*honestum*). The theological virtues of hope and charity perfect the will according to each of these inclinations. On the natural plane, if the will were not free (had not the *affectio iustitiae*) it would love nothing except for itself. Hope perfects this natural love of self. See Scotus, *Lectura III In Sent.* d. 26, q. 1, in *Opera omnia*, vol. 21 (Vatican City, 2004), 194: 423–430.

[6] See Scotus, *Ord.* I, d. 17, p. 1, q. 2, n. 26, in *Opera omnia*, vol. 5 (Vatican City, 1959), 149, and Hoffmann, "Distinction," 223. Interestingly, Scotus even argues that one would not be truly free if one could not but elicit an act. That is, if by one's will one could not "not elicit" the act of some habit with which one is endowed (even the habit of charity), one would not be free. He concludes that the habit of charity cannot so dominate man that he cannot sin, lest he not be free. Since freedom is essential to love and charity, it would be a contradiction to suggest that the habit of charity could dominate a man. Therefore, it cannot be the sufficient cause of the act of love. See Scotus, *Ord.*, I, d. 17, p. 1., q. 2, n. 25, in *Opera omnia*, vol. 5 (Vatican City, 1959), 148.

[7] See Hans Reiner, "Beatitudo und Obligatio," 236–66 and 306–28.

character of lovability.⁸ It is simply that the affection for what is fitting must be moderated by a higher principle. Moreover, Scotus speaks of the "fittingness" of the act of love of another, especially love of God, because the *affectio iustitiae* gives the will this "correspondence" to such an act as its ultimate perfection.⁹ These qualifications indicate the divergence of Scotus from later viewpoints at odds even with his. Notwithstanding, Scotus portrays a love of God that is purely "objective," not grounded in any perfecting relation of creature to God. He writes, "Even our reason tells us that God is the greatest thing to be loved by the *affectio iustitiae*, insofar as He is the greatest good, even if, *per impossibile*, He were not our good."¹⁰ The passage should be startling for a Thomist. More startlingly, Scotus contends that, viewed in the mode of our understanding, God loves even Himself by two affections, the *affectio commodi* and the *affectio iustitiae*. God's greatest love is that whereby He loves His good as the infinite good in itself, *not* as His own good. So, even God treats Himself as an "objective person" out there, to be loved infinitely.¹¹ As we shall see, this conception of things is entirely divergent from the view of Thomas.

This discussion of Thomas's critics is of course by no means exhaustive. It is, however, exemplary. In this chapter, I will show that Aquinas in fact upholds a love of the other for his own sake, and above all, love of the Divine Other. It is not difficult to establish this contention from the texts. How to relate this love of others to the self-love treated in the second and third chapters is more difficult. Is love of another simply juxtaposed to self-love? Are there two fundamental, irreducible affections of the appetite? If there is neither juxtaposition nor collapse of one into the other, how are the two loves related? The present chapter treats Thomas's understanding of the genesis or development of love of others from the love of self. It treats both love of neighbor and love of God. It treats each with regard to a non-elected or natural love and with regard to an elected or chosen love.

---

⁸ See Scotus, *Lectura III In Sent.*, d. 27, q. 1, n. 31, in *Opera omnia*, vol. 21 (Vatican City, 2004), 209: 215–16.
⁹ See Scotus, *Ord.* III, d. 26, q. 1, n. 17, in *Opera omnia*, vol. 15 (Vivès, 1894), 341a.
¹⁰ Scotus, *Lectura III In Sent.*, d. 27, q. 1, in *Opera omnia*, vol. 23 (Vivès, 1894), 480b.
¹¹ This appears in Scotus's examination of charity under the light of the very character of its formal object. Scotus, *Lectura III In Sent.*, d. 27, q. 1, n. 27–28, in *Opera omnia*, vol. 21 (Vatican City, 2004), 208: 171–85.

Love of Neighbor

Expansion of Self

Aquinas depicts love of other rational creatures as having its genesis in love of self. He insists, however, that genuine love of another does not reach out to the other so as to "direct" the other to the self as to its end. That is, genuine love of another involves love of friendship (*amor amicitiae*) that terminates in the other and that includes love of concupiscence (*amor concupiscentiae*) for the other's good *as* that of the other. A love that would reach out to the other so as to direct the other to the self would be only self-love. The other would be treated as instrumental to one's own end, included in a series of means directed ultimately to the perfection of the self. For example, I may love another for his wealth, and his wealth as means to my pleasure.[12] Notwithstanding, Thomas's thesis remains: love of others is generated from love of self. Thomas finds his thesis pithily expressed by Aristotle: "Things pertaining to one's friendship with another come from things pertaining to one's 'friendship' with oneself."[13] How does Thomas reconcile the other-directed character of true love of another with the refrain that love of the other is generated from love of self?

Thomas distinguishes two kinds of order: that of genesis and that of finality. Self-love is the root of love of another in the genetic order but not in the order of finality. It indicates the soil, as it were, in which love of another creature arises and not a secret, ulterior purpose of love of another. In the order of finality, the friend is loved for his own sake. How, according to Aquinas, does love of another emerge from love of self?

Thomas expresses the genesis of love of a neighbor in self-love in two ways. He writes of love of one's good (*bonum suum*) as being the root of love of another. He also notes that one loves something insofar as it is one with oneself. These ways are related, for something that is more one with oneself is closer to one's own. It is more proper. Let us take oneness first.

Besides the substantial unity one has with oneself, there is possible a union of similitude with another.[14] On the basis of a union of simili-

---

[12] See *DDN* 4.10, pars. 428–32 and *ST* 1-2.28.3. See also, Peter Kwasniewski, "St. Thomas, Extasis, and Union with the Beloved," *The Thomist* 61 (1997): 587–603.

[13] *Sent.* 3.29.3, ad 3. See also *ST* 1.60.3, sc; *ST* 2-2.25.4; *DC* 7, ad 11; *Quodl.* 5.3.2; and *Eth.* 9.4. See also Aristotle, *Nicomachean Ethics* X, 4 (1166a1–1166b25) in *The Complete Works of Aristotle: The Revised Oxford Translation*, trans. W. D. Ross, revised by J. O. Urmson; ed. Jonathan Barnes, no. 70.2 Bollingen Series (Princeton University Press, 1984).

[14] See *ST* 1-2.28.1, ad 2, which draws upon *ST* 1-2.27.3.

tude with another, rational love of other persons can arise. In order that one may be in a position to love another, one must be aware that another person exists and judge there to be a correspondence or similitude or fittingness (*convenientia*) between that person and oneself.[15] If another person has this ontological correspondence through similitude, one can love him.[16] Essentially, similitude bespeaks communication in a form, as though two distinct beings shared one form.[17]

As we saw in Chapter Two, similitude is twofold, actual and potential.[18] If a neighbor actually (*in actu*) has some similitude with me, he is already in a manner one with me. For this reason, Aquinas holds, I can love him as a friend, willing to him the honest good I will for myself. In short, the love that arises can be a love of friendship. If he has a similitude with me only potentially (*in potentia*), I can love him by intending to provide something for him.[19] If, conversely, I have a similitude with him only potentially (*in potentia*), I will on these grounds love him with *amor concupiscentiae*, seeking his assistance to attain what he already has. Of course, the very hope I have of attaining my good through this person disposes me also to love him for his own sake with *amor amicitiae*, as we shall see.[20]

When one loves another with *amor amicitiae*, one affectively takes that other to be "one" with oneself. The other affectively becomes in a way an "other self."[21] Or, one could say the self doubles[22] or undergoes an affective expansion.[23] Thomas writes, "When someone loves someone else by a love of friendship, he wills good to him as he does to himself: so, he appre-

---

[15] See Nicolas, 18 and 34–35.
[16] See *ST* 1-2.27.3 and *DDN* 4.9, par. 406.
[17] See *ST* 1-2.27.3 and also, Egenter, 14ff, and note (a).
[18] Again, see *ST* 1-2.27.3 and also Egenter, 15 and 18ff.
[19] See *DDN* 4.9, par. 407.
[20] See *ST* 2-2.17.8.
[21] See *Sent.* 3.27.1.1; *Eth.* 9.10; and *SCG* 3.158. See also Egenter, 19.
[22] See Egenter, 23. Egenter correctly articulates Thomas's understanding of the affective expansion of self through love. However, he misunderstands Thomas's pairing similitude in act with love of friendship and similitude in potency with love of concupiscence. Egenter thinks that if I already possess some good, then I love it by a love of friendship as a "part" of my entire "I" (see *Gottesfreundschaft*, 23–24 and 25–26). Egenter translates "love of concupiscence" as "desiring love" (*begehrende Liebe*).

This reading is incorrect. Love "of concupiscence" or love of desire does not, in its most precise sense, signify "desire." If I possess the good that I will to have, I rejoice. This delight is precisely an effect of love of concupiscence, a partial efficient cause, together with possession and knowledge of possession.

[23] See Gallagher, "Desire for Beatitude," 27–34, and Osborne, *Love of Self*, 95.

hends this person as another self, insofar, namely, as he wills good to him as to himself."[24] When in act, love for another makes the lover disposed towards his beloved *as* he is towards himself. Thus, he rejoices with his beloved's happiness, weeps with his sadness, procures good things for him, and wards away evil things.[25] For Thomas, this affective union of lover and beloved, formally constituting love, is based on similitude.[26]

The deeper foundation for the volitional expansion of one's own good lies in fellowship in truly common goods. A good is truly common because it is sharable or communicable.[27] As Benjamin Smith notes, because communicable, such a good can unite several hypostases with reference to itself, perfecting each. Finally, because it perfects the many and not just the one, it is more universal.[28] The common good is thus distinct from the "proper" good (in the narrow sense of the term "proper good" as being the property of an individual). In some sense, the strictly "proper good" as such is opposite to the common good: my steak is not your steak, nor your wisdom mine. However, we should not push this contrast to a breaking point: "To make a sharp distinction between an individual good and the common good is to misunderstand the dependence of the individual good on the common good."[29] The very good of the part is *ordered* to that of the whole. In the case of a truly common good, this complementarity is exemplified. If you take the guitar while I sing, together we share the good of the music we make. The symphony is a common good. In fact, the symphony is the kind of common good that cannot be good unless commonly held, for it cannot *be* unless it is participated in by the many played instru-

---

[24] *ST* 1-2.28.1. See also, *SCG* 3.153, par. 2; *ST* 1.20.1, ad 3; *ST* 1.60.1, ad 2. *ST* 2-2.25.4 reads, "As unity is a principle of union, so the love by which someone loves himself is the form and root of friendship. For in this way we have friendship with another, that we bear ourselves towards others as we do towards ourselves." For the Aristotelian connection in this regard, see K. Hedwig, "Alter ipse: Über die Rezeption eines Aristotelischen Begriffes bei Thomas von Aquin," *Archiv für Geschichte der Philosophie* 72 (1990): 253–74.

[25] See *ST* 1-2.28, arts. 3–5.

[26] See Nicolas, 35–36.

[27] See Charles De Koninck, *The Primacy of the Common Good Against the Personalists* and *In Defense of St. Thomas: A Reply to Fr. Eschmann's Attack on* The Primacy of the Common Good, trans. Ralph McInerny, in *The Writings of Charles De Koninck*, ed. Raph McInerny (Notre Dame: University of Notre Dame Press, 2009), 63–108 and 205–363. See also Osborne, *Love of Self*, 87–94.

[28] See Benjamin Smith, "The Meaning and Importance of Common Goods," *The Thomist* 80 (2016): 587ff.

[29] Osborne, *Love of Self*, 90.

ments. The excellence of the parts and that of the whole go hand in hand, although that of the former is ordered to that of the latter.

These foundations in union and similitude show that love of another is not the result of a herculean overcoming of tendencies that are naturally evil, as though aliens strove to will good to each other without any connection to desire, happiness, and fellowship. As Charles De Koninck puts it, "The common good does not have the note of an alien good."[30] So, love of another is naturally good for oneself, just as it inclines towards acts of fellowship. Still, the common good is not the precisely *proper* good of the individual; it is a greater good, and the individual is greater for loving it.

Regrettably, the theme of the common good cannot be studied in great depth in this monograph. I will return to it at other key junctures. At this point, a citation of Olver's fine study must suffice:

> To love something as a common good is to love it as a good whose proper subject is not oneself. We necessarily desire to share in this good, but it is not our own possession of the good that we primarily desire or are pleased by; what we primarily desire or are pleased by is the possession of the good by its proper subject. If, however, the common good that we love is one whose proper subject is a whole of order, our wish that the whole might possess the good is essentially the wish that we might possess the good together with those others who belong to this order. To love a common good is to wish that it be shared by those others who are similarly ordered to it.[31]

Love requires the perception of an ontological fittingness of beloved with the lover. Common goods certainly satisfy this *ratio* of fittingness. We shall see this more starkly in the next section, in which we treat the part-whole analogy in the love of God above self. However, the common good itself is not the love but the union of similitude that is a precondition of love. Nor is recognition of the common good the essence of love. Rather, a volitional act is love. Thus, for there to be love-in-act there must be an affective expansion of the lover himself, so that "he" becomes, affectively, "he and his beloved": "For this reason love is called a 'uniting force,' because it attaches another to the self, bearing itself towards the other as it does towards itself."[32]

---

[30] See De Koninck, *Primacy*, 76 and 85ff. See also Jordan Olver, "Love of God above Self," *The Thomist* 80 (2016): 125f.
[31] Olver, "*Bonum*," 692. See *ST* 1.60.5, ad 3.
[32] *ST* 1.20.1, ad 3.

As we see, the path to love of others entails neither the negation of self-love nor self-love's domination. Instead, love of another involves volitional expansion of self. Hence, love of another involves an expansion of one's good (*bonum suum*). One loves the other as one loves one's good. Indeed, the other becomes part of one's good, or, rather one's good expands so as to be inclusive of the other.

Thomas's linking of any object of love to the *bonum suum* can raise an understandable concern. At first blush, it may seem to imply that the lover simply annexes the "other" as an empire might annex a neighboring state, subjecting the state to its "own good." Nygren has just this concern: "'Amor amicitiae sive benevolentiae' constitutes no threat to the doctrine that all love goes back ultimately to self-love and that man can only love that which is a 'bonum' for himself. But at the same time, the place where Christian Agape-love, the love that seeketh not its own, was to find a refuge has disappeared."[33] If Nygren is correct, Thomas's discussion of love of the other remains unfounded. The fine scholar Richard Egenter unfortunately lends support to such a reading, conceiving the expansion of self in terms of the neighbor as a good "for me (*für mich*)."[34] I would argue that Nygren's reading is inaccurate. Thomas employs the phrase "one's good" (*bonum suum*) in many ways. It can signify the good of the self narrowly defined, one's neighbor, and even God. In this section, we treat only the first two senses. I would note that Aquinas even employs the phrase "proper good" (*bonum proprium*) in several ways.[35]

On an initial and straightforward reading, the phrase "one's good" or "our good" naturally suggests the good that is strictly one's own. Taken in such a way, it would be synonymous with "proper good," signifying one's "property." Even this sense of the term is rich, however, for human goods are many. So, taken narrowly, the phrase (whether *bonum proprium* or *bonum suum*) can target different kinds of good. Sometimes, the concrete content of this good is not specified.[36] Sometimes, it indicates lower level goods of the lover, the love of which ought to and can be referred to

---

[33] Nygren, 645.
[34] Egenter, 46.
[35] See *ST* 2-2.19.6; *SCG* 3.24, par. 7. De Koninck also recognizes that "proper good" is not always opposed to "common good," although he stresses the primary use of these terms as opposed. Indeed, Thomas often uses *bonum proprium* as synonymous with *bonum privatum* (see *ST* 2-2.47.10 and *ST* 1-2.109.3), and this is what De Koninck understandably takes the term *bonum proprium* properly to signify.
[36] *ST* 1.60.5, ad 1 and ad 2; *ST* 1.63.1, ad 4; *ST* 1-2.109.3; *ST* 2-2.47.10 and 11, corp.; and *ST* 2-2.132.1.

the higher end that is God.³⁷ It can indicate one's good in opposition to another's good.³⁸ In this sense, love of the proper good, taken precisively, can indicate pride.³⁹ It can also refer to one's own spiritual good.⁴⁰ It can refer to one's share in beatitude.⁴¹ Thus, there is a range of meaning even in its initial, narrow meaning. There is also a wider sense of *bonum suum* and *bonum proprium*.⁴²

Bonum proprium and *bonum suum* can be used to signify the good of a friend whom a man takes to be one with himself. That is, these phrases can signify a horizontal expansion of one's own good to include or encompass, as it were, another person with whom one shares some similarity. There are various ways in which something can be one's good.⁴³ On the one hand, this expansion of one's own good involves a certain union in the good. It does not involve leaving the (true) self behind.⁴⁴ So, Thomas writes, "A man loves [someone] from this, because he apprehends him as his good."⁴⁵ Indeed, the greater the union, the greater the love: "Everything naturally has an appetite for its own good and from the fact that something is one with it, it follows that it loves that thing; therefore, we love more those things that are more united with us."⁴⁶ On the other hand, the love in this union in the good is not self-centered but truly other-centered: "We love our neighbors insofar as we find in them our good by similitude. Here we are speaking of the love of benevolence."⁴⁷ In short, love of another consists in an affective expansion of the lover so that the lover wills for his friend the same ultimate perfection he wills for himself.

A key effect and sign of this expansion in love of friendship for another is appetitive ecstasy. "Ecstasy" means "standing outside." In this context, it implies the affection's targeting an external good and remaining therein, not turning that good back towards the self:

---

³⁷ *ST* 2-2.19, arts.6 and 10.
³⁸ See *ST* 2-2.37.1.
³⁹ See *DM* 8.2, ad 15.
⁴⁰ See *ST* 3.65.3, obj. 1. *Ad Hebr.* 13.3, par. 769, and *Ad Col* 1.3, par. 11, use "*bonum nostrum*" to indicate human sanctification. Of course, this private spiritual good is ordered to the common spiritual good: see *ST* 3.65.3, ad 1, and *DC* 2.
⁴¹ *SCG* 1.100, par. 2.
⁴² For Thomas explicitly taking "proper good" in various ways, see *DC* 2.
⁴³ See *DDN* 4.9, par. 406 (*bonum nostrum*), and *DC* 2 (*bonum proprium*).
⁴⁴ McEvoy portrays something more like an abandonment of self in his "Amitié," 390.
⁴⁵ *ST* 1-2.62.4.
⁴⁶ *DDN* 4.11, par. 449.
⁴⁷ *Sent.* 3.29.6.

When something is loved in the first mode of love (i.e., by love of friendship), thus the affection is brought to the thing loved, which the lover does not return back to himself, because he wishes good to the thing loved itself and not for the reason that something might accordingly come to himself from the beloved. Thus, such love causes an ecstasy, because it places the lover outside himself.[48]

In the *Summa theologiae*, Aquinas expands on this theme, linking a relative kind of ecstasy with love of concupiscence for some external thing and a simple or true kind of ecstasy with love of friendship for another person:

In love of concupiscence, the lover is carried out of himself, in a certain sense; in so far, namely, as not being satisfied with enjoying the good that he has, he seeks to enjoy something outside himself. But since he seeks to have this extrinsic good for himself, he does not go out from himself simply, and this movement remains finally within him. On the other hand, in the love of friendship, a man's affection goes out from itself simply; because he wishes and does good to his friend, by caring and providing for him, for his sake.[49]

Love of friendship for another involves true ecstasy, whereas love of concupiscence for some external thing involves only a relative kind of ecstasy. Nevertheless, love of friendship for a created person does not beget a completely ecstatic movement, whereby one orders all that one is and has to the beloved. No created person orders itself to any fellow creature in a total manner, since no other individual created thing can be loved as an ultimate end above oneself. Hence, the lover "does not will the good of his friend more than his own good."[50] Although in self-love there is real love of friendship, its natural form does not admit an ecstatic character. The reason is evident: In self-love the lover's affection remains for his own good. Thus, although self-love may be said to consist in a lover's being with himself in a manner not identical with the self-identity of substance, operatively as it were, this being with oneself does not constitute ecstasy. Of course, this is no mark against self-love.

As we see, *bonum suum* and even *bonum proprium* do not always signify the lover himself or his inhering perfection. In genuine love of another,

---

[48] *DDN* 4.10, par. 430.
[49] *ST* 1-2.28.3.
[50] *ST* 1-2.28.3, ad 3.

one wills good for the other by a love of concupiscence grounded in a love of friendship *for the other*.[51] The other, not the self narrowly defined, is the target of the love. Since through love the *bonum suum* expands, and since love *actualizes* the lover, there is the indirect consequence of greater perfection of self. Nonetheless, it would not be love *of the other* were such augmentation the end of the love. The genetic order is not the order of finality. As Peter Kwasniewski puts it, "Such reflexive perfection is not the *radix amoris* but the *fructus amoris*: it follows upon but does not constitute the essence of love directed to another's good."[52]

Natural and Elected Expansions

The volitional expansion of oneself and one's own good can occur either naturally (in a non-elected manner) or by choice. The difference depends on how things stand in reality, the apprehension of which is the aim of the intellect.[53] It depends on whether the lovers are united by nature or not: "If [the lover] be one with [the beloved] by natural union, he loves him with natural love; but if he be one with [the beloved] by a non-natural union, then he loves him with non-natural love."[54] Here, "natural" union and love are opposed to "elected" union and love. Natural union between the two gives rise to natural love. For example, children have a natural love of parents, and vice versa. All humans, as humans, have a natural union, which serves as the reason for a natural human fellowship. Of course, for such natural loves to be humanly lived, they must also be freely chosen and prudently executed.

In addition to such natural loves, elected loves of various kinds are possible according to the various kinds of possible non-natural unions.[55]

---

[51] "We are by no means entitled [in this case] to take *bonum nostrum* as if it meant *perfectio nostra*. My neighbor may be my good; he is not my perfection. What then does it mean to speak of my neighbor or fellow citizen (or for that matter, my self, my hand, my God) as my good? He is good as a subsistent good, and therefore is such as to have good wished for him. To say that he is 'my' good indicates a relatedness to me." Mansini, "*Duplex Amor*," 169.

[52] See Kwasniewski, 593.

[53] Errors, willful or not, are of course possible. Nonetheless, just as ideology cannot paint over a dairy allergy to make ice cream really someone's good when it is in fact an evil, so in the end no amount of ideological wishful thinking can establish true happiness.

[54] *ST* 1.60.4 (my translation). For a good account of this affective expansion in Aquinas's thought, see David Gallagher, "Self-love," 29–35.

[55] Non-natural here indicates what can happen in a manner consonant with nature, but only if it is elected or chosen. It does not imply something contrary to nature.

Each of two young girls who seek common activities can recognize in the other a possible sharer in friendship; thus, they can establish a union of friendship, each choosing the other as another self. They consequently share joys and sorrows. The mutual targeting of each other as a good loved for her sake gives rise to a common good of friendship.[56] Two men who love fishing can establish a kind of friendship associated with the activities of fishing. Each truly wishes the success of the other; further, each takes the other to be another self, rejoicing for the other as though for what regards his own self. A teacher can choose to love his students and thus make their good to be his own; rather, he allows his own good to be stretched unto theirs. A man and a woman can take each other for life as spousal friends open to life and thus enter a marital union. In short, while a man naturally loves his own beatitude or *bonum proprium*, through love his affective concern can expand so as to include the neighbor's own good as well. The tent pegs of his affection for his own good are moved outward, so as to include his neighbor.

The critic might still suspect that Thomas presents a portrait of expanded egoism. I suggest several reflections in response. First, we might reverse the angle from which we pose the difficulty. Instead of thinking of how *I* am able to *freely love* another, perhaps I might think of how I should like to be loved.[57] Do I want my friend to be pained by my pain and rejoice over my happiness? Do I want my friend to consider such happenings to me as though they were happenings for him? Do I want him to be happy in my presence because he finds something to delight therein? Or, rather, do I want him to be happy in my presence simply because *he* wills to act thus, despite the absence of anything in me that might evoke such happiness? Do I want him to make a strenuous act of sympathy when he sees me in pain, not because the wound touches his very good (which has expanded so as to include mine) but because, though it does not, he wills to have sympathy? Surely, we wish our friend to treat us as so united with himself that our pains and joys become in a way his own. This perspective enables us to deflate false expectations concerning our own supposed obligation to achieve a purely disinterested love of another as alien. Consider a wife. She does not want her husband to love her despite his not finding anything in her attractive. Nor does she want him to rejoice with her good only by a strenuous act of sympathy that overreaches a native alienation of two juxtaposed hypostases. The very word "compassion" (*com-passio*) suggests

---

[56] See Kwasniewski, 594.
[57] I was inspired to frame the situation in this way by David Gallagher.

undergoing the same emotions or passions together.

Secondly, Thomas draws out other-centered consequences of the other-centered love of another. These further signal the genuine sense of this love as targeting the other's good for his own sake. We can discover Thomas's thought on the further consequences of love of another by examining the passions set in motion by this love. To do this, we must retrace our steps from Chapter Two. With respect to self-love, the possession or non-possession of the loved good results in joy or desire: we desire what we love but do not have, and we rejoice in having what we love. From these basic passions emerge all the others.

Now, the pattern of love that a man has for his neighbor is modeled on the pattern of love that he has for himself. He wills good to his neighbor just as he does to himself because he takes his neighbor to be another self.[58] Love of friendship for another leads one, further, to desire the other to have the absent good one wills for him and to rejoice in his possession of that good. So, in this case, desire and joy arise with respect to the *friend's* possession or non-possession of the good loved for his sake. Thus, Aquinas writes, "We love him for whom we wish some good, as is proper to a friendship for a noble person; but not as the good which we wish for ourselves, as is proper to a friendship for a pleasant or useful person."[59] One can even delight in a friend's virtuous actions as though they were one's own "from the fact that another's actions, if they be good, are reckoned as one's own good, by reason of the power of love, which makes a man to regard his friend as one with himself."[60] Likewise, one can rejoice in the good effects of one's own actions for a friend precisely because these effects benefit the friend: "Inasmuch as through being united to others by love, we look upon their good as being our own, we take pleasure in the good we do to others, especially our friends, as in our own good."[61]

One of the more notable and cherished instances of compassion is mercy. For Aquinas, mercy is not pity for an alien undergoing suffering but taking upon oneself sadness for the evil afflicting one's beloved, as though it were afflicting oneself: "Someone is called merciful as though having a

---

[58] See *Sent.* 3.28.6.
[59] *DC* 8, ad 16. The English is taken from Thomas Aquinas, *On Charity (De Caritate)*, trans. Lotti H. Kendzierski, Mediaeval Philosophical Texts in Translation, no. 10 (Milwaukee: Marquette University Press, 1993). This work was likely written between 1271 and 1272 (Torrell, 336); yet, Sherwin would place it earlier (see Sherwin, *By Knowledge*, 199ff, n192).
[60] *ST* 1-2.32.5.
[61] *ST* 1-2.32.6.

sorrowful heart (*miserum cor*) because, that is, it is touched with sadness at another's misery as though it were his own."[62] Similarly, since zeal results from the intensity of love, an intense love of friendship for another issues in the zeal by which one is moved to ward off anything hindering the good of the beloved, just as one naturally has zeal for one's own good.[63]

In his treatment of Christ's satisfaction for sin, Aquinas highlights the depths of mercy. Clearly, God shows his compassion for us in sending His Son to die for our salvation, who bears our pains.[64] This bearing of pain is not substitutionary, however, but inclusive. Suffering alone in His redeeming act, He works to awaken love in us. We, in turn, suffer with Him, who has made us His friends. Since we suffer with Him, we share in the (subjective) redemption. Christ's mercy extends to the point of enabling us to pay with Him through suffering for love of Him who suffered.[65]

We can pursue the implications of these Thomistic principles further. The ultimate good one wills for a friend is true beatitude. In the case of true friendship, the friend also virtuously wills true beatitude for himself. Closer perusal allows us to discern something more than basic, a beautiful, manifold union between the friends. The friends are one in loving, for the first wills the good of the second, just as the second wills his own good. The second person is joyful or desirous, sorrowful or fearful, depending on his own situation with respect to the loved good or hated evil. Because of the genuine union of love, the first also experiences these passions for his friend's sake: "In the love of friendship, the lover is in the beloved, inasmuch as he reckons what is good or evil to his friend, as being so to himself; and his friend's will as his own, so that it seems as though he felt the good or suffered the evil in the person of his friend."[66] Conversely, since true friendship is mutual, a similar union of passions is had with respect to the situation of the first person vis-à-vis the second. The first person loves his own good, and the second loves the first person's good. As a net result, each loves in various ways that are similar to those of the other. The two breathe forth similar loves, becoming one in love.[67] Further, each wills the good of the friendship, the very communion of the two. The net result of the society established is the genuinely common holding of

---

[62] *ST* 1.21.3.
[63] See *ST* 1-2.28.4.
[64] See *SCG* 4.54 and 55.
[65] See *SCG* 3.158, par. 7.
[66] See *ST* 1-2.28.2.
[67] These and numerous other elements of friendship can be gathered from meditation on the profound study of mutual indwelling in *ST* 1-2.28.2.

a good as communicable, a common good (*bonum commune*). Those who share a common good can be extremely zealous for love of this common good. Since a common good is by definition sharable or communicable, such zeal does not hinder but preserves and promotes true friendship. Zeal for a non-communicable good hinders friendship, but zeal for a communicable good protects it.[68]

Further consideration helps us discover signs of the ecstatic, other-centered orientation of the loves. Ultimate beatitude is one and the same for all men, that is, union with God. God is the same for all and is most communicable of all.[69] Although my attaining God is not your attaining God, neither of us hinders but each fosters the other. If we examine lesser goods, we can notice the ecstatic character of love more distinctly. Lesser goods constitute real, even urgent, goals in the pilgrimage of human life. For instance, one person strives for musical skill, another for poetic grace, another for a job, etc. A good friend embraces all the known, virtuous aims of his beloved. So, he truly wills his beloved's fruition in these matters. However, different people seek different goals. Not all share the same aims in these lesser but non-negligible matters. So, the good friend, because of his love for his friend, has concern for goods that would not be of concern to him otherwise. Here, we put our finger on signs indicative of the genuine character of love for another. The affective expansion calls one to take interest in the beloved's virtuous interests, whether or not they are of interest to one's narrowly defined *bonum proprium*. The expanded sense of *bonum suum* and even *bonum proprium* embraces these goods not included in the *bonum proprium* narrowly construed. So, expansion of one's *bonum suum* is by no means annexation, much less ego-enlargement.[70] The expansion of

---

[68] See *ST* 1-2.28.4, ad 2.

[69] On this, see esp. De Koninck, *Primacy* and *Defense, passim*.

[70] I would stress the difference between something being good "for me" (Egenter, 46) and something being "my good" in an expanded sense. In love of neighbor, I take the other to be my good in an expanded sense, so that I genuinely undergo an *ecstasy* towards him, willing his good for him. That I become a "greater I" in this love does not mean that I integrate my neighbor into myself but rather that I now enjoy an "expropriated," truly social existence. The patterns of my passions regarding my friend manifest this fact. When my friend is suffering, I, though richly blessed, suffer with him, for I too am wounded with him because of my love. Once again, see the majestic depths of our incorporation into Christ as co-sufferers with Him, succinctly and deftly traced in *SCG* 3.158, par. 7.

The spontaneity of my wounded love for a friend indicates how much I have taken my friend's good, his independent existence, to be radically pertinent to me. It may be that Egenter's appeal to the distinction between metaphysical analysis and ethical

one's *bonum suum* consists in or constitutes communion. Human society is built up through these expansions. Thus, society is not established by beings, intrinsically alienated at first, which overcome a natural egoism by a love of others as unrelated to self.[71] Rather, society is established by the accomplishment of affective expansion and union in common goods.

A final comment is in order. Precisely because in true friendship the beloved is loved for his own sake, the lover wants to be with, live with, and act together with the beloved. These are the proper acts of friendship.[72] In laying out the effects of love, Thomas begins by noting the three kinds of union associated with love. The substantial union is the basis or potency for love, the affective union is the essence of love, and the real union is the aim of love. Since in love the beloved is the end, real union is desired. The end of love of another is not the love itself by which the other is loved, but the beloved himself. For this very reason, the lover "is not satisfied with a superficial apprehension of the beloved, but strives to gain an intimate knowledge of everything pertaining to the beloved, so as to penetrate into his very soul."[73] Since the lover is moved by love of friendship, this hunger for knowledge is not merely a love of the private good of the lover, but is rather the fruit of the love for the other.

If this is the way Thomas views things, he has carved out space for love of neighbor. Has he carved out sufficient space for love of God for His own sake, for which we ought to "strain every nerve"?[74] If by love I take complacency in another as though in a second self, and thus undergo an

---

experience alleviates this difficulty I have with his text (see ibid., 47). Egenter rightly insists that in truly selfless love of another, all consciousness of the (perfecting) relation of the beloved to my "I," conceived in the narrow sense, must fall away, lest the selfless character be endangered (see ibid., 50).

Still, even metaphysically one must sharply distinguish social existence, social personhood, from self. The expanded self is not simply a "greater I"; it is an *affectively* expanded self, which in essence entails that things afflicting or enriching another, but not me, afflict or enrich me through my genuine affective union with this other, who is a self-standing being. On social persons, see Russell Hittinger, "The Coherence of the Four Basic Principles of Catholic Social Doctrine: An Interpretation," in *Pursuing the Common Good*, Acta 14, ed. Margaret S. Archer and Pierpaolo Donati (Vatican City: Pontifical Academy of Social Sciences, 2008), 105f.

[71] Osborne, *Love of Self*, 104: "It is a mistake to see the perfection of either immaterial or material beings as merely the perfection of an individual which is unrelated to the rest of the universe."

[72] See *Eth.* 8.5, par. 1600. See also *Sent.* 3.27.2.1; *Sent.* 3.32.1.2; *SCG* 4.22, par. 2; *SCG* 4.54, par. 5; *ST* 2-2.23.1; *ST* 2-2.24.9; *ST* 2-2.25.3; *ST* 2-2.180.7; and *ST* 3.75.1.

[73] *ST* 1-2.28.2.

[74] Aristotle, *Nicomachean Ethics* X, chap. 7 (1177b34), 1861.

affective "expansion" of my own good, bearing myself towards the beloved as I do towards myself, it seems that the beloved is lovable *insofar* as the beloved is one with oneself. If God is also lovable on this account, will He not be loved on account of (*propter*) man? But this is repugnant to faith and, according to Aquinas, also to reason.

Love of God

Non-Elected Love of God

According to Christians and Jews, in the right order of things, God should be loved more than self. This obligation is enshrined in the *Shema* and in the New Law. For Thomas, this is not merely an obligation but natural to human nature as such. If we prescind from the condition of sin into which children of Adam are born, the love of God above all things and more than oneself is possible to human nature.[75] There exists, Thomas holds, a natural inclination to this act.[76] In this contention, Aquinas parts ways with some of his masters.[77] If there were no such inclination, he argues, "[n]atural love would be perverse."[78] Charity, then, would not elevate natural principles but destroy them. This inclination is as it were a natural justice, remaining as long as human nature remains, even though, according to Aquinas, original sin vitiates man's capacity to act on this natural inclination. The vigor to achieve the promise of the seeds of virtue necessarily present in nature has collapsed into weakness.[79]

At this point, Thomas's principles force us to countenance a difficulty. Although he traces the contours of love of another, he holds that others are lovable only inasmuch as they are related to or one with the lover. Clearly, every creature is more united to itself than to any other creature, and its

---

[75] See especially Osborne, *Love of Self*, 70–86, which demonstrates the falsity of Henri de Lubac's reading of Aquinas on the natural love of God.

[76] By contrast, Thomas's predecessors thought that the natural tendency of a being in the state of integral nature was to love self more than God. See Alexander of Hales, *Summa theol.* P II, Inquis. II, tract. III, sect. II, q. II, Tit. I, dist. II, memb. 1, cap. 1, art. 2, probl. II, partic. II, n. 166 (Quarachi, p. 217 and 227); Saint Albert the Great, *II Sent.*, d. 3, art. 8; Albert the Great, *Summa theol.* II P., q. 14, memb. 4, art. 2. References found in Santiago M. Ramírez, *De caritate*, q. 26, art. 3, par. 708, n. 1, p. 487.

[77] See St. Albert echoing his predecessors in *Summa theol.* P. II, Tract IV, q. 14, memb. 4, art. 2, in Albert the Great, *Summae theologiae Pars secunda (Quaest. 1–67)*, vol. 32, *Opera omnia* (Paris: Ludovicum Vivès, 1895), 200.

[78] *ST* 1.60.5. See also *ST* 1-2.109.3; *ST* 2-2.26.3; and *Quodl.* 1.4.3.

[79] See *DM* 16.2, ad 17, and *ST* 1.109.2–3.

own good is more proper to itself than to any other creature. So, it seems that no one can love another human person more than himself. Would it not be the same with regard to love of God? Am I not more one with myself than with God? Is not my own good more proper to me than to God? It seems that love of God above love of self is not possible on Thomas's principles.[80] In order to respond to this difficulty, Thomas appeals to the relationship of part and whole while further elaborating his differentiated sense of *bonum suum* and even *bonum proprium*.[81] As we shall see, Thomas compares the creature to God as part to whole, since the creature is something belonging to God (*Dei est*).[82]

To follow Thomas, we must first appreciate those senses of the part-whole relationship that are closer to home. For Thomas, every part of an organic whole or substance has a natural inclination to preserve the whole more than itself. The reason is that the very nature of such a part is oriented towards the whole; it exists only *as* so oriented. Such parts are, after all, articulations or embodiments of the intelligibilities virtually contained in the substantial form. Thus, unlike subsistent parts of an accidental whole, which sometimes are only violently ordered to the good of the whole, their very existence depends on or derives from that of the whole. This ordering finds expression in the sacrifice an organic part makes for the good of the whole. The example Aquinas adduces is the movement of a hand to fend off a blow. A hand is part of the body. So, it exposes itself for the welfare of the whole body when a beating is threatened.[83]

So far, we have considered organic parts in relation to substantial wholes. We find the part-whole relationship also in an extended sense. If something subsists of itself, it cannot be an organic part. It can nevertheless be considered part of some non-organic whole. If the non-organic whole is artificial, the relationship might not be so profound. For example, the door of a car is a part of the whole car, an accidental whole. However, the door derives nothing from the whole, and it has its own rate of decay, whether or not it is attached to the car. The goodness of unity in an artifact such as a car is simply that of the function of the accidental whole. There seems to be no discernible orientation of the part to the whole in such cases, except that which is imposed by the artist. Hence,

---

[80] See *Sent.* 3.29.3, obj. 3.
[81] For a treatment of the early interpretations of this doctrine, see L.-B. Gillon, "L'argument du tout et de la partie après saint Thomas d'Aquin," *Angelicum* 28 (1951): 205–23 and 346–62.
[82] See *ST* 1.60.5.
[83] See *ST* 1.60.5.

the orientation is extrinsic or violent.⁸⁴

If, however, a subsistent thing derives its being, nature, or well-being from that of others, it can be considered a part in relation to the others, which can be considered, unitedly, to be a non-organic whole. For example, children receive their life, sustenance, and education through the family; so, they can be considered parts of the family. Further, if the very good of the subsistent thing is found more perfectly in others, it can in this sense be considered part of the others, which can unitedly be considered as a kind of whole. Thus, every man is part of the whole human race. Finally, if a subsistent good can attain a good that is sharable to many, it relates to this common good as a part relates to a whole.⁸⁵

This differentiated set of part-whole relationships allows Thomas to explore a differentiated sense of the *bonum suum*:

> [Now the *bonum suum* of anything can be understood in many ways]. One way depends on what is appropriate to the essential character of the individual. It is thus that an animal seeks his good, when he desires the food whereby he may be kept in existence. A second way depends on what is appropriate to the species. It is in this way that an animal desires his proper good, inasmuch as he desires the procreation of offspring and the nourishment of the same, or the performance of any other work that is for the preservation or protection of individuals belonging to his species.⁸⁶

The *bonum suum* is not simply and only a narrowly defined good. Further, as the *bonum suum* admits an extended understanding, so Thomas's dictum that everything loves its *bonum suum* can be understood in extended senses. It is evident that everyone loves his own good, defined restrictively, that is, his substantial being and happiness. Yet, since every person is of the human race, each also naturally loves that which conduces to the common good of all men. Both of these loves are natural tendencies; that is, they are not chosen. The individual man is naturally ordered to the common good of all men more than he is ordered to his own private good.⁸⁷ Whether he acts on this in the realm of freedom is another matter.

---

⁸⁴ This is a classical sense of violent inclination, having nothing to do with unjust force. In short, such violent inclination has its sole impetus from without, not from within. By contrast, natural inclination is from within.
⁸⁵ See De Koninck, *Primacy*, 76–86.
⁸⁶ *SCG* 3.24, par. 7.
⁸⁷ See *ST* 1-2.94.2 and *SCG* 3.24, par. 7.

We are at length prepared to grasp Thomas's application of the part-whole relationship to that of creature to God. Since every creature belongs to God, it relates to God somewhat in the way that a part relates to its whole. Of course, God is unlike each of the kinds of wholes considered above. God is not a subsistent that is composed of parts. So, the creature is not an organic part of God. Nor is God a community inclusive of created persons. So, created persons are not parts of a divine social collective. Nor is God an artifact that is put together. Rather, God exists essentially of Himself and is the very source of being and good for all His creatures. As Thomas puts it, God is a whole "before parts and without parts."[88] The "part," conversely, is a being that subsists in itself, a human hypostasis or individual man, while God is outside of all creaturely being. It might seem, then, that the analogy of "whole and part" has been extended so far as to be only improper or metaphorical. The proper meaning of the analogy appears broken.[89]

On closer inspection, Thomas is utilizing the foregoing examples as pedagogical introits to something more profound.[90] He is guiding us to

---

[88] See *DDN* 2.1, par. 113, and Gregory Stevens, "The Disinterested Love of God According to Saint Thomas and Some of His Modern Interpreters" (PhD diss., Angelicum, 1951), 171.

[89] Olver refers to Gilson's remarks on this very topic. Olver, "Love of God," 99. Gilson calls the part-whole analogy a "mere metaphor" by which Aquinas leads us by the hand to something more. Etienne Gilson, *The Spirit of Mediaeval Philosophy*, trans. A. H. C. Downes (Notre Dame: University of Notre Dame, 1936), 283ff. Gilson, a good Thomist, is right to see *manuductio* as the path to follow Aquinas. As I read Aquinas, that path leads to discovery that the "metaphor" is actually a "proper analogy"; I concur with Stevens on this point (Stevens, "The Disinterested Love of God," 316). Olver is right to criticize Gilson for reading Aquinas on the part-whole analogy as reducing love of God to love of self by instrumentalizing God as the mere condition for one's own existence (Olver, "Love of God," 115ff).

[90] Those who have closely studied his treatment of the Holy Trinity will recognize a similar pattern therein. At first blush, terms such as "father" and "generation" seem only metaphorically applicable to God, at best. On closer inspection, one can isolate pure perfections embedded distinctly in such terms. Hence, they can be said properly of God. Moreover, since God is the noblest Being, pure perfections are said more properly of God than of any creature. I find this procedure of initial discovery flowering into a mature restatement to be widespread in Aquinas.

Olver has studied the various texts in which Thomas employs the analogy and holds for a significant shift in Aquinas's thought, namely, that beginning with *ST* 1-2.109.3, Aquinas depicts the whole as the universe itself, of which each creature is part and of which the extrinsic good is God. My reading is not necessarily in conflict with Olver's. I aim to be discipling Thomas's method of digging round a matter, unearthing a core insight into a pure perfection, and judging its analogical fittingness to various things.

discern *participation* as central to the part-whole relationship. In short, every part "participates" in its whole. Nor is this sense of participation an empty term without causal account. Its notion is this: participation is to have in a limited way, from another, what the other has in plenary fashion. Efficient causality is the explanatory foundation for the participatory relation of existing goods.[91] Once we achieve this notion of participation, our understanding of the part-whole relationship undergoes a shift, a deepening; our definition has been enriched. In light of this shift we can return to the examples that first occasioned reflection on the part-whole relationship, evaluating them in light of the new definition. The examples adduced do not live up entirely to the mature notion they nonetheless somewhat instantiate. They approach it but do not fulfill it.[92] In fact, only one case of the relationship perfectly instantiates the notion, namely, that of creature to Creator. Every creature derives its being, nature, and well-being *entirely* from the Creator, who has in Himself all perfections in unlimited fashion, simply and undividedly. Most precisely, every creature is a "part" ordered to the whole universe, which itself is ordered to the (extrinsic) good of the

---

[91] I concur with Osborne on these points. See Osborne, *Love of Self*, 98ff.

[92] It should be noted that when Thomas draws the analogy (the higher is to the lower as the whole is to the part), he has a participatory framework in mind. He does not have in mind simply a comparison of greater to lesser status in being. That which is higher is as whole to that which is lower for two reasons. First, the lower derives its perfections or benefits in some way from the higher. Second, that which is higher contains the perfections of that which is lower but without the limits and fragmentedness proper to the lower level of existence. We should, finally, acknowledge that it is not simply true, according to Thomas, that that which is higher exhaustively has the perfections of that which is lower.

The "hierarchy of being" attests to the deficiency of any creature on any level of existence to represent the divine goodness. Hence, in order the best to represent his goodness, God created not merely a set of highly noble beings but an unspeakably vast range of beings, from slime to the supreme angelic substances. An angel in some ways is a "whole" including whatever perfections there are in lower beings, but in other ways the lower beings represent the divine in ways that elude even the angels, as the flowers of the field are more splendid than Solomon. A universe with both higher and lower creatures better represents the divine bounty.

Moreover, as Charles De Koninck argues, the very order of the universe is itself the immanent, created end that God intends in creating. By creating a multitude of diverse creatures, God is able to bring about a universal order, and the subsistent things in this order find it to be a good greater than themselves. The good of order is something in which each participates, and thus it is the good of each *qua* part of the whole universe. *A fortiori* is each thing ordered more to God than to its own private good. See De Koninck, *Primacy* and *Defense, passim*.

universe, God.⁹³ Thus, the part-whole relationship, in the sense of participation, applies perfectly *only* to the creature-Creator relationship and is therefore said most properly of this relationship.⁹⁴

Consequently, the creature's inclination to its own good has the character of a part's orientation to its good. The part does not incline simply to its own limited good; it inclines by nature more to the good of the whole than to its own good.⁹⁵ So, too, every creature inclines not merely to its own good but to those wholes to which it is ordered. Ultimately, the universe of creatures constitutes an ordered whole; so, each creature inclines, further, to the good of the entire universe, which is composed for this unity of order. Finally, the entire universe is ordered to God as to the extrinsic common good. Hence, each creature has a natural inclination to love God more than it loves itself.⁹⁶ Jordan Olver describes this lucidly:

> Each creature attains and shares in this good through its likeness to God, but representation of the divine good is better attained by the universe of creatures acting as a whole (like soldiers working for victory together rather than separately), and it is for this reason that Aquinas identifies the order of the universe as the greatest created good. The representation of the divine good exhibited by the universe as a whole is, consequently, the intrinsic common good of the universe, and God is the universe's extrinsic common good because he is that towards which the intrinsic good is ordered.⁹⁷

The love of God above self does not strike against the principle that unity founds love. Yet, in the case of a part's relation to its whole, the very identity of the part includes its reference to or dependence upon the whole.

---

⁹³ See *ST* 1.103.2; *ST* 1-2.109.3; *ST* 2-2.39.2, ad 2; *DP* 1.2, ad 1; and *In librum De causis*, lectio 10. God is a "certain (*quoddam*)" common good (*ST* 1.60.5, ad 5).

⁹⁴ See *In Phys*. 3.11, par. 385 and Ezra Sullivan, "Natural Self-Transcending Love According to Thomas Aquinas," *Nova et Vetera* 12 (2014): 941.

⁹⁵ I concur with Olver's analysis on this point. Olver, "Love of God," 118. Olver's hearty quip that the heart does not pump blood so as to remain alive, instrumentalizing the body to its own end, is a limpid illustration of the impertinence of standard objections to the analogy of part-whole ("Love of God," 121ff).

⁹⁶ This is the argument in *ST* 1-2.109.3, well articulated by Olver in his "Love of God." As for other objections to this rich analogy, Olver has amply refuted them ("Love of God," 120–26). Sullivan also points to *ST* 1.65.2, which elaborates the order of lesser parts to higher parts as well (Sullivan, "Self–Transcending," 922).

⁹⁷ Olver, "Love of God," 128. See also Olver, "*Bonum*," 691ff.

Its good is *that* it be ordered to the whole as to its end.⁹⁸ Hence, it would not suit a part to love itself in precision from its whole. In the love of God, the lover bears this ontological truth out affectively, undergoing an affective expansion.

There is, nonetheless, a difference between the expansion of self with regard to love of neighbor and that with regard to love of God. It is not simply a case of "becoming a larger, more extended I" in both cases, as some scholars at times imply.⁹⁹ Rousselot, for example, writes: "When I

---

⁹⁸ See Olver, "Love of God," 118, and Sullivan, "Self-Transcending," 923.

⁹⁹ Rousselot divides medieval theories of love into two types: physical and ecstatic. By "physical" he means natural. According to this theory, one must base "all real or possible loves on the necessary propensity of natural beings to seek their own good. For such authors, although hidden, there is between the love of God and the love of self a fundamental identity" (Rousselot, *The Problem of Love*, 78). He has Thomas principally in mind. According to Rousselot, Thomas reads the famous Aristotelian dictum about friendly feelings for others coming from friendly feelings for oneself as indicating "the *formal reason* of love." As a result, "one can maintain that an appetition is conceivable only as a seeking of oneself. This not only makes the altruistic inclinations derive from self-love, but also reduces them to it" (Rousselot, 83). He will explain the "manner" in which this reduction can be understood later in the text. Self-love is the "measure, model, and ground" of all loves and "surpasses them all" (Rousselot, 84–85). At this point, it sounds as though Rousselot approvingly regards Thomas's theory as egocentric.

Rousselot goes on to explain the matter in light of unity in part-whole relations. The part is but fragmentary, having its entire ordination to the whole; so, in its very self-love it more truly loves the whole of which it is but part (87–92). According to Rousselot, Thomas would find fault with the following question: whom ought one love more, God or self? "Instead of reducing the love of God to a mere form of the love of self, it is the love of self that is reduced to a mere form of the love of God" (94). That is, "To the extent that a being is a spirit there is an exact coincidence between its individual good and the good of God, but to the extent that a being is associated with matter the coincidence is looser" (Rousselot, 99). In the end, Rousselot's reading of Aquinas involves conflation of love of self and love of God, and his rhetoric frequently leads one to think of Aquinas as promoting ego-expansion. By contrast, Aquinas distinguishes but relates these loves.

Egenter, on the contrary, states that Thomas solves the problem of unselfish love of God by appealing to the expansion of one's concept of self (see *Gottesfreundschaft*, 26). Egenter appears to imply that love of God is but a form, albeit the highest form, of self-love (26 and 65). On the other hand, the conflation can be taken the other way, love of self being but a form of love of God (27). Egenter does differentiate self-love's relation to love of God from its relation to love of neighbor (44–45).

Bujo sounds an important warning here: "One must stress especially here that the fact that Thomas speaks of an *alter ipse* in *ST* 1-2.28.1, does not mean that he subsumes the otherness of the beloved under the *ipse* of the lover; rather, he rightly preserves this otherness on the basis of the act—act relationship" (*Die Begründung*, 155). Nicolas stresses that in friendship, neither the self nor the friend is the sole center of reference;

seek my pleasure and I believe that I am loving myself, in reality, more profoundly and more truly, it is God whom I love."[100] Such a conception involves a misconception of love and a misreading of Aquinas.

First, Rousselot misconceives love. He conflates the reason that everything has an attractive character—the divine good—with the good intended by this or that act of love Even in sinful loves, Rousselot opines that "the love of God remains the formal reason and as it were the heart [*l'âme*] of all our other loves."[101] This conception of love of God as the root of all appetition leads Rousselot to say, "Nothing is estranged from God; all things endeavor to unite with Him."[102] Rousselot hereby undercuts what is most profound in man, explicit rational love. Do the demons endeavor to unite with God? For Thomas, one does not really love God as God except when one intentionally loves *Him*. Since humans alone of all earthly creatures are capable of analytically arriving at knowledge of God and of believing in His providence, humans can and ought to love God explicitly, with the love that depends on knowledge. Rousselot bypasses this most significant and distinctive feature of human love and stresses non-conceptual love as more profound. This way of evaluating the relation between natural love and rational love is inverted. Indeed, this kind of inversion has been endemic in recent theology. The conscious life of man is relegated to a second-class, befuddled attendant to the non-rational but supposedly more profound "depths."[103]

Now, a Thomist surely must affirm the metaphysical truth behind Rousselot's claim that nothing has an attractive character except by its likeness to God, for God alone is goodness itself.[104] Thomas puts this most strongly as follows: "Something is assimilated to God insofar as it is good. Now, this or that particular good has the character of being appetible insofar as it is a similitude of the first goodness. Therefore, a thing tends to its own good on account of this, that it tends to the divine similitude, and not conversely."[105] Thomas goes on immediately to describe four ways in which something can be taken as "one's own good." In this exposition, he clearly

---

rather, the two in communion together are the reference, and the reference is singular insofar as they are united in the good they have in common ("Amour de soi," 38).

[100] Rousselot, *The Problem of Love*, 92.
[101] Rousselot, 123.
[102] Rousselot, 94.
[103] What comes especially to mind is Karl Rahner's disastrous application of the probably mistaken division of the categorical and transcendental aspects of human action.
[104] See *DV* 22.2, and *SCG* 3.17 and 19.
[105] *SCG* 3.24, par. 6.

shows that beings of different grades tend to their "own good" in these different ways. The imperfect tend to their singular good; the perfect tend to the good of the species; the more perfect tend to the good of the genus; and the most perfect (God) causes all good in everything. Although each thing finds its own good attractive because it is a divine similitude, yet each does so in its own way. The least profound way is that among things lacking life. The more profound is that among intellectual beings. Indeed, Thomas elsewhere says that, whereas nature intends pleasure for the sake of operation, yet the particular animal intends pleasure.[106] Indeed, Thomas distinguishes the power governing the whole, *natura naturans*, from the distinct inclinations of each thing. Whereas the governor of all intends the death of this for the life of that, each thing intends to be. The inclination of the form is to be, not to perish, although matter is intrinsically open to another form. Therefore, from the inclination of matter, living physical things "tend" towards their deaths.[107] Regarding these different levels of inclination, Nicolas states, "[i]t is undeniable that for [Thomas] sensible love and rational [spiritual] love are simply the superior forms of the inclination of nature."[108] Further, "[e]licited love is the superior form of the natural appetite."[109] Nicolas is correct, and Rousselot is misguided, although Rousselot's thesis concurs with Nicolas's reading of the movement of rational appetite from self-love to love of God: both hold that this involves transition from the indeterminate to the determinate.[110]

Rousselot's reading of Aquinas is also mistaken. As Mansini notes, the perfect realization of the part-whole relationship entails an *inversion* of the way "similitude" as cause of love is determined. We have seen that similitude is a cause of love: a lover loves what has some similitude with itself. The standard that measures similitude in the case of love of a creature is the lover, not the beloved. In love of neighbor, I am the principle or measure of the similitude. In the case of God as object of natural love, it is the reverse. The creature is likened to God, not God to the creature.[111]

---

[106] See *ST* 1-2.4.2, ad 2.
[107] See *ST* 1-2.85.6.
[108] Nicolas, "Amour de soi," 17.
[109] Nicolas, "Amour de soi," 17.
[110] See Rousselot, *The Problem of Love*, 97.
[111] "So, while God's friendship for us can be said to involve a similitude, our likeness to him, our friendship for God does not mean we love him because he is like us. In charity, *our* friendship for God, the principle of likeness is suspended, or perhaps we could say, *aufgehoben*," Guy Mansini, "*Similitudo, Communicatio,* and the Friendship of Charity in Aquinas," in *Thomistica*, ed. E. Manning (Leuven: Peeters, 1995), 1–26, vol. 1, *Re-*

So, every creature has a natural tendency to God more than to its own private good. In particular, a man is ordered to God above all things since God is entirely the source of his being and goodness. Indeed, God is the source of the entire good of the universe:

> [W]here one is the whole cause of the existence and goodness of the other, that one is naturally more loved than self.... Now God is not only the good of one species, but is absolutely the universal good; hence everything in its own way naturally loves God more than itself.[112]

Although a man indeed tends towards his own good, he also tends towards God's good *more* than he tends towards his own good narrowly defined. Aquinas even claims that each thing tends to its own good on account of tending to the divine likeness, and not conversely.[113] With regard to intellectual creatures, the comparison at work must be that of two loves of friendship, love of self and love of God. We must now be more precise in what we mean by loving God "more" than self.

The question of "more" admits of two considerations, the good "object" willed for the beloved and the "degree" of intensity of the love itself. In his *Commentary on Galatians*, Thomas writes,

> Love can called greater or lesser in two ways. In one way, with regard to the object; in another way, with regard to the intensity of the act. For, to love someone is to will good to him. Thus, someone can love one person more than another, either because he wills the one a greater good as an object of love or because he more wills him good [than he does the other], that is, by a more intense love.[114]

The object concerns the good we will to the one we love. In love of another, we will good to our beloved, and there should be a proportion, actual or potential, between the good we will and the person for whom we will it. In

---

cherches de théologie ancienne et médiévale, Supplementa, 20. See also Sullivan's study of the part-whole relationship and Capreolus's astute reading of Aquinas (Sullivan, "Self-Transcending," 917ff).

[112] *ST* 1.60.5, ad 1.

[113] See *SCG* 3.24, par. 6. Still, this is a natural order; this does not mean that in the realm of free choice and human action, that every act of love is in fact love of God.

[114] *Ad Gal.* 6.2, par. 364. See also *ST* 2-2.26.7.

113

this sense, we love someone more to whom we will a greater good. The intensity of a perfection is a measure of the subject's "sharing" in some form to a greater or lesser extent. An act or operation is in a way a form; one "enters" this form more or less by performing the act more or less intensely. Or, we can say that an operation and its habit take root more or less deeply in some subject.[115] Consequently, intensity concerns the relation of the operation to the subject operating; it has to do with the *principal* of action. In the case of love, there is the following consequence. That object is lovable which is somehow one with oneself. So, that is more lovable, in terms of the intensity of love, which is more one with oneself. Intensity of love is in proportion to the nearness of the object to the lover himself.

Let us apply this distinction to the question at hand. As regards the object, one man can readily will another a greater good than he wills himself. For instance, a just person wills the most talented and virtuous person, rather than always himself, to be chosen as the leader of a group. An unconfused sports fan wills the athletic hero to gain the victory. Now, since God is infinite, clearly any sane person should will God a good greater than he wills himself. It would be literally suicide to be jealous of God's perfection.[116]

What about the intensity of love? Can one love a neighbor more intensely than one loves oneself? Thomas answers in the negative. Each created person is closer to himself than he is to any other created person. One is close to another created person by way of the other being similar to oneself.[117] Thus, each created person loves himself more intensely than he does any other created person.

When it comes to God, however, Thomas holds that every rational creature naturally tends to love God's good for God's sake more intensely than it inclines towards its own good. The reason has to do with the more perfect instantiation of the part-whole relationship, with the expanded sense of the *bonum suum*:

> There have been some who maintained that an angel loves God more than himself with natural love, both as to the love of concupiscence, through his seeking the divine good for himself [more] than his own good; and, in a fashion, as to the love of friendship, in so far as he naturally desires a greater good to God than to him-

---

[115] See *ST* 1-2.112.4.
[116] See *Sent.* 2.5.1.2; *SCG* 3.109, par. 8; *ST* 63.3; and *DM* 16.3.
[117] See *Sent.* 3.29.5, ad 2.

self; because he naturally wishes God to be God while as for himself, he wills to have his own nature. But absolutely speaking, out of natural love he loves himself more than he does God, because he naturally loves himself [more intensely and more principally than he loves God].

> The falsity of such an opinion stands in evidence, if one but consider whither natural movement tends in the natural order of things; because the natural tendency of things devoid of reason shows the nature of the natural inclination residing in the will of an intellectual nature. Now, in natural things, everything which, as such, naturally belongs to another, is [more] principally and more strongly inclined to that other to which it belongs, than towards itself. Such a natural tendency is evidenced from things which are moved according to nature: because *according as a thing is moved naturally, it has an inborn aptitude to be thus moved*, as stated in *Phys.* ii, text. 78. For we observe that the part naturally exposes itself in order to safeguard the whole; as, for instance, the hand is without deliberation exposed to the blow for the whole body's safety. And since reason copies nature, we find the same inclination among the social virtues; for it behooves the virtuous citizen to expose himself to the danger of death for the public weal of the state; and if man were a natural part of the city, then such inclination would be natural to him.
>
> Consequently, since God is the universal good, and under this good both man and angel and all creatures are comprised, because every creature in regard to its entire being naturally belongs to God, it follows that from natural love angel and man alike love God [more and more principally than they do themselves]. Otherwise, if either of them loved self more than God, it would follow that natural love would be perverse, and that it would not be perfected but destroyed by charity.[118]

Here, Aquinas uses not only the expression "more intensely" but also "more principally." What is the distinction? It is difficult to say. This is one of the very few texts in which both expressions are used together. There are, as Thomas's *Commentary on Galatians* suggests, two points of

---

[118] *ST* 1.60.5.

measurement: the object targeted (the good willed) and the relationship of the operation to the subject (the lover). Both "more intensely" and "more principally" appear to regard the relationship of the operation to the subject. Thus, if there is a pertinent distinction, these characteristics would seem to be ordered, one to another. Perhaps intensity is a consequence of principality: that is "more principal" which causally underlies something "less principal." If some love causes another love, it will be more intense than the love it causes. So, it seems that Aquinas is arguing that the natural love of self arises on the basis of the natural love of God for His own sake and above all things.[119] However, Aquinas elsewhere speaks of love of God as emerging from love of self. We shall treat these texts in the next section on elected love of God.

There are two senses in which the previous passage employs the word "naturally" in the phrase "naturally loves." First, naturally means that the inclination is from natural principles, not from those of grace. The final sentence makes this clear by distinguishing such love from that of charity.[120] Secondly, such love is natural in the sense that it is the natural inclination of the will, not due to free choice.[121] This meaning becomes evident in the middle of the response, wherein Thomas compares the will's natural inclination to the movements of natural bodies. Thomas's reply to the fifth objection makes this all the more evident. The objection argues that those who sin cease to love God more than they love themselves. Thomas responds that the will has a natural movement towards the universal good, which movement is ineradicable: "So far as [God] is the universal good of all, every thing naturally loves God more than [it loves] itself."[122] Of course, original sin obstructs the further realization of this natural inclination in an elected love of God.[123] We shall treat elected love in a moment.

In summary, we have encountered Thomas's further development of the order of loves laid out in Chapter Three, which treats the twofold end. Chapter Three regards the ultimate perfection man seeks, by a love of con-

---

[119] See, e.g., *ST* 1-2.109.3 and *SCG* 3.24, par. 6.

[120] On the plane of *natural* inclination, in the sense of innate disposition, every creature, even a demon, inclines to this love of God above self. On the plane of free choice, such love does require grace because of original sin.

[121] "If as we saw in the *Names* commentary the two loves are two kinds of *complacentia boni*, it is relevant for us to understand as well that the *bona* that provoke the two loves may be indifferently either what we are naturally ordered to such that we cannot not love it, or what we are by nature free to love or not love." Mansini, *"Duplex Amor,"* 176.

[122] *ST* 1.60.5, ad 5. For further confirmation, see also *ST* 1.63.1, ad 3 and 4.

[123] See *ST* 1-2.109.3.

cupiscence, for himself whom he loves by love of friendship. Thomas notes in *ST* 1-2.2.7, ad 2, that what is at stake in the inquiry on beatitude is the good one wills for oneself. There, he leaves unresolved the question whether one does (or should) love another, namely, the Divine Persons, more than himself. Thomas refers us to the argument found in his treatment of charity.[124] A text that can help us bring both considerations together is *Sent*. 4.491.2.1, ad 3:

> Whatever is loved by love of concupiscence cannot be the ultimate thing loved (*ultimum dilectum*), since it is referred to good of another, of the one, namely, for whom it is desired, but that which is loved by love of benevolence can be the ultimate thing loved. Therefore, created beatitude which is in us is not loved except by love of concupiscence. Whence we refer the love of it to ourselves and thus to God, since we must also refer ourselves to God.

We naturally love ourselves and thus seek the state of beatitude; however, we also have a natural tendency to love God more than ourselves. Thus far, I have treated the ordering of loves but not as explicitly free acts, to be examined in the next section.

I have followed Aquinas's analysis of the expansion of one's *bonum suum* all the way to the love of God by love of friendship. This path does not involve the denial of the starting principle, that love of self is first in the order of generation.[125] Here, Thomas attempts to walk a middle path. On the one hand, God is not to be referred to oneself in an ultimate act of love that places self above God. Rather, God must be loved for His own sake or on account of Himself: "To love one [on account of himself] can be understood in two ways. First, in such a way that one is loved as a final end; and thus only God should be loved [on account of Himself]."[126]

On the other hand, a man could not love God if He were not related to his own good narrowly defined. The logic of the expansion from self-love to love of God requires that there be a connection of the creature to God for God to be lovable with greater intensity than self. God is loved as the person's good, albeit as something more proper to the person than he is to himself. One does not simply love God because God is better than oneself in a sheerly objective but unrelated way. If He were simply bet-

---

[124] He returns to the question in *ST* 2-2.26.3.
[125] By contrast, see Avital Wohlman, "L'élaboration," 256–61.
[126] *DC* 8, ad 6.

ter in this way, one could perhaps will Him the infinite good in a remote and wishful way, but one would not love Him more intensely than one loves oneself. We see Thomas express this point in his consideration of a counterfactual situation: if *per impossibile* (if, supposing that the following impossible assumption were true) God were not related to the proper good of the creature as the whole cause of its being and goodness, God would not be the whole reason for the creature's love, "for it would not be in the nature of anyone to love God, except from this—that everything is dependent on that good which is God."[127] The creature could, perhaps, admire such a God's goodness and greatness. But such admiration would not be tantamount to loving God more than itself. Rather, it would be akin to someone marveling at a beautiful piece of art or an exquisite landscape in which he has no fervent interest. In Newmanian terms, this might be a merely "notional love." Perhaps in some respects, a man's love for some angel X belongs in this category. A man naturally loves angel X less intensely than he does himself, even though the angel is far superior in the natural order.[128] On the other hand, the analogy also fails, for the angel supports the human good. Further, the angel is connected with man in the communion of persons. Hence, a man indeed loves the angel; they are, finally, bound together in the communion of the saints. The very analogy of being shows the impossibility of the assumption. However, just such an assumption underlies certain readings of "pure love." Although such readings can be well intended, they rest on an ideology of metaphysical alienation. Premising such originate alienation, they attempt to bridge the chasms between persons by a love disconnected from self-love. For Aquinas, by contrast, communion in the good links together both self-love's relation to the love of other created persons and self-love's relation to love of God. Fellowship in a sharable good binds the sharing members together. Each finds his good in the fellowship. God, of course, only diffuses and does not gain from this fellowship.

It is noteworthy that Aquinas returns to this notion of the importance of communion in the good as foundation of love when he treats the order of charity. Without unduly anticipating chapters to come, I would

---

[127] *ST* 1.60.5, ad 2. See Gallagher, "Self-Love," 38 and Rousselot, *The Problem of Love*, 92f. For contrary readings of this passage, see Spaemann, "Die Lehre," 90–91 and Geiger, *Le Problème*, 22. Thomas subtly teaches the same in *Sent.* 3.29.5, maintaining that the "proper" good is measured by closeness to oneself. No creature is closer to another than each is to itself. God, however, as intimate and total cause of any creature's *bonum proprium*, is more proper to it than it is to itself.

[128] See *ST* 2-2.26.4.

like to attend briefly to a similar *per impossibile* reflection on charity. In heaven, Aquinas writes,

> God will be to each one the entire reason of his love, for God is man's entire good. For if we make the impossible supposition that God were not man's good, He would not be man's reason for loving. Hence it is that in the order of love man should [most love himself after God].[129]

The statement is quite pointed: were God not man's good, God would not be man's reason for loving. One could will such an alien God to be the Infinite *Esse* (in a remote and unrelated sense), but one could not love Him in the way one actually can love the God in whom one partakes. So, although God is loved more than oneself naturally, self-love is naturally first in the order of generation, for it is from the natural inclination to one's good that the person also has a greater inclination to God Himself as to what is more properly and excellently his own good.[130]

Elected Love of God

The natural love of God above self, present in every rational creature, makes possible an elected or freely chosen love of God above self. It is in this realm of freedom that the problem of love appears in all its profundity. When it comes to a decision of free will, the most significant consideration is the ultimate end. Does a man seek his ultimate end in riches, in pleasures, in himself, or in God?[131] More precisely, does he love God more for His own sake than for the beatitude found by union with God? As we shall see, choice of the ultimate end is the object of consideration in the first moral act. According to Aquinas, as there is natural dilection for God above self, so there is possible free love of God that is more intense than love of self.

---

[129] *ST* 2-2.26.13, ad 3.

[130] The point regarding alienation is crucial. It serves both to correct misbegotten articulations of eudaimonism and to ward off the nihilism of voluntaristic, disinterested altruism.

[131] Failure to choose God involves both intellectual and volitional dimensions. The detailed treatment required for just treatment of this matter is beyond the scope of this work. On the topic, see Lawrence Dewan, "The Real Distinction between Intellect and Will," *Angelicum* 57 (1980): 557–93; Cornelio Fabro, "La dialettica d'intelligenza e voluntà nella costituzione dell'atto libero," *Doctor communis* 30 (1977): 163–91; Hoffmann; and Sherwin.

Clearly, only rational creatures can achieve free acts. Hence, only rational creatures can have elected dilection. Further, only rational creatures can have knowledge of and thus explicit love for God:

> To reduce conclusions to their principles or secondary causes to their first causes belongs only to the power of reasoning. Hence only a rational nature can trace secondary ends back to God by a sort of analytic procedure so as to seek God Himself explicitly. In demonstrative sciences a conclusion is correctly drawn by a reduction to first principles. In the same way the appetite of a rational creature is correctly directed only by an explicit appetitive tendency to God, either actual or habitual.[132]

We now come to the significant question. In the state of integral nature, is it possible to love God more and more intensely than one loves oneself? Thomas unequivocally answers "yes." If there were no natural, non-elected love of God above self, natural love would be perverse: "Otherwise, if one loved self above God naturally, it would follow that natural love would be perverse and that it would not be perfected but destroyed by charity."[133]

Does Aquinas, further, teach that an elected, natural love of God above self is possible in the state of integral nature? His thought necessarily implies it. He explicitly states that the aforesaid natural inclination must be present in any state of nature, including that of damnation.[134] Thus, when he contends that the love of God above all things, more than self, is not possible without the help of grace for those in the state of original sin, he is not referring to the mere inclination to love but to freely elicited love of God.[135] Therefore, in the state of integral nature, it must be possible to elicit a free act of love of God above self.[136] Another argument can be made. Right order demands that God be loved more than oneself. Thus,

---

[132] *DV* 22.2, corp.

[133] *ST* 1.60.5. See, again, *DDN* 4.9 and 10; *ST* 1.60.1, ad 3; *ST* 1-2.62.1, ad 3; *ST* 1-2.109.3; *ST* 2.2.26.3; *Quodl*. 1.4.3; *Ad 1 Corin*. 13.4, par. 806. Thomas's conviction in these texts represents a development from an earlier reticence (see *Sent*. 3.29.3). For an excellent treatment of natural love, see M.-R. Gagnebet, "L'amour naturel de Dieu chez saint Thomas et ses contemporains," *Revue thomiste* 49 (1948): 424–46, and Gagnebet, "L'amour naturel de Dieu chez saint Thomas et ses contemporains II," *Revue thomiste* 49 (1949): 31–102. More recently, Thomas Osborne has competently addressed this matter (see Osborne, *Love of Self*, 70–86).

[134] This claim is evident in *ST* 1.60.5, ad 5.

[135] See *ST* 1-2.109.3.

[136] See *ST* 1-2.109.3 and also *DV* 22.2.

the just man is one who chooses to direct himself to God: "Therefore, according to right reason and the instinct of nature everyone refers himself to God, as the part is referred to the good of the whole."[137] Hence, failure to love God above self by elected love entails moral fault. Now, Aquinas teaches that in the state of integral nature it would be possible not to sin either venially or mortally throughout life.[138] So, Thomistic principles imply that an elected love of God above all things is possible in the order of integral nature without supernatural grace.

It goes without saying that such a free act, a reduction from potency to actuality, requires the help of God as Source and End of being. It does not, however, require grace. Not all divine help (*divinum auxilium*) is grace properly so-called. Some divine help is in the order of nature, and some is in the order of grace. In each order, in fact, God works in two ways to bring about achievement. Thomas articulates this twofold divine work in *ST* 1-2.109.1–2. In the order of nature, God bestows forms or proximate principles of operation and also moves things to their operations. For instance, God gives man an intellect and moves him to the operations of thought. Likewise, He gives man a will and moves him to acts of will. Thomas calls God's action as Prime Mover "help" (*auxilium*); this is help in the order of nature. Thomas argues for a similar twofold help in the order of grace throughout his treatise on grace: God not only produces supernatural operations but bestows the forms whereby such operations are connatural and sweet to the human person.[139]

Now, election involves freedom of choice, which entails the possibility of the opposite choice. Hence, if an elected love of God is possible, it remains possible for a free pilgrim constituted in the state of integral nature to choose *not* to love God above self. Elected love is *electable* and thus allows the possibility of failure. That failure, Thomas describes in *SCG* 3.109, comes from not ordering one's own good to the ultimate end itself, which is God. It is impossible, he holds, not to will one's proper good (narrowly construed). So, if one's proper good is not identical with God, then moral failure is possible. Hence, he concludes, every agent except God is able morally to fail:

---

[137] *De perf.* 13.
[138] See *ST* 1-2.109.8. See also *DM* 3.1, ad 9.
[139] See esp., *ST* 1-2.110.2–3. Shields errs in taking the special help that would be given in a state of integral nature for grace properly so-called (see Shields, "Will," 116, 133, and 138–42).

> Every will naturally wishes what is a proper good for the volitional agent, namely, perfect being itself, and it cannot will the contrary of this. So, in the case of a volitional agent whose proper good is the ultimate end, no sin of the will can occur, for the ultimate end is not included under the order of another end; instead, all other ends are contained under its order. Now, this kind of volitional agent is God, Whose being is the highest goodness, which is the ultimate end. Hence, in God there can be no sin of the will.
>
> But in any other kind of volitional agent, whose proper good must be included under the order of another good, it is possible for sin of the will to occur, if it be considered in its own nature. Indeed, although natural inclination of the will is present in every volitional agent to will and to love its own perfection so that it cannot will the contrary of this, yet it is not so naturally implanted in the agent to so order its perfection to another end, that it cannot fail in regard to it, for the higher end is not proper to its nature, but to a higher nature. It is left, then, to the agent's choice, to order his own proper perfection to a higher end. In fact, this is the difference between those agents who have a will, and those things which are devoid of will: the possessors of will order themselves and their actions to the end, and so they are said to be free in their choice; whereas those devoid of will do not order themselves to their end, but are ordered by a higher agent, being moved by another being to the end, not by themselves.
>
> Therefore, it was possible for sin to occur in the will of a separate substance, because it did not order its proper good (*proprium bonum*) and perfection to its ultimate end, but stuck to its own good as an end.[140]

As I read this passage, it regards all intellectual creatures in any order, whether in the state of (pilgrim) grace or in the state of integral nature. According to my reading, Thomas teaches that every such creature is confronted with a choice, whether or not to order itself to the ultimate end, which is God. In ordering itself to God, it would love the ultimate end by

---

[140] *SCG* 3.109, pars. 7–8. The English text is taken from Thomas Aquinas, *Summa Contra Gentiles, Book Three: Providence (Part II)*, trans. Charles J. O'Neil (New York: Doubleday, 1957).

a love of friendship more than it loves its own good and perfection. While a certain natural inclination conduces to this choice, it does not make the choice inevitable, even for an angel.

However, reputable scholars would understandably object that the scope of Thomas's claim is not as broad as I have made it. They hold that, for Thomas, angels created in the state of integral nature would be factually impeccable; that is, such angels would not sin. They hold, further, that all angels are "peccable" in the sense that they are not necessarily impeccable in every order.[141] Such scholars can refer to a number of texts that imply that an angel can sin only in view of the offer of grace.[142] According to such texts, an angel would sin by willing to attain the good end (beatific vision) in an evil way, that is, by its own power apart from the promise of grace.[143] The objection is significant. I offer the following comments in response.

First, the above citation from this text constitutes the heart of Thomas's response (*SCG* 3.109) to a question about the possibility of angelic sin, nestled in the context of objections (*SCG* 3.108) and replies (*SCG* 3.110). None of the arguments makes any appeal to the offer of grace as the condition for the possibility of angelic sin. Perhaps, then, this text (*SCG* 3.109) simply differs from those adduced by the respectable scholars who would object to my reading. Second, Thomas draws an analogy here between human and angelic sin. Humans can sin by following their lower appetite against the order of reason; angels are not capable of this misfortune. However, he argues, humans and angels alike can fail to order their proper good to God. None would disagree that man can sin in this way in the state of integral nature. So, the very analogy suggests that the scope of the claim includes angels in the state of integral nature; else, why not further differentiate capacity for sin in angels and men, likening them only with respect to the offer of grace? Third, *SCG* 3.110 indicates that the angelic sin consisted in failure to love a good, namely, the higher good. Instead, the angel simply loved his own good and perfection. In this regard, it clear-

---

[141] See C. Courtès, "La peccabilité de l'ange chez saint Thomas," *Revue thomiste* 53 (1953): 158n5.

[142] See *DM* 16.3; *ST* 1.63.1, ad 3; and *ST* 1.63.3. Gagnebet offers a powerful analysis defending this thesis in "L'amour II," (1949), 72–86.

[143] Proponents of this reading include Gagnabet and Courtès. In addition to their above-cited works, see also Courtès, "Le traité des anges et la fin ultime de l'esprit," *Revue thomiste* 54 (1954): 155–65. For more reading on the significant but elusive topic, see Serge-Thomas Bonino, *Angels and Demons: A Catholic Introduction*, trans. Michael J. Miller (Washington, DC: The Catholic University of America Press, 2016), 197–201, esp. 197ff, n25.

ly differs from *DM* 16.3, which lays the fault with the *way* the angels loved the supernatural end. Fourth, other texts share elements of the argumentation and of the scope of the claims in *SCG* 3.109,[144] and some reputable scholars defend the reading that I defend.[145]

It remains to consider *how* the transition to this elected love of God is effected, at least as it occurs in man. On the one hand, God remains the end of elected love and is not turned back towards the lover, as though loved by the love of concupiscence merely as source and object of beatitude.[146] On the other hand, this love of God emerges from self-love.[147] One discovers that the best way to love himself is to love God precisely for His own sake.[148]

Does Aquinas's claim, to be discussed presently, that elected love of God emerges from love of self conflict with his claim that each thing loves its own good on account of the divine likeness?[149] I do not think so, for the former claim involves the genesis of elected love and the latter involves the natural order imposed by God. As will be explained, in the genetic order and from the point of view of the human person, elected love of God emerges from love of self. Because the order of the Creator's intention is from A to X does not mean that the intended order of the creature is always identical. The genetic order may be from X to A. True, no good is desirable except because it participates in the divine good. True, God orders all things to Himself as to the ultimate end. However, a cow seeks a particular blade of grass, not God. Similarly, human love on the conceptual

---

[144] See *DV* 24.7 and *Sent* 2.5.1.1.

[145] See Jacques Maritain, *The Sin of the Angel: An Essay on a Re-Interpretation of Some Thomistic Positions*, trans. William Rossner (Westminster, MD: The Newman Press, 1959) and Tobias Hoffmann, "Aquinas and Intellectual Determinism: The Test Case of Angelic Sin," *Archiv für Geschichte der Philosophie* 89 (2007): 122–56.

[146] Olver charges Gallagher with violating this principle (Olver, "*Bonum*," 685). Olver sides with Wohlman and Geiger, against Gallagher, in contending that "love of others for their own sake is impossible if we make love of self the foundation of our affective acts" ("*Bonum*," 686). Gallagher, however, identifies a *generational* priority. It is as though a particular act of self-love is *occasion* for the conversion to maturity. While in general I find I concur with Olver's recent analysis, on this issue I find I concur more with Shields.

[147] One of the clearest texts on this point is *DS* 3. See Gallagher, "Self-Love," 24–25. Of course, to love God above self also constitutes the realization of man's own good, but this realization is not the final cause of the love of God above love of self. If it were, God would ultimately be referred back to oneself.

[148] See Gallagher, "Self-Love," 38–39.

[149] See *SCG* 3.24, par. 6.

plane (*voluntas ut ratio*) naturally inclines to the lover's proper good narrowly defined and from this basis is converted to the love of God above self.

Thomas touches upon the generational priority of self-love in his description of the first moral act.¹⁵⁰ The inquiry is whether it is possible for someone in the state of original sin to sin venially while not sinning mortally. Thomas answers in the negative for the following reason. All mortal sins regard the end, for every mortal sin involves a rejection, either explicit or implicit, of the ultimate end. Now, a person who has already made any choice has either oriented himself rightly to the last end or not. If he has done so, God has justified him by grace, and so he is in the state of grace and no longer in the state of original sin. If he has not, he has sinned mortally and is thus in the state of mortal sin. This inquiry leads Thomas to inquire about the first moral act. The end is the first thing in the order of intention even though it may be the last thing attained in the order of execution. What then happens in the first moral act, the first free act? It will be recalled that all choice rests on natural love of beatitude. However, this natural love reaches out not to a particular good but to the perfecting good in general. The perfecting good in general names the aspect of appetibility in whatever can be rationally lovable. One always chooses something under this aspect.¹⁵¹ Still, among choices and among the objects of free choice, there is an order. The choice of means is always subordinate to a loved end; if love of that end is chosen, it is prior to love of the means chosen out of an intention for it.¹⁵² In the order of intention, the end is first. Conversely, for pilgrims and the needy, the order of execution begins with the last of the means to be chosen. If I choose to eat, I must then choose what to eat, where to eat, and how to get there. The first action I undertake is the last chosen in the order of intention. Clearly, the most crucial object of choice in terms of the macropicture is that *wherein* one's ultimate end lies.¹⁵³ This choice leads to sundry other choices in its service. As Aquinas contends, this choice of the good which one takes to be the instantiation of one's ultimate end is at stake in the first choice to be made by any individual, since one subsequently directs other chosen things towards this chosen end. This chosen end will be either God or something else. If it is not God, one sins mortally and remains in the state of sin until by

---

¹⁵⁰ See J. Maritain, "The Immanent Dialectic of the First Act of Freedom" in *The Range of Reason* (New York: Charles Scribner's Sons, 1952), 66–85.
¹⁵¹ See *ST* 1-2.2.8.
¹⁵² For Thomas's complex study of intention and choice, see especially *ST* 1-2.12 and 13. See also the fine study in Sherwin, *By Knowledge*, 81–94.
¹⁵³ See *ST* 1-2.1.4.

grace one converts to the love of God above self in charity. Further, one's habitual orientation is towards this idol of choice, be it money or power or pleasure, etc. Nonetheless, since one's will still has the good in universal as its object, it remains possible to commit free acts not ordered to the idol, acts that target legitimate particular goods in ways, in principle, open to the true ultimate end though not actually ordered thereto. In short, it is possible for one in the state of sin to commit free acts that are not even venial sins.[154]

What criteria inform the choice of the thing one takes to be the ultimate end, the instantiation of the good in universal? According to Thomas, the person on the cusp of freedom considers first himself: "The first thing that occurs to a man to think about then, is to deliberate about himself."[155] In thinking about himself, he is thinking about his good. How could things be otherwise? Love follows knowledge, and we first know things close at hand before we know their cause: "*As each thing knows itself before it knows something else, even God, so also the love which someone has for himself is prior to that love which he has for another in the way of generation.*"[156] The deliberation begins with the self and thus involves also ordering other things to oneself as end, since "the end is the first thing in the intention."[157] The question at stake is, in what object should one place one's ultimate end? If the consideration concludes with the self as end, one will order all things to oneself. If one takes God as the ultimate end, one will order even oneself to God as to the ultimate end.[158] Clearly, Thomas is describing a query deeply embedded in natural love of self.

According to David Gallagher,

> [T]he turning to God, the decision to love God above all else, is taken precisely in view of what will be best for the person himself. In other words, it is precisely on the basis of his self-love that the person chooses to love God more than himself. On the basis of wanting what is best for self—self-love—a person chooses to love God above self.[159]

---

[154] See *ST* 1-2.109.8.
[155] *ST* 1-2.89.6.
[156] *Sent.* 3.29.3, ad 3, emphasis mine. Aquinas held to the opinion that God is not the first thing known. *ST* 1.88.3.
[157] *ST* 1-2.89.6, ad 3.
[158] See *ST* 1-2.89.6 and Gallagher, "Self-Love," 39.
[159] Gallagher, "Self-Love," 39. See the surrounding discussion in "Self-Love," 35–39. Of course, once one loves God, one does achieve an augmentation of one's well-being. Yet,

Perhaps expressing something similar himself, Thomas writes, "A man truly loves himself by ordering himself to God."[160] Still, as we saw above, the just man will choose God himself as ultimate end. Aquinas refers to such a choice in his treatment of the first moral act: "If he then direct himself to the due end, he will, by means of grace, receive the remission of original sin."[161] Should he fail to do this, he would sin mortally. Hence, Aquinas answers the initial question in the negative: A person cannot be in the state of original sin with only venial sin. Venial sin requires a free act, and anyone who has acted freely is *either* in the state of grace *or* in the state of mortal sin.

This first moral act, performed rightly, involves two loves of friendship. There is a natural free love of friendship for oneself and a *free* love of friendship for God more than oneself. Love of friendship for oneself necessarily involves love of concupiscence for one's own beatitude. Love of friendship for God involves willing God to be the good that He is, uncreated beatitude.

As we saw an expanded sense of *bonum suum* in our treatment of love of neighbor, so we encounter a third sense of *bonum suum* and even *bonum proprium*, namely God Himself as our good:

> God is a good greater than anything else, and He is more proper to each thing than is anything else, for He is more intimate to the soul than it is to itself, as is said in the book *On the Spirit and the soul*. Thus, God is more to be loved than anything else.[162]

We can link our earlier consideration of the part-whole relationship with this expanded sense of *bonum suum*. Just as participation is most perfectly found in the creature-Creator relationship, so is God most perfectly one's *bonum suum*.[163] That is most one's proper good which is both one's greatest good and most one's own. God, of course is the greatest good, for He is the First and Noblest Being. More intimately, He is also most one's own, since as Creator His plan of wisdom and causal power are more deeply active in the created spirit than is the created spirit itself. Indeed, whereas created spirits are free, God alone inclines their wills naturally to the final

---

the love of God is not maintained "in order that" but rather "with the result that" thereby one achieves one's greatest perfection. See Bujo, *Die Begründung*, 171.

[160] *ST* 1-2.100.5, ad 1. See also *ST* 2-2.25.4, ad 3.
[161] *ST* 1-2.89.6.
[162] *Sent.*, 3.29.3, sc 2.
[163] Once again, this is not to take *bonum proprium* in the sense of *bonum privatum*.

end; they have not competence to do this.¹⁶⁴ Since God is greater than any other good and is more proper to any spiritual being than it is to itself, He can be called even the *bonum proprium* more properly than anything else. In the order of knowing, *bonum proprium* is more natively said of what is identical with or belongs to oneself. In the order of excellence and being, we discover that the very expression has its most perfect realization in God.¹⁶⁵ Thomas's commentary on Psalm 32 brings this out explicitly: "Therefore the beatitude of man is to inhere in God. For each thing is perfect if it inheres in its proper good. But the proper good of man is God."¹⁶⁶ Consequently, joy is true "when it regards the proper good of man, which is not something created but God."¹⁶⁷ Thomas states the same in the *Prima secundae*: "[Just men] seek to inhere in God as in the proper good."¹⁶⁸

The law of action follows the law of being. Thus, precisely because God is most perfectly one's proper good, one should refer one's own proper good narrowly defined to God as to an end. Indeed, Thomas holds that one should *entirely* refer one's own good to God. That is, in the love of God there should be not only a partial ecstasy, as there is in love of neighbor, but a thorough and complete ecstasy:

> When the affection of the lover is brought to a beloved [which is] superior, to whom the lover himself belongs, the lover orders his very own good to the beloved. Thus, if a hand could love a man, it would order what it itself is to the whole. It would, therefore, be placed totally outside itself because in no way would something of itself be left for itself, but the whole [of it] would be ordered to the beloved.¹⁶⁹

Now, a hand has a certain kind of relative independence of status, being an imperfect hypostatic part and not an ordinary "accident." Further, a hand

---

[164] *ST* 1.105.4.

[165] If we rank the various things to which its *res significata* properly applies, we find God at the acme, for the *res significata* applies to God without restriction. Hence, *bonum proprium* signifies God preeminently. In the order of knowing, of course, the matter is somewhat the reverse, since we discover lesser goods, such as sensible goods, first. I say "somewhat" because some lesser goods are discovered later, such as the good of dopamine for the brain.

[166] *Psalm*. 32.11.

[167] *Ad Phil*. 4.1, par. 153.

[168] *ST* 1-2.109.6.

[169] *DDN* 4.10, par. 432.

has sundry elements and structures that "virtually" have their own intelligibility and being. Thus, the hand is *less* the human hypostasis's than any creature is God's. Consequently, we should take Thomas's claim all the more strongly with regard to the creature's relationship to God. In subsequent chapters, we will explore this ecstatic character as it is exemplified in the love of charity.

If perhaps Thomas's stress on ecstasy satisfies concerns of some who seek a kind of purity in love, it may conversely worry others. Perhaps Thomas has robbed man of his primal thirst for happiness? Not so. If God is most properly one's good, subjecting oneself to God must be the creature's good as well: "In this consists our whole good: that we be subjected to God."[170] The subjection is not slavish but natural (in accordance with nature, in accordance with one's creaturely status) and good:

> Everything that is naturally subject to something has its good in this: that it be subject to that thing. So, the good of the appetite for sensible things in man is that it be regulated by reason. Now every will, both of an angel and of a man, is naturally subject to God. The good of the angelic and human will, therefore, is that it be regulated by the divine will.[171]

Cleaving to God is a perfection of man as an ultimate operation uniting him to God.

In this chapter, we have waded into the realm of grace in our analyses. Does this spoil our findings? This calls for some comment. First, the basic points concerning natural love of God, both innate and elected, have been established. A purely natural order is possible, since grace is a gift the gratuity of which is distinct from the gratuity of creation itself. However, in a purely natural universe, an elected love of God must be possible, or else it would be necessary for rational creatures to be unjust.

Second, in the concrete order in which we find ourselves, free love of God takes place in a situation of both grace and sin. The first moral act does not take place in a purely natural state; rather, the human person coming to the use of reason is in the state of original sin but offered graces. As all are aware, Aquinas judges it to be impossible for one in such a state to love God above self by way of freely chosen natural dilection. Original sin involves the loss of sanctifying grace and a wound to nature's vigor for

---

[170] *Sent.* 4.15.4.1.3, ad 3.
[171] *DDN* 4.19, par. 537.

right action.[172] In His mercy, God calls, through operating graces, those in such a state to salvation by way of justification. Hence, the concrete expression of this first free choice is inseparable from an acceptance of offered grace.[173] Each person, begotten in a corrupt state yet target of God's actual operative graces, is faced with the choice between ordering himself to God and choosing himself as ultimate end.

Conclusion

Love of other created persons is rooted in and modeled after love of self. Thus, there is a genetic priority to love of self. Yet, genuine love of another does not subject the other's good to that of the self but involves the willing of the other's good for his own sake. Because for Aquinas all love involves union, in the love of another the self does not will the other's good in a remote or disinterested way, as though the other is an alien to whom one wills a separated good. Instead, the lover's own good expands through the affective expansion entailed in, or constitutive of, love of friendship for another. This expansion is not an overcoming of metaphysical alienation, although in the context of human weakness and sin it is an overcoming of selfishness. There is a metaphysical basis for this expansion, because the potency for it is the substantial good of the other, with either its promise or a real possession of the perfecting good, as bearing similitude to that of the lover. By the union of love, the lover bears himself towards the beloved as he does towards himself. This description is not to the detriment of the distinction of lover and beloved, for the ecstasy of love is genuine and lasting. It would cease to be love of another were it not. The ecstasy and the mutual indwelling are preserved in and entailed by each other. Thus, love of another is not the union of unrelated goods, not the anonymous willing of another's good, but the intimate bond of two in the common good of friendship.

Love of God involves a similar but different expansion of one's own good. In the case of love of God, one's own good is not the measure of the similitude; rather, God's good is the measure, since one's own good is entirely from and modeled on God's good. Further, in the case of love

---

[172] Natural here is distinguished from supernatural. See *ST* 1-2.109.3. Whether Thomas's position is correct is another matter. I read the "corrupt state" as do most Thomists, namely, as the state in which anyone begotten of Adam remains until justified. Would it be possible to read "corrupt state" as more precisely indicating the state of one who has deliberately fallen into mortal sin without yet being justified?

[173] More precisely, such an act is already supported by operative actual grace.

of God, the ecstasy is not only true but entire or complete. Such love of God has a natural, non-elected root in the human person. In the order of integral nature, it would be possible to execute a well-lived life the apex of which would be love of God the First Cause above all things and more intensely than oneself. In our concrete sinful situation, however, such love is according to Thomas impossible without grace. Moreover, even were it executed and expressed in prudent action, such love is not the limit of man's capacity. The divine power can awaken in man an intimate and covenantal friendship for himself, one grounded on the supernatural communication of divine good to the human person. To this love of charity we now turn.

CHAPTER 5

Charity and Love of Beatitude

CHARITY PERFECTS THE NATURAL LOVE OF GOD, both as elected and as non-elected.[1] Based upon the gratuitous communication of divine beatitude, charity is a friendship with God.[2] As are all friendships, charity is a rich and manifold reality. Central among its acts is love of friendship for God as Supernatural Friend, with reference to which one wills, by love of concupiscence, God to "have" the beatitude He is. Thus, this central act involves benevolence, or willing good to another, yet this willing is colored with the fervor proper to love. This fervent love of the other is mutual, God's for man and man's for God. Finally, this fervent love drives towards fellowship or real union. Although natural love of friendship for God is possible in the state of integrity, charity is the noblest possible love for God. Charity grows during earthly life and is perfected in the life of glory, in which one attains the greatest beatitude and also loves God perfectly above all things and loves all things, including oneself and created beatitude, in perfect subordination to God. The relationship between self-love and love of God for His own sake is thus best grasped through consideration of heavenly charity. Since, however, such a consideration requires an

---

[1] There is, to repeat, a natural love of God present in any rational creature. Realization of an elected love of God cannot, Aquinas argues, occur in the fallen world except by the aid of healing grace in the justified man.

[2] For secondary work on this topic see Leo M. Bond, "A Comparison between Human and Divine Friendship," *The Thomist* 3 (1941): 54–94; Anthony W. Keaty, "Thomas's Authority for Identifying Charity as Friendship: Aristotle or John 15?," *The Thomist* 62 (1998): 581–601; Fergus Kerr, "Charity as Friendship," in *Language, Meaning and God: Essays in Honour of Herbert McCabe*, ed. Brian Davies (London: Geoffrey Chapman, 1987), 1–23; G. Mansini, "*Similitudo*"; McEvoy, "Amitié"; McEvoy, "*Philia* and *Amicitia*: The Philosophy of Friendship from Plato to Aquinas," *Sewanee Mediaeval Colloquium Occasional Papers* 2 (1985): 1–23.

understanding of charity in general, we first investigate the general relationship between charity and the love of beatitude. In the present chapter, we will discuss charity itself and its manifold relation to love of beatitude.

Charity as Friendship with God

Famously, Thomas defines charity as "a certain friendship of man to God."[3] Thomas's notion is rich, lean though his poetry is. Without wishing to simplify his thought, I hope to identify its core elements so as to discuss the problem of love in light thereof. It is not possible to treat his notion comprehensively here, although hopefully it can be done justice.

Two key passages succinctly present Thomas's thought on charity as friendship. In *ST* 1-2.65.5, Thomas judiciously adumbrates the features of charity treated in this and the next two chapters:

> Charity signifies not only the love of God but also a certain friendship for Him. Friendship adds, in addition to love, a certain mutual return of loving affection with a certain mutual communication, as is said in *Ethics Book VIII*. That this pertains to charity is evident from what is said in 1 Jn 4:16, "Who remains in charity, remains in God, and God in him" and from what is said in 1 Cor 1:9, "God is faithful, by whom you were called into fellowship with his Son." Now, this fellowship of man towards God, which is a certain familiar intercourse with him, indeed begins in this life by grace but is perfected in the future life by glory. The truth of each of these [realizations of friendship] is held by faith and hope. So, as someone cannot have friendship with one whom he disbelieves or with whom he despairs to have any fellowship or familiar intercourse, so someone cannot have friendship for God, or charity, unless he have the faith by which he believes in this kind of fellowship and intercourse of man with God and unless he hopes to attain to this fellowship.[4]

In this passage, we discover several key elements of charity as friendship; we also glimpse charity in the twofold perspective of its inchoate state on pilgrimage and its perfected state in glory. The better-known passage in *ST* 2-2.23.1 further explicates some of these elements. Thus, with the help

---

[3] *ST* 2-2.23.1 (my translation and emphasis).
[4] *ST* 1-2.65.5 (my translation).

of the latter, we will unfold the elements of charity as friendship.

Elements of Charity as Friendship

The first key element to note is the foundation of the friendship. Friendships are founded on a good held (loved) in common. Here, Thomas speaks of a "communication." This is a variegated concept. It is sufficient at present to note that the term involves a sharing of the good. At least once, Thomas speaks of communication in the natural goods of creation as laying a foundation for a natural friendship of man to God:

> Now, we have a twofold relationship with God. One is with respect to the goods of nature, which we participate presently from Him.... According to [this] first communication, there is a natural friendship with God, according as each thing, insofar as it is, has an appetite for God as the first cause and highest good, and desires Him as his end.[5]

Even were God not to offer intellectual creatures grace, their existence would not of itself, apart from sin, be meaningless and wretched. Notwithstanding, such a friendship would be very limited and remote. Charity is not sufficiently founded on this basis. Instead, charity involves a radically higher communication with God. It is founded on gifts totally exceeding the formal object of natural reason and will; it is founded on the communication of supernatural goods:

> The [second relationship] is with regard to beatitude, insofar as we are presently partakers by grace of supernal felicity, insofar as this is presently possible, while we also hope to arrive at the perfect attainment of that eternal beatitude and to be made citizens of the heavenly Jerusalem.... According to [this] second communication there is the love of charity, by which only the intellectual creature loves God.[6]

The formality of charity's friendship, or the formal object of the love ingredient in this friendship, is God as (supernatural) beatitude. By His

---

[5] *In Corinth*. 13.4, par. 806. Sullivan also refers to this text and this reality of natural friendship (see Sullivan, "Self-Transcending," 943).

[6] *In Corinth*. 13.4, par. 806.

grace, God offers this friendship to man now, with a promise of its fruition hereafter. Elsewhere, Aquinas remarkably notes that, when such communication has taken place, "it is necessary that some friendship is founded upon it."[7] If the communication occurs, friendship arises. The claim is remarkable.

The elements of charity, however, all stand together. We cannot consider this communication adequately until we first take cognizance of the other elements. After treating these, we will return to elusive aspects of the communication.

The second key element to note is love. If charity signifies "not only the love of God,"[8] it surely signifies the love of God. What kind of love does it signify? A number of points are in answer to the question. First of all, we must consider the object of charity. Its object is the Most Noble Being, God. Not only is the material object noblest, but the formal object or the aspect under which God is targeted is the noblest possible, God as Triune Beatitude.[9] This formality is a crucial determinant distinguishing the love of charity from a purely natural love of God for His own sake.[10] Thomas writes,

> Now the proper object of love is the good, as stated above (*ST* 1-2.27.1), so that wherever there is a special aspect of good, there is a special kind of love. But the Divine good, inasmuch as it is the object of [beatitude], has a special aspect of good, wherefore the love of charity, which is the love of that good, is a special kind of love. Therefore charity is a special virtue.[11]

That Thomas identifies charity's object with God as object of (supernatural) beatitude demonstrates that he would not accept a reading of charity as either disinterested or opposed to self-love. When we appreciate the connection of Thomas's "treatises," we are compelled to specify the formal object as the Triune God, for God cannot be man's supernatural beatitude except as He is in Himself, the Triune God. The gift of charity tends towards the full presence of God in vision. In consequence of charity's noble

---

[7] See *ST* 2-2.23.1.
[8] *ST* 1-2.65.5.
[9] If the prophets of old had charity without having the Triune faith, it is possible to have charity without believing God to be Triune. And so it is. However, the gift of charity tends towards the vision, and the vision necessarily has the Triune God as its object.
[10] See *ST* 1-2.109.3, ad 1.
[11] *ST* 2-2.23.4.

formality is the nobility of its efficient cause. God as Triune Beatitude surpasses all natural powers. There is no created natural principle sufficient to elicit such an act so as to develop a virtue for it. God alone can infuse the virtue of charity and His supernatural help is required to elicit the act of charity. In the next chapter we shall treat also the necessity of faith for the pilgrim's possession of charity.

Secondly, the love of charity involves real benevolence towards the beloved. Benevolence is willing the good of the beloved for his own sake. All loves reach out toward the good; however, not all loves involve willing the good of the loved object. Some objects are loved only for the good they bring the lover. One loves ice cream not for itself but for its delightful taste. Charity comes with the note of benevolence, since who has charity loves God for His own sake. Charity thus includes a love of friendship for God, with reference to which one wills God to have the supernatural good that He is. So, in the love of charity, there is clearly an ecstatic element; the lover's affection goes out to God for God's sake. This point is central, but it is not sufficient.

Importantly, not all benevolence is even real love. As we have seen, genuine love is an affective union that by its character aims at real union with the loved good. Thomas observes that there is a kind benevolence that does not involve such an aim. He describes it as a kind of "well wishing" that does not incline the one who wishes well to seek company with the object of benevolence. For instance, someone might casually will good to one of two competitors without seeking the presence of either. Whereas love that reaches out to another only to obtain something from him runs against genuine benevolence, genuine love of another is not sheer benevolence. Genuine love stretches towards the beloved, zealously and stably seeking union with him:

> [Benevolence] properly speaking is that act of the will whereby we wish well to another. Now this act of the will differs from actual love, considered not only as being in the sensitive appetite but also as being in the intellective appetite or will. For the love which is in the sensitive appetite is a passion. Now every passion seeks its object with a certain eagerness. And the passion of love is not aroused suddenly, but is born of an earnest consideration of the object loved; wherefore the Philosopher, showing the difference between goodwill and the love which is a passion, says (*Ethic.* ix. 5) that [benevolence] *does not imply impetuosity or desire*, that is to say, has not an eager inclination, because it is by the sole

judgment of his reason that one man wishes another well. Again such like love arises from previous acquaintance, whereas [benevolence] sometimes arises suddenly, as happens to us if we look on at a boxing match, and we wish one of the boxers to win. But the love, which is in the intellective appetite, also differs from [benevolence], because it denotes a certain union of [affection of the lover to the beloved], in as much as the lover deems the beloved as somewhat united to him, or belonging to him, and so tends toward him. On the other hand, [benevolence] is a simple act of the will, whereby we wish a person well, even without presupposing the aforesaid union of the affections with him.

[Therefore, benevolence is certainly included in rational love, according as it is an act of charity. But *dilectio* or love adds the union of affection. On account of this addition, the philosopher says that benevolence is the beginning of friendship].[12]

This passage brings together several aspects of charity, most notably, its benevolent character and its "engaged" or "interested" character. The love of charity includes the will's complacency in the divine beatitude as a good towards which the just man wants to tend. Together with benevolence, there is a love for God in charity. In *ST* 2-2.23.1, Aquinas points to the engaged aspect of love in stating "neither does benevolence suffice for the notion of friendship; there is also required a certain mutual affection (*mutua amatio*)." In *ST* 1-2.65.5, he states that charity adds to love a certain "mutual return of affection (*mutuam redamationem*)." Finally, love involves a vehement movement of the appetite of the lover towards the beloved; love cannot, then, be mere whim. In these respects, love is more than or other than sheer benevolence.

We can draw together these various notes of charity. First, its object is God as Triune Beatitude. Second, it comes with benevolence. Third, it is a genuine *love*, including an affective fervor and involving the judgment of reason (elevated by grace), that seeks union with the beloved. Fourth, foundational to charity is the communication from God to man of supernatural beatitude. I would like to return to this foundational element, enigmatic as it is.

R. Egenter argues with some force that Thomas adapts and applies Aristotle's insight that friendship is founded on a *communicatio* to his the-

---

[12] *ST* 2-2.27.2.

ory of love. For Aristotle, *communicatio* means *convivere*, the act itself of friendship being its basis. According to Egenter, Aquinas interprets *communicatio* in an ontologically rich way, according to a Platonic conception of sharing, participation. Similitude, in the Platonic conception of things, bespeaks a sharing of form not simply in the order of predication but in the order of real communication. Thus, *communicatio* or ontological sharing of a form grounds friendship. As it grounds friendship, so it grounds love, according to Thomas, who applies this element of Aristotle's theory of friendship, reading it metaphysically, to his theory of love.[13] When treating of the foundation of charity as the *communicatio* of properly divine goods to man, Egenter takes to task those who, failing to see its ontological depths and jumping straight to operations, read *communicatio* as simply *convivere*.[14] The term "charity" refers to a habit and an act. As a habit divinely infused, charity has a stable entitative aspect, elevating the volitional power to the supernatural level by specifying its formal object to be God in His own supernatural being. This habit of charity is also ordered to its realization in particular acts.[15] Egenter's suggestion makes sense of Thomas's phraseology: "Now, the love that is founded upon this communication is charity."[16] If "friendship" names the relationship in its entirety of man to God in grace, to be consummated in glory, then acts of love form part of this relationship.[17]

Charity as a Created Habit

A friendship between two earthly pilgrims is not simply the sum of acts of love and conversation. It includes an element of stability that continues even when the acts do not occur. One aspect of this stability is the virtues associated with the friendship *as* they have a concretized order to the particular friend. For Thomas, there is a set of habits and virtues in charity's friendship with God.

Most foundationally, there is the habit of grace in the essence of the soul. By this habit of grace, the human person formally participates in a si-

---

[13] See Egenter, *Gottesfreundschaft*, 38–44.
[14] See Egenter, 55. Here, Egenter targets M. Th. Coconnier.
[15] See Egenter, 61–62.
[16] *ST* 2-2.23.1 (my translation).
[17] There is a "dilection" that is charity. See *Sent.* 3.27.2.4.4, ad 2; *Sent.* 3.28.1.7; *DV* 25.3, ad 5; *SCG* 3.158; *ST* 2-2.25.2, ad 1; *ST* 2-2.26.1; *ST* 2-2.31.2; etc. For a comparison of *amor*, *dilectio*, and *caritas*, see *ST* 1-2.26.3.

militude of the divine nature.[18] Whereas in virtue of his natural principles, a man is ordered to a connatural end, in virtue of the supernatural habit of grace in the soul, he is ordered to a supernatural end.[19] That end is living the life that is proper to God, insofar as this is possible through grace and glory. As God knows Himself immediately and loves Himself accordingly, with the infinite act that He is, so man's end according to God's promise is to know God immediately and love Him accordingly. The foundation of man's relationship to God in nature is augmented or further actualized by this gift of grace in the soul, together with other habitual graces and sundry actual graces. This further actualization is not the simple development of a natural orientation, as though a bare refinement of it. The actualization is the bestowal of the higher formality in the relationship, God as object of beatitude and not simply as source and end of nature.

With respect to this elevation of human nature, operative habits of grace are also in order. That is, the theological virtues and the gifts of the Spirit are in order. As operative habits, these are stable dispositions to the performance of an act that is good for the actor. Aquinas notes that virtue has reference to essence or nature: an action can be described as good for the actor only if it accords with his nature as being perfective of him. Whereas the four cardinal virtues are perfective of man as man, the theological virtues are perfective of man as an adopted child of God called to supernatural beatitude. These virtues enable God's child to act in a manner befitting his adoption.[20]

Before treating the theological virtues distinctly, we may note the two common aspects of each. First, they are called "theological" for three reasons. (a) They have God as their direct object, since by them one is ordered immediately to God. By contrast, in the state of integrity one could only have inferential and indirect knowledge of God. To know God immediately would not be one's end. (b) These virtues are not acquired but infused by God alone. (c) Our knowledge of the existence of these virtues comes through divine revelation.[21] Second, they are "virtues" as being stable operative habits. They are in the category of accident, each being a certain infused "quality" that inheres in or further actualizes an operative power. As such, they incline the power to a certain act.

Of the theological virtues, the first that is required, without which

---

[18] See *ST* 1-2.110.3.
[19] See *ST* 1.62, arts. 1 and 2 and *ST* 1-2.62.1.
[20] See *ST* 1-2.110.3 and *DC* 2.
[21] See *ST* 1-2.62.1.

the others cannot be (in the pilgrim state), is faith. The reason faith is required is that in order freely to journey towards an end, one must will the end so as to order the means to it. Now, one cannot will what one does not know, and "[n]atural knowledge cannot attain to God according as He is the object of beatitude." So, "[a]s the ultimate end is indeed in the will through hope and charity, but in the intellect through faith, faith must be the first of all the virtues."[22]

Through hope, the second theological virtue, the will is strengthened to desire attainment of such a surpassing end. The obstacles of natural limitation and sin present threats to this desire. Only by manfully facing these threats and the ardor of attaining glory can we possibly make the journey. The strength required is divine. Hope leans with absolute confidence on God's strength and mercy in order that we may through divine help make this journey in a fitting manner.[23]

We come at last to the created habit or virtue of charity. First, we should consider whether there is such a thing. Thomas Aquinas famously argued against Peter Lombard concerning the existence of a created habit of charity. Lombard held that acts of charity are immediate effects of the Holy Spirit wrought in a man without a created medium or principle. For Lombard there is no created virtue of charity, although there are virtues of faith and hope. Instead, the Holy Spirit's effective power produces the acts of charity in the human heart. As Aquinas notes, correctly, Lombard did not hereby deny that the justified person has created acts of charity. Acts of charity are human acts: it is really the man who is loving God. What Lombard denied is that any created principle disposes to these acts. He asserted this in order to uphold the transcendent character of acts of charity.[24]

---

[22] *ST* 2-2.4.7 (my translations). Another crucial point being made here is that the theological virtues rank above the cardinal virtues, since the theological virtues order one to the ultimate end. We should not think that because grace builds on nature we should first work on a purely natural foundation only subsequently to establish a supernatural foundation. Such would be a mistaken conception, misleading in its direction and founded on pride.

[23] See *ST* 2-2.17, arts. 1 and 2.

[24] Lombard holds that the Spirit so communicates Himself to the human person that that person is made a true lover of God and neighbor: "Unless the Holy Spirit is so communicated to someone that he be made a lover of God and neighbor, he is not brought from God's left hand to his right hand" (Lombard, *I Sent*, dist. 17, chap. 4, 145:17–19). Further, Lombard claims that charity alone distinguishes the children of the kingdom from the children of darkness (*I Sent*, dist. 17, chap. 4, 145:14–16). Consequently, there is no ground for seeing Lombard as precursor to Martin Luther's theory of justification

Thomas affirms Lombard's defense of created acts but argues that in order for there to be created acts of charity the will must be adequately disposed.[25] Thomas's argument is unremitting. First, he argues remotely from the way God moves all things. God moves each thing to its due end, not simply as an efficient cause moving an exterior thing but as a bestower of forms, whereby each is inclined to the end to which it is ordained.[26] Thus, God disposes all things sweetly for the purposes He has in mind for them. If God so disposes all things in the order of nature, how much more does He dispose those things He loves in a special way, His own adopted children.[27] Second, the very character of an act of rational love demands that it be voluntary or in accordance with an intrinsic principle of inclination. Dilection is an act of will and thus voluntary. So, it is intrinsically contradictory to hold that something is an act of will and that there is no intrinsic inclination to the act.[28] Thomas then poses this dilemma: if there is no created virtue of charity, one of two impossible results follows, "Either that act of charity is not voluntary, which is impossible because to love something is to will it; or it does not exceed the capability of nature, and this view is heretical."[29] Third, unless there is an intrinsic principle of the act of charity, then in the act of charity man would only be moved as an instrument and not moving as a coworker. In such case, the act of charity would not be meritorious. Since without charity merit is impossible, there would be no human merit at all, which is false.[30] In light of the Council of Trent, we can note that this argument makes appeal not simply to a loosely held tradition of merit but to the dogma of faith.[31] Finally, Thomas even adds an argument from experience. It is clear from the experience of the saints that acts of charity are the sweetest of acts. Thus, they conform to a saint's disposition. Since human nature does not dispose a man to acts of charity, a created

---

by faith alone.

[25] See G. Hibbert, "Created and uncreated Charity: A Study of the Doctrinal and Historical Context of St. Thomas's Teaching on the Nature of Charity," *Recherches de théologie ancienne et médiévale* 31 (1964): 63–84; J. Stufler, "Petrus Lombardus und Thomas von Aquin über die Natur der caritas," *Zeitschrift für katholische Theologie* 51 (1927): 399–408; F. Zigon, "Der Begriff des Caritas beim Lombardus und der hl. Thomas von Aquin," *Divus Thomas* 4 (1926): 404–24.

[26] See *ST* 2-2.23.2.

[27] See *DV* 27.2; *ST* 1-2.109.1; *ST* 1-2.110.1; and *DC* 1.

[28] See *ST* 2-2.23.2 and *DC* 1.

[29] *DC* 1.

[30] See *ST* 2-2.23.2 and *DC* 1.

[31] See Trent VI, chapter 16 and canon 32.

habit must be added to make them pleasing[32] and virtuous.[33]

Charity is also infused directly by God. Having God as supernatural beatitude as an object of one's act is not possible to any created power. Much less so is having a stable disposition to such an act. Thus, "[c]harity can be in us neither naturally, nor through acquisition by the natural powers, but by the infusion of the Holy Ghost, who is the love of the Father and the Son, and the participation of Whom in us is created charity."[34] In sum, Thomas accounts for the gratuitous and volitional traits of charity by rooting its act in a created habit, by tracing that habit back to the free gift of grace, and by stressing the constant need of actual grace for acts of charity.[35]

The net result of the transformation of man by habitual and actual graces is a stable relationship of man to God. This relationship is the friendship of charity. Before turning to a consideration of the various ways in which the love of beatitude is related to charity, we should now consider one difficulty concerning charity as a love.

A Difficulty

We have suggested that charity is like love, and we noted that for Thomas love regards its object whether present or absent. It would seem, then, that charity does not necessarily require the presence of God. Richard Egenter, however, points to texts wherein Thomas maintains the opposite of this claim.[36] In a discussion of the theological virtues, Thomas asks whether charity is the greatest of the three.[37] Although each virtue has God as its object, faith and hope regard the object as not possessed. The love of charity, on the other hand, "is of that which is already possessed: since the beloved is, in a manner, in the lover, and again, the lover is drawn by

---

[32] See *DC* 2, ad 15 and *ST* 1-2.110.3.
[33] See *ST* 2-2.23.2.
[34] *ST* 2-2.24.2.
[35] For crucial teaching concerning actual grace, see *ST* 1-2.111.2. Lonergan's study of this element in Aquinas is quite good. See Bernard Lonergan, *Grace and Freedom: Operative Grace in the Thought of St. Thomas Aquinas*, ed. Frederick Crowe and Robert Doran, vol. 12, *Collected Works of Bernard Lonergan* (Toronto: University of Toronto Press, 2000).
[36] See Egenter, *Gottesfreundschaft*, 79–80.
[37] The following remarks are not meant to divert the topic to charity but to discuss a difficulty in order to bring greater clarity to a reading of Thomas's doctrine of love as a passion.

[his affection] to union with the beloved."[38] Here, Thomas claims that charity is of what is already possessed. This statement offers the only other apparent exception to Thomas's mature teaching on love in general, which regards its object, whether possessed or not possessed.

Egenter attempts to solve the apparent contradiction by adverting to the indwelling of the Holy Spirit.[39] Because the divine indwelling occurs through sanctifying grace, it enjoys a natural priority to the created love of charity, which is an effect of that grace. Therefore, the love of charity is of something that is already possessed, namely, the Holy Spirit who dwells within the justified person. Egenter then concludes that Thomas identifies love with real, not merely affective, union:

> Further, [this indwelling] signifies not merely a union according to natural affection, and not merely a union of similitude, but rather a union according to reality. To be sure, this is not to be taken in the pantheistic sense of a mingling of beings, but rather in the sense of a real personal presence precisely through indwelling.[40]

If Egenter is correct, then the love that is charity does not share the general property of love as of what is either present or absent.

On the other hand, we should also advert to Thomas's insistence that charity is the one theological virtue that belongs to both wayfarer and blessed. Beatific vision and the mystical indwelling that pilgrims enjoy on earth are not identical; otherwise, all pilgrims would be finally blessed. The passage Egenter cites continues: "Again, the lover is drawn by desire to union with the beloved."[41] Undoubtedly, desire is of that which is not yet possessed. Thus, the charity of the wayfarer must also be of that which is not yet possessed. So, even in this text Thomas teaches that charity can be (and, for the wayfarer, is) of what is not had. Indeed, in a subsequent question Aquinas contends, "Charity is love, the nature of which does not include imperfection, since it may relate to an object either possessed or not possessed, either seen or not seen."[42] Egenter's insistence that Thomas

---

[38] *ST* 1-2.66.6 and *ST* 2-2.23.6, ad 3. Thomas also distinguishes hope and charity by the fact that hope involves a person tending to the end, whereas charity involves the a certain transformation of the person into the end. See *ST* 1-2.62.3.
[39] See *ST* 1.37.1.
[40] Egenter, *Gottesfreundschaft*, 79. Recall Thomas's distinction at *ST* 1-2.28.1, ad 2.
[41] *ST* 1-2.66.6.
[42] *ST* 1-2.67.6.

holds charity to be a "union of real presence" cannot be sustained without qualification.[43] The solution may lie in the character of charity as an infused theological virtue. Although a created habit making man both formally just and also capable of eliciting meritorious acts, charity is not acquired by human action, requires the constant divine infusion from above, and, most importantly, ever has as corollary the divine indwelling which on earth anticipates beatific union.[44] All this notwithstanding, anticipation is not consummation: all creation groans.

Charity and Love of Beatitude

Charity and love of beatitude are neither antithetical nor merely juxtaposed. The matter has a certain complexity to it, both on account of the creaturely realities concerned and on account of the pilgrim or developmental stages. I advert to this complexity somewhat in this chapter and more pointedly in the next chapter, which treats the charity of the wayfarer. Chapter Six examines the simplicity of charity in heavenly life.

Charity has a manifold relationship to the love of beatitude. Moreover, there are various kinds of love of beatitude. I treat, first, the ways in which the love of beatitude rooted in self-love can lead towards charity. Second, I take stock of a threefold relationship of self-love to charity: as incompatible, as included therein, and as juxtaposed thereto. Third, I suggest yet one more way in which love of beatitude is included in charity, that is, as an ecstatic attraction.

Love of Beatitude Leading to Charity

Thomas in various ways articulates how charity can have developmental roots in love of beatitude. To be sure, one does not mount up to a perfect act of charity by way of nature.[45] Nor does one mount up to charity by way of gifts of grace that are not already formally effective for sanctifica-

---

[43] Egenter recognizes that these and other like statements offer some difficulties for his reading, but his interpretations of these are more relevant to the discussion of the problem of love in particular.

[44] See *ST* 1.43.3.

[45] By perfect we mean that the act is one of true and stable charity, at least in its issue, although it may be the first such act. By contrast, an act that has some of the elements of a true act of charity, one that is inchoate or whose issue is fleeting and not integral in perfection, is an imperfect act of charity. In short, perfect charity means actual charity; imperfect charity means only charity in potency.

tion. The first act of charity must be the result of God's further action on an as yet unjustified man, even if this person has been increasingly open to the calling of grace.[46] Notwithstanding, certain factors in the man whom God is calling are dispositive towards this divinely given yet freely willed act of charity.

As we have seen in the previous chapter, one way in which Thomas summarily puts this is to appeal to the order of generation. In the *Sent.*, an objector argues that because love of others, even love of God, is rooted in self-love, the other will never be loved more than oneself. Thomas replies:

> The friendly relations that are towards another come from those that are for oneself, not as from a final cause, but as from that which is prior in the order of generation. For as anything belonging to oneself is known before something else, even God, so too the love that someone has for himself is prior to that which he has towards another, *in the way of generation*.[47]

The order of finality is not the order of generation. In the order of freely elected loves, self-love comes first because self-knowledge is, as it were, connatural to the acting subject. In the order of finality, the other is loved for his own sake. Out of charity, God is indeed loved for His own sake, and more than oneself, but self-love can lead towards such transcendent love in the way of generation.

Thomas explores this path of generation most clearly in his treatments of hope as prior to charity. In each treatment, Aquinas at least implicitly compares the foundation of hope to charity as imperfect love relates to perfect love. He identifies a transition from the one to the other. There is an aspect of this transition that is, as it were, spontaneous or fluid, and there is an aspect that involves deliberate conversion and decision.

In a kind of natural way, the theological virtue of hope, founded on the natural love of beatitude, leads to the recognition of God as related to one's good (*bonum suum*). Since one loves one's good, this recognition disposes one to love of God for His sake. This occurs as follows. Hope precedes charity in the order of becoming because a man first seeks his own good. Beatitude, so elusive for frail mankind, requires hope in order to

---

[46] See *ST* 1-2.111, art. 2 and *ST* 1-2.112.2. Besides Lonergan's work, another fine work on the topic is Joseph Wawrykow, *God's Grace and Human Action: 'Merit' in the Theology of Thomas Aquinas* (Notre Dame: University of Notre Dame Press, 1995).

[47] *Sent.* 3.29.3, ad 2 and ad 3.

overcome the obstacles to its attainment. The man who believes in God as the giver of all good can, with God's help, come to hope in Him for eternal beatitude. Further, this hope leads to the love of charity:

> [A] man loves a thing because he apprehends it as his good. Now from the very fact that a man hopes to be able to obtain some good through someone, he looks on the man in whom he hopes as a good of his own. Hence for the very reason that a man hopes in someone, he proceeds to love him: so that in the order of generation, hope precedes charity as regards their respective acts.[48]

The description here makes the transition from unformed hope to charity seem somewhat connatural or spontaneous. When we hope, we can come to see God as our good, since He is source of all our good and mercifully promises to bring us to perfect happiness. Once again, we encounter the expansion of the *bonum suum* from self to God: "Because by the very fact that we hope that good will accrue to us through someone, we are moved towards him as to our own good; and thus we begin to love him."[49] So, hope can lead to charity. Conversely, charity in turn stimulates and strengthens hope:

> As stated above (Q. 40, A. 7), in treating of the passions, hope regards two things. One as its principal object, viz., the good hoped for. With regard to this, love always precedes hope: for good is never hoped for unless it be desired and loved. Hope also regards the person from whom a man hopes to be able to obtain some good. With regard to this, hope precedes love at first; though afterwards hope is increased by love. Because from the fact that a man thinks that he can obtain a good through someone, he begins to love him: and from the fact that he loves him, he then hopes all the more in him.[50]

In the order of becoming, hope precedes charity because one first hopes to attain certain goods. Then, one comes to look upon the provider of these goods as one's own good; thus, one comes to love the provider. Finally, love of the provider enkindles greater confidence in His help and thus greater

---

[48] *ST* 1-2.62.4.
[49] *ST* 1-2.40.7.
[50] *ST* 1-2.62.4, ad 3. See also *DS* 3.

hope. Now, the love of the goods one hopes to attain is part of self-love. Thus, charity increases self-love.[51]

Hope and faith can also dispose us to be converted to charity by way of confronting us with the promise of a great good and the threat of a great evil. Faith and hope can bring us to take sober stock of our future. A good self-regard, informed by the gifts of these theological virtues, can spur us towards adopting the divine good itself as the reason for action, for example, for converting to God as our ultimate end to be loved for His own sake. This latter explanation more visibly portrays the paradoxically self-interested character of the transition from self-love to love of God. Hope incites one to undertake whatever is necessary to avoid the punishments and obtain the rewards that faith reveals. The initial motivation is self-interest, not *as* ignoble but certainly *as* self-regarding. However, the condition for the realization of this interest is the love of God for His own sake.

Of course, faith informs the sinner that he cannot achieve this conversion unless God brings it about. Thus, hope opens a weak man to trust in God for the grace to obtain and accomplish what he cannot do on his own power, namely, to love God out of charity with all his might. It is as though Thomas is commenting on the parable of the rich young man: "What good deed must I do, to have eternal life?" (Matt 19:16). The rich young man is concerned for his own welfare: what must I do *so as to attain eternal life*? The desire is not evil, although it is not the love that saves. Thomas compares it to an imperfect love:

> Now there is a perfect, and an imperfect love. Perfect love is that whereby a man is loved in himself, as when someone wishes [good to someone]; thus a man loves his friend. Imperfect love is that [by which a man loves something not in itself but so that this good may come to himself]; thus a man loves what he desires [*concupiscit*]. The first love of God pertains to charity, which adheres to God [in Himself]; while hope pertains to the second love, since he that hopes, intends to obtain possession of something for himself.

Hence in the order of generation, hope precedes charity. For just as a man is led to love God, through fear of being punished by Him for his sins, as Augustine states (*In primam can-*

---

[51] In this respect, Wohlman and Dom Gregory Stevens rightly describe the love of God as leading to love of self. They neglect the root of natural and supernatural love of God in self-love.

on. *Joan., Tract.* ix), so too, hope leads to charity, in as much as a man through hoping to be rewarded by God, is encouraged to love God and obey His commandments.[52]

In *DS* 3, Aquinas adds also the role of fear of punishment. Such fear is grounded in the faith that makes one certain that what pagans vaguely and divergently suspect to be the case is indeed the case, a future of eternal woe for those who rebel against God's love. This fear can thus be present with or without hope. Perhaps the most comprehensive elaboration is in the *Tertia pars*, wherein Aquinas narrates six acts by which, under God's grace, we are converted from mortal sin. First, God operates in us, calling us. Second, one comes to believe that God exists, that He is who He is (Triune, Father of Jesus, etc.), that He loves man, and that He will judge him in the end. Third, there is a "movement of servile fear" whereby one fears being punished for sins. Fourth, there is a "movement of hope," by which one hopes to obtain mercy from God and thus determines to emend one's life. Fifth, there is a "movement of charity" by which the person detests sin because it is offensive to God and not because it will bring punishment. Finally, there is the "movement of filial fear" by which he freely or spontaneously makes satisfaction to God.[53]

These narratives of the movement from self-love to love of God resemble Thomas's treatment of the deliberation involved in the first moral act. Although the life of charity may appear arduous, hope can urge a man to venture the risk of love. If the offered charity is, through grace, received and acted upon, its own logic begins to operate so that the lover no longer seeks his private good as primary.

Moreover, the interesting and vital connection between self-love and love of God does not stop here. The love upon which hope is based is not usurped by charity. Rather, the latter perfects the former: "On the other hand, in the order of perfection charity naturally precedes hope, wherefore, with the advent of charity hope is made more perfect, because we hope chiefly in our friends."[54] Self-love continues to exist, and is even reinforced, with the advent of charity. In what precise senses can self-love and charity coexist?

---

[52] *ST* 2-2.17.8. See also *DS* 3. The published translation of this passage called for some greater precision, which appears in brackets. *Secundum se* and *sui gratia* are not exactly identical. *Secundum se* is usually pitted against the *per accidens* or the *secundum aliud*. See *DDN* 4.10, par. 429.
[53] See *ST* 3.85.5.
[54] *ST* 2-2.17.8.

Threefold Relationship of Self-Love to Charity

Thomas observes that there are three forms of self-love in relation to charity. He analyzes these forms while inquiring whether he who has charity still fears the divine punishment that threatens his particular good. Fear presupposes love. So, fear of the loss of one's own loved good presupposes self-love. The text, quite lengthy, is worth citation:

> Servile fear comes from love of self because it is a fear of the punishment which is harmful to one's own good. Thus, the fear of punishment can remain with charity in the same way as self-love does, for it is for the same reason that a man loves his own good and that he fears to be deprived of it.
>
> Now self-love can relate in a threefold manner to charity. In one way, it is opposed to charity. This happens when a man places his end in the love of his own good. In another way, it is included in charity. This occurs when a man loves himself on account of God and in God. In a third way, it is indeed distinct from charity, but is not opposed to charity. This happens when someone loves himself by reason of his own good, although he does not place his end in his own good. This also happens when someone can have for his neighbor another special love besides charity, which is founded on God. This occurs when a neighbor is loved either by reason of blood ties or of some other bond coming from the human condition. But these loves are referable to charity.
>
> Accordingly, fear of punishment is included in charity in one way, for to be separated from God is a certain punishment which charity greatly flees. This belongs to chaste fear. But in another way, fear is opposed to charity, according as someone flees from the punishment that is opposed to his natural good as from the principal evil contrary to the good which he loves as an end. [Such a] fear of punishment cannot exist with charity. In another way the fear of punishment is indeed distinct in substance from chaste fear because a man fears the penal evil not by reason of separation from God but insofar as it is harmful to his own good. But he does not place his end in this good; nor does he dread this evil as being the principal evil. Such fear of punishment can exist with charity. But this fear is not called servile except when punishment is dreaded as a principal evil as is evident from what has been said.

Thus, fear, insofar as it is servile, does not remain with charity. But the substance of servile fear can remain with charity just as love of self can remain with charity.[55]

This text calls for careful analysis.[56]

There are two kinds of self-love and two ways in which one kind is related to charity.[57] There is a self-love not included in charity and there is a self-love that is included in charity as an elicited act. The self-love not included in charity can be deliberately embraced as making the self the ultimate end. In this way, self-love is embraced in a manner mortally sinful and thus is incompatible with charity.

The difference between the second and third forms of self-love is subtler than may at first appear. These loves are similar in that each (the second and third forms of self-love) involves willing a good for oneself, ultimately, the good of beatitude. In this respect, they are similar.

We must consider the matter more deeply. As a deliberated act, natural self-love (the third form Aquinas notes) is certainly affected by the lover's hope in God's covenantal promises and reaches out to the supernatural end. We may say, with recent scholars, that it is modalized by grace.[58] So, as chosen, the same material object of beatitude is loved both by natural self-love (the third form, modalized by grace) and also by charity (the second form). Nevertheless, the loves target the same material object distinctly. Just as one and the same exterior act is susceptible of being willed on account of two distinct ends, so the vision of God is susceptible of being willed on account of two reasons.[59] Natural self-love targets it as one's own perfection. Charity targets beatitude because one is a child of God, whom one loves for His own sake as beatific Friend. This form of self-love, the

---

[55] *ST* 2-2.19.6.

[56] For an exemplary reading, see Gallagher, "Self-Love," 39–43.

[57] Actually, the argument below shows that there are two kinds of self-love but that one of these kinds has a twofold relation to charity: a relation of opposition and a relation of compatibility. The second form of self-love is simply identifiable with charity itself because it is a love of self as a secondary object of charity.

[58] On this concept of the modalization of nature by the call of grace, see Steven Long, "On the Loss, and the Recovery, of Nature as a Theonomic Principle: Reflections on the Nature/Grace Controversy," *Nova et Vetera* 5 (2007): 146; see also 147–50 and 153. See also Malloy, "Supernatural Existential," 417.

[59] See *ST* 1-2.18, arts. 4–7. There is great difficulty and much debate in the interpretation of these articles. In my opinion, these debates do not affect the basic claim I am advancing. I can love the beatific vision simply because I happen to be one of the many children of God, for each of whom I will this good. I can also will it as my own perfection, having

second form included in charity, targets one's own good precisely as it target's a neighbor to be loved in charity. The same act of charity targets a neighbor's good and the divine good:

> Now since the species of an act is derived from its object, considered under its formal aspect, it follows of necessity that it is specifically the same act that tends to an aspect of the object, and that tends to [an] object under that aspect: thus it is specifically the same visual act whereby we see the light, and whereby we see . . . color under the aspect of light.
>
> Now the aspect under which our neighbor is to be loved, is God, since what we ought to love in our neighbor is that he may be in God. Hence it is clear that it is specifically the same act whereby we love God, and whereby we love our neighbor.[60]

In this act, the *reason* for loving both God and neighbor out of charity is God Himself, loved for His own sake as beatific Friend. Now, one of the "things" in the world that belongs to God as beloved by Him in a special way is the very person who has charity. Hence, one who has charity loves himself just as he does all who are specially loved by God. Aquinas writes,

> We can speak of charity according to its proper character, namely, as it is a friendship of man principally to God and consequently to those things that belong to God. Among these is even the man himself who has charity. Thus, among the other things which he loves out of charity as pertaining to God, he loves also himself out of charity.[61]

Hence, this second form of self-love is a love necessarily consequent to the principle act of charity and having the same object or reason for loving. In this regard, the self-love is not distinct in species from the love of charity whereby one loves God. The *ratio diligendi* or reason for loving in this

---

believed it through faith and trusting through hope that it is really, concretely possible. Insofar as I *actually* pursue it in this latter mode, it is not adequately integrated into my life as a child of God endowed with charity. Insofar as I *actually* pursue it in the former mode and in the mode of ecstatic attraction, it is integrated into my life as a child of God.

[60] *ST* 2-2.25.1, ad 1. See also *ST* 2-2.23.1, ad 2.
[61] *ST* 2-2.25.4.

self-love is the beatifying goodness of God loved for its own sake, the very object itself of charity.[62] It is as though the man with charity loved himself in an objective kind of way, as something "outside" himself but connected to his beloved, God.[63] He is a secondary object of charity, just as are all God's children, potential or actual.

The *ratio diligendi* of the third form of self-love is distinct from that of the second form. Further, this third form of self-love is somewhat identifiable with the first form of self-love. Both target the proper good of man on account of himself, and both emerge from natural self-love. What distinguishes the first and third forms of self-love, however, is whether one chooses God or oneself as ultimate end. If one chooses God as ultimate end, the natural self-love is, at least habitually, referred to God because one refers one's very self to God as ultimate end. If a freely acting person has not chosen God as ultimate end, he has chosen himself as ultimate end. His self-love is not simply present but is freely embraced (or ventured upon) as an ultimate orientation incompatible with charity.[64]

Does charity tend towards the annihilation of the third form of self-love? Well, as an innate inclination, such self-love is inalienable. Even though a man loves God out of charity, he still has a natural inclination of the will to love his own goods of life, health, natural activities, beatitude, the proper objects of each power, etc.[65] Thus it was that Jesus wept over Lazarus and naturally found death repugnant in His bloodied sweat on the Mount of Olives.[66] Thus it is that martyrs should accept death only insofar as it is ordered to an end higher than the good of earthly life.[67] Still, there is a dynamic development towards integration, and the third form of self-love, as described, is not integrated.

---

[62] *Ratio diligendi* refers to the reason for loving something or that on account of which something is loved. If three distinct things are loved on account of one thing, there is only one *ratio diligendi* for the love of these things. Conversely, there can be more than one *ratio diligendi* for the same material object. The *ratio diligendi* corresponds to the formal object of love (*quo*) and the material object refers to the actual thing loved (*quod*). See *Sent.* 1.17.5.

[63] I drew attention to this in my dissertation in 2001. Recently, Shields has drawn attention to it. See Shields, "Will," 129.

[64] Indeed, the intellect and being remain primary. So, it is the *self* that one embraces as ultimate end, not the love of self. Hence my formulation: embraced as an ultimate orientation.

[65] See *ST* 1-2.10.1.

[66] See *ST* 3.14.2. Further argumentation for the claim that the third form of self-love remains in heaven is provided in the following chapters.

[67] *ST* 2-2.124.3.

The more that charity informs and imbues the life of a pilgrim, the more intimately is he united with God in his deliberate actions. Charity, as love of the ultimate end, can order all licit loves in due proportion so that a man's life becomes more and more suffused with and expressive of divine love in its details. This ordering takes place through charity eliciting and commanding various acts.

One who has the habit of charity can freely "elicit" acts of charity for God, neighbor, and self. An act is elicited by the power, through some habit, from which it flows immediately, actualizing that power. The person with the habit of charity can elicit an act of charity for himself. This is the second form of self-love noted above, one "included" in charity.

One who has charity can also command (*imperare*) various human acts. In the strict sense, an act is commanded by the will if it is accomplished through the mediation of another power. Such acts are freely chosen expressions of the inner affections of charity through the mediation of some other power such as motor control. Bending the knee in adoration, kissing one's spouse, and helping a neighbor can all be commanded acts of charity, if they are chosen with a view to the end of charity. Commanded acts that involve the mediation of some other power can be interrupted by a non-willful failure. Motor control, public worship, and physical communion are not always in the power of the human agent.

There is a further sense in which one with charity can "command" acts. In a broad sense, an act is commanded by one habit if it is accomplished through another habit, albeit in the same power. Precisely in this way, charity is the mother of the acts of other virtues.[68] For instance, by the virtue of charity, I might choose to make an act of hope.[69] Similarly, I might choose to love my bodily health, as St. Francis apologized to brother ass. By an act of charity, I can also choose an act of love of beatitude, the formal species of which is that of the natural inclination, albeit as modalized by grace. Unlike commanded acts properly speaking, self-love as a volitional act does not involve the mediation of another power. In this sense it is somewhat like an elicited act because it too is under the immediate control of the agent. In another sense, however, it is more like a commanded act, for it differs in species from charity itself.[70] That is, in its own nature, it does not share the *ratio diligendi*, or formal object, of an act of charity, which is God as beatific Friend. Charity's elicited acts do share

---

[68] See *DC* 5, ad 2.
[69] These acts differ in habit (see *ST* 2-2.28.4, ad 2).
[70] For this reason, the habit through which the act is imperated is distinct from the habit

charity's *ratio diligendi* and are, consequently, in themselves not distinct in species from charity itself, although they can entail different consequent volitions. For instance, charity for a wayward neighbor occasions sadness and desire, whereas charity for God always causes joy. The *rationes diligendi* of other rational loves, which charity can command, include such formal objects as kinship, citizenship, comraderie, spousal bond, etc. Charity can order these distinct rational loves to itself. Thereby, it can command the acts of other virtues.

The different *rationes diligendi* provide the specific distinctions between charity and other rational loves. Charity's control over the acts of these loves is comparable to the ordering of an architect or master builder who orders the sundry ends of sundry workers in such a way as to bring about the ultimate end, the marvelous edifice. In one sense, this ordering involves an extrinsic principle. As the builder is not this or that carpenter, so charity is not self-love. In another sense, this ordering involves the *integration* of man's sundry wants and needs into the simplicity of a saint's life. Insofar as charity commands an act, it impresses the act with its own finality as the *ultimate reason* for the act. So, although the act has of itself a *ratio diligendi* not identical to charity, it becomes more and more pliable to charity's own *ratio diligendi*. Divine love more and more permeates one's life so that one's gestures and actions become more and more expressive of charity. Even so, grace does not destroy nature. So, charity does not obliterate the distinctiveness of the other loves insofar as these are licit, that is, orderable to God.[71] Rather, charity commands and directs licit loves towards one simple end, communion with God.[72]

The point is quite practical. Charity cannot by itself accomplish the full range of human action. The complexity of being human requires the complexity of skills adequate to the accomplishment of the human good. In his treatment of penance as a virtue, Thomas gives us an example of charity commanding the acts of various other virtues:

> An act springs from charity in two ways: first as being elicited by charity, and a like virtuous act requires no other virtue than charity, e.g., to love the good, to rejoice therein, and to grieve for what is opposed to it. Secondly, an act springs from charity, being, so to speak, commanded by charity; and thus, since charity commands

---

through which the act is accomplished. See *ST* 2-2.23.4, ad 2.
[71] See *ST* 2-2.23.7.
[72] See *ST* 2-2.23.8.

all the virtues, inasmuch as it directs them to its own end, an act springing from charity may belong even to another special virtue. Accordingly, if in the act of the penitent we consider the mere displeasure in the past sin, it belongs to charity immediately, in the same way as joy for past good acts; but the intention to aim at the destruction of past sin requires a special virtue subordinate to charity.[73]

There is necessity of a virtue whereby one removes sins by acts of satisfaction. So, charity commands the act of the virtue of satisfaction in restitution for sins.

In commanding the acts of other powers and other habits, charity does not obliterate but builds up. It is the mother, giving birth to the many acts of the virtues, specifically those of the infused cardinal virtues.[74] In shaping a man, it is the bond integrating his sundry tendencies towards one ultimate end. In fact, it thereby perfects these various acts and preserves their distinctness, since the life of saints continues everlastingly for the good. As ordering each to the common good of the fellowship of the saints, charity builds up the body of Christ.[75]

We return to our question. Does charity tend towards the annihilation of the third form of self-love? The third form of self-love is, as defined, distinct and un-integrated into charity. Thus, insofar as it involves the realm of deliberate acts, it indicates immaturity. Spiritual growth renders self-love more and more pliable to the movements of the Holy Spirit so that the love is more and more conformable to and expressive of charity. If self-love is more and more commanded by charity, it more and more bears the stamp of charity's order to God as to its end, as though the self-love were but a means.[76] In short, natural self-love retains its distinct *ratio diligendi* as a habit, but its act acquires the character of a means to the end of charity, as Gallagher contends:

> The natural self-love one has for oneself remains; it is part of one's nature. What does happen, however, [is] that this love tends to be

---

[73] *ST* 3.85.2, ad 1. For other examples of this qualified kind of imperation, see *Sent.* 2.38.1.2, ad 5 and 2.44.2.1, ad 4; *ST* 1-2.114.4, ad 1 and *ST* 2-2.88.6; and *DC* 3.

[74] For a more detailed consideration of these relationships, one attentive to the cardinal role of prudence in the execution of acts of charity, see the fine study by Sherwin, *By Knowledge*, 170–184.

[75] See *DC* 2.

[76] See again *ST* 2-2.26.7.

less and less actual; that is to say, the person adverts less and less to his good in these terms. . . . Thus the seeming replacement of love of self focused on self as opposed to love of self focused on the common good, should be seen as an exchange between the habitual and actual states of the two loves.[77]

Gallagher's analysis does justice to Thomas's central principle that grace elevates but does not destroy nature.

The spiritual transition just narrated is a process of growth. Thomas identifies three stages in this growth as found in pilgrims. A certain dominating act or object marks each stage, although each stage has the acts of all stages:

> [T]he diverse degrees of charity are distinguished according to the different pursuits to which man is brought by the increase of charity. For at first it is incumbent on man to occupy himself chiefly with avoiding sin and resisting his concupiscences, which move him in opposition to charity: this concerns beginners, in whom charity has to be fed or fostered lest it be destroyed: in the second place man's chief pursuit is to aim at progress in good, and this is the pursuit of the proficient, whose chief aim is to strengthen their charity by adding to it: while man's third pursuit is to aim chiefly at union with and enjoyment of God: this belongs to the perfect who *desire to be dissolved and to be with Christ*.[78]

Beginners focus on fighting sin, from which they have just been delivered. Those in the second stage focus on advancing in charity, on becoming better friends of God. Finally, the proficient simply aim at union with God. Of course, these three stages are not fast and neat. The "perfect" pilgrim does not retire from previous stages as though beyond them. So too, beginners strive for union with God. What differs from stage to stage is the chief occupation, the chief task in one's daily plan. These three stages involve the lover's progressive shift of attention away from himself and towards his ultimate end, God. This shift most emphatically does not involve a movement from self-interest to disinterest. It involves transition to a God-centered life that is even more interested than before. Such interest can be called an "ecstatic attraction" for God. To this we now turn.

---

[77] Gallagher, "Self-Love," 43.
[78] *ST* 2-2.24.9.

Charity's Ecstatic Attraction to Beatitude

First, what is the "ecstatic attraction" to God rooted in charity? It is charity's spontaneous interest in union with God (hence, "attraction") precisely on account of God's goodness in itself (hence "ecstatic"). Charity draws a man towards the vision of God precisely because it is love of the divine good for God's sake. This is an attraction to the vision of God not identifiable with the natural love of beatitude, even as modalized by grace. Nor is it identifiable with the way in which one loves oneself because one happens to be a child of the God Whom charity loves. This attraction is nobler than the first love and more personal or intimate than the second; it forms a constituent dynamism of the very nature of charity's love for God. This attraction does not draw God to the lover, as in the natural love of beatitude based on self-love. The lover is so possessed by his beloved's goodness that he is drawn outside himself and towards his beloved, being attracted towards the beloved's presence on account of His beauty.[79]

As will be recalled, love is ecstatic when the lover intends the good of the other for the other's sake. The affection is not borne towards something outside so as to bring it back to one's proper good narrowly defined. Rather, one undergoes an affective expansion of self, so that one's love circulates around the beloved for the sake of his good. In this sense, there is a straining to uphold the other's good. Yet, this is not love of another considered as alien to oneself; instead, one's very good expands so that there is a union of two. In the *ST*, Thomas further develops this notion of ecstasy from the *DDN*. A love is ecstatic if it involves willing the good of another for his sake. Thus, one does not turn one's neighbor back towards oneself but truly wills that the neighbor be well.[80] Aquinas also relates ecstasy to the mutual inhesion of lovers. Love causes lover and beloved to inhere in one another. By this mutual inhesion the lover desires to fathom the depths of his beloved.[81] Now, no matter how strong the bond of union, the distinction of persons remains, and love does not thwart but upholds the distinction. Because the beloved is not identical with the lover, love of the beloved causes the lover's affection to go outside of itself and remain intent on the beloved's good. The affection which zealously seeks union with the beloved is nonetheless extended outwardly towards the beloved's good for the latter's sake. Mutual inhesion couples with ecstasy so that love achieves its full measure.

---

[79] See Ramírez, *La esencia*, 282–86 and 364–68. See also Egenter, 42.
[80] See *DDN* 4.10 and *ST* 1-2.28.3.
[81] See *ST* 1-2.28.2. See the fine treatment of this subject in Peter Kwasniewski, "Extasis," 592–603. See also, Ramírez, *La esencia*, 365–68.

Of all loves, charity is the most ecstatic because in charity a man refers himself totally to God for His own sake, leaving behind nothing in himself that he does not at least habitually refer to God as to its ultimate end. Hence, he gives himself to the needy: "A man is made to be outside of himself when he does not seek those things that are his own but those things which redound to the good of others, and this is what charity does."[82] Simultaneously, charity is also the most zealous, involving the greatest desire of the lover seeking to plumb the depths of his beloved. Thus, charity drives a man towards the vision of God, just as any real love of another does.[83] From love of another emanates a desire for the other's presence precisely on account of the goodness of the other and not simply on account of the beatitude and delight that the other's presence brings to the lover.[84] Because this love of the other's presence does not refer the other to the lover as means to an end, the love of the other's presence remains true to authentic love of friendship for the other. Since it terminates in the other and not in the lover's own perfection, this type of love for the other's presence can be described as "ecstatic." The two aspects of love of others, ecstasy and the quest for inhesion, are encapsulated by the single phrase "ecstatic attraction."

While it is my claim that Thomas upholds this distinct, ecstatic attraction to the vision of God, it is not a simple matter to establish the textual evidence. Most of Thomas's presentations of love of the beloved's presence describe such love as a love of concupiscence based upon self-love. Careful analysis reveals, however, that Aquinas upholds an ecstatic attraction based upon love of others. Both love of friendship for God and that for a fellow man impel one towards the presence of the beloved. Now that I have described our concept of "ecstatic attraction," I hope to show that this concept corresponds to Thomas's own depiction of charity.

Thomas's various analyses of love provide three indications that from love of friendship for another there arises an ecstatic attraction towards the presence of one's friend, whether a neighbor or God. First, the very nature of love involves attraction to the good loved. Love of friendship requires but is not reducible to sheer benevolence.[85] In benevolence, one wills the other good for the other's sake. The structure of benevolence

---

[82] *In II Cor.*, 12.1, par. 447.
[83] *ST* 1-2.4.2, ad 3.
[84] See *ST* 1-2.28.2.
[85] See *ST* 2-2.23.1 and *ST* 2-2.27.2. As Ramírez nicely puts it, for Thomas sheer "benevolence" is but a spontaneous sympathy for someone. Ramírez, *De caritate*, q. 27, art. 2.

therefore underlies all love of friendship. However, it is possible to have a detached benevolence for someone. If we see a ship on the horizon, we will it to come safely to port, but we might not wait to meet any of the passengers or crew. Love, at play in love of friendship, involves also a union of affection for the beloved.

Now a union of affection, or love, is constituted by the lover's appetite being proportioned to the beloved good.[86] This appetitive proportioning is the proximate principle whereby some good is actually embraced by some lover. This embrace immediately issues either in desire or in delight, depending on whether or not the loved good is absent or present to the lover (in the case of love of concupiscence) or to the beloved (in the case of love of friendship). I contend that Aquinas holds that, even in the case of love of friendship for another, the lover tends towards the beloved. The reason is that love formally constitutes an inclination in the will for the loved good. Since the appetite is a power of orientation or inclination towards the good, when the rational appetite is proportioned to the good, the good "exists" in the will of the lover "as the end of motion in the proportionate motive principle by the suitability or proportion the will has for it."[87] By love, the lover "already participates" in something of the beloved.[88] Of its very nature, therefore, the union of affection that is love causes the lover to tend towards the beloved, desiring the union of real presence or rejoicing therein.[89] Thus, because his appetite is proportioned to the loved good, the lover has an inclination towards this beloved precisely from the very love of friendship that he has for the sake of the beloved. This inclination constitutes the ecstatic attraction to the presence of the beloved on account of the beloved's goodness.

Being the noblest form of love of friendship, charity likewise cannot be reduced to benevolence. Charity is a supernatural love of God. Further, it includes, among other things, a certain note of mutual affectionate love. As such, far from being sheer benevolence, charity of its very nature causes an inclination towards the beloved's presence.[90] The following passage bears repeating: "The love that is in the intellectual appetite also dif-

---

[86] *ST* 1-2.25.2.
[87] *SCG* IV.19, par. 4. The final phrase could be translated "which the term has for the principle." Both senses are true to Thomas's thought. First, the object of love must be ontologically proportionate to the lover, suitable to love. Second, love itself *is* the proportioning of the appetite towards the object of love.
[88] *ST* 1-2.25.2, ad 3.
[89] For a marvelous text on this, see *Sent.* 1.10.1.3.
[90] Javier Prades speaks of charity, in particular, as begetting a tendency towards God.

fers from benevolence. It implies a certain affective union of the lover for the beloved, insofar as the lover judges the beloved to be in a certain way one with him or pertaining to him. Thus, the lover is moved towards the beloved."[91] A similar comment appears in Thomas's commentary on Hebrews: "Charity is love. Now, the proper mark of love is to unite, because, as Dionysius says, love is a unitive power."[92] Thus, charity impels each saint towards the vision of God precisely because it is an ecstatic love of friendship for God.[93]

Second, it is intrinsic to friendship that friends will to converse and have fellowship with one another. Friendship is the comprehensive relationship of friends, inclusive of much more than sheer benevolence. Now, Thomas agrees with Aristotle that "[n]othing is so characteristic of friends as living together.... [T]he principal act of friendship is to live with one's friends."[94] By the phrase "living together," Thomas and Aristotle imply the full range of activities that friends can enjoy, including the following: conversation, common pursuit of projects and aims, play, artistic endeavor, eating together, upright sexual relations between validly married spouses, fraternal competition, etc. Living together is proper to friendship in several respects. First, friendship consists in a mutual sharing of selves, which occurs most properly in living together.[95] In addition, common activities allow one to take greater delight in a friend because of greater appreciation of his many aspects.[96] Finally, friendship is built around common pursuits, and spending time in one another's company allows friends to en-

---

Charity conforms man to the Holy Spirit and therefore arouses a desire for union with God. The reason for this is that like is attracted to like, and those who are like the Holy Spirit in love are therefore necessarily attracted to the Holy Spirit. See Javier Prades, "Deus Specialiter," 296–97. See also *SCG* 3.150–152.

[91] *ST* 2-2.27.2.
[92] *Ad Hebr.* 10.2, par. 512.
[93] Gallagher, "Desire for Beatitude," 44–45: "Thus while union with the loved one is an effect of *amor amicitiae* and the tendency toward such union is essential to it, the union does not constitute the end to which the love as a means is ordered.... We should also note that here again the tendency toward union and the consequent joy which belong to the essential structure of love make a 'purely disinterested' love impossible for Thomas. Love, by its very nature includes an inclination towards a union of the lover with the loved." By contrast, see Drost, "Realm of the Senses," 56.
[94] *Eth.* 8.5, par. 1600. The English is taken from Thomas Aquinas, *Commentary on Aristotle's Nicomachean Ethics*, trans. C. I. Litzinger (Notre Dame: Dumb Ox Books, 1993). See also *Sent.* 3.32.1.2; *ST* 2-2.23.1; *ST* 2-2.25.3; and *ST* 3.75.1.
[95] See *Eth.* 9.14, par. 1946.
[96] See *Eth.* 9.14, par. 1947.

joy such pursuits together.⁹⁷ Even though the genuine lover does not treat his friend's delightful presence as the end to which his friend is a means, actively being with one's friend forms the heart of the acts of friendship. The mutual expansions of the *bonum suum* of each friend towards the other entails their common enjoyment of a greater *bonum suum*, that of their social person.⁹⁸

Since charity is not only a love of friendship but also *friendship*, it too inclines the human friend to God's presence. Recall that friendship adds something in addition to love, namely, "mutual return of affection with a certain mutual communication."⁹⁹ If friendship involves communication, the friendship that is charity involves the noblest of communications, that of God to man and, reciprocally, of man to God. Such communication involves conversation, which begins in this life and is perfected in the next life.¹⁰⁰ Although mutual interaction and conversation form the dynamism of every friendship, including charity, every true friend loves his friend for the latter's sake and not for privately held benefits of this interaction. Moreover, such love leads one towards union with the beloved:

> Although a friend takes delight from the presence of his friend, yet it is not on account of this that he seeks the presence of his friend: in order to delight in him. Rather, he seeks his friend's presence on account of his friend himself, to whom he wishes to be united insofar as it is possible.¹⁰¹

The way in which a false friend chokes delight from his "friend" should not obscure from our vision the whole aim and culminating act of friendship, communication in the good. Indeed, if one did not long for a friend's presence in his absence, one would not truly love him: "if anyone be willingly and easily deprived of the friend's presence and be more pleased with other things, this proves that he loves the friend either not at all, or only a little."¹⁰²

Third, a contemplative act itself is loved in a twofold way, both as a perfection of the lover willed for himself and as a strict result of love of the

---

⁹⁷ See *Eth.* 9.14, par. 1948.
⁹⁸ The notion is inspired by the ideas of Russell Hittinger conveyed at The First John Paul II Lecture at The University of Dallas (February, 2007).
⁹⁹ *ST* 1-2.65.5.
¹⁰⁰ For the passage and the other elements noted here, see *ST* 1-2.65.5. See also *ST* 2-2.23.1.
¹⁰¹ *Sent.* 3.34.2.3.1, ad 2.
¹⁰² *DC* 11, ad 6.

other for his sake. The beatific vision is the ultimate contemplative act. As such, it is an operation perfecting the one contemplating and targeting its object. There are, as we have seen, two poles of the act, the operation itself as operation of a subject and the object of the operation. Aquinas finds there to be two reasons for or ways of loving any contemplative operation as it targets its object. One can love the act out of self-love and one can love the act out of love of the object (the other):

> A cognitive operation can be affectively sought on two accounts. In one way, it can be loved insofar as it is a perfection of the knower. Thus, one's affection for the cognitive operation proceeds from the love of self. This was the affection in the contemplative life of philosophers. In another way, this operation is loved insofar as it terminates in the object. Thus the desire for contemplation proceeds from love of the object, because where love is, there are one's eyes. . . . The contemplative life of the saints has this kind of affection.[103]

In this treatment of the love of contemplation, we see another accounting for what we have designated "ecstatic attraction." One is drawn, by the very love that targets the beloved's good for his sake, towards the vision of his beauty.

Thomas's principles do not permit us to read the aforesaid ascriptions of the two loves—one to philosophers and one to saints—to be mutually exclusive. These two ways of loving beatitude are compatible; indeed, the love of saints includes that of philosophers, since neither grace nor glory abolishes self-love. If actual philosophers loved their contemplation more than Truth, this was no fault of nature but of pride. Recall that the self-love upon which the virtue of hope is based tends towards the vision of God by love of concupiscence (grounded in self-love).[104] Now, although hope does not remain in heaven, the love upon which it is based does remain.[105] Charity, however, is the ecstatic love of God for His own sake, and such love engenders a love of the beatific vision: "The contemplative life consists especially in contemplation, towards which charity moves."[106]

Charity impels the lover towards the vision of God precisely because

---

[103] *Sent.* 3.35.1.2.1. See also *ST* 2-2.180.7.
[104] See *ST* 2-2.17.8 and Ramírez, *La esencia*, 317.
[105] See *Sent.* 3.31.2.1.2, ad 3.
[106] *ST* 2-2.180.7.

of His goodness as loved for His sake. St. Paul so loved God that he wished to be dead and with Christ already because the proper affection of charity is that "the soul desires to be with Christ."[107] St. Thomas explains that charity itself drove Paul to long for Christ's presence:

> And there is the motion of grace, which charity implies, which moves one toward the love of God and of neighbor. This affection moves to the love of God in order that we may be with Christ. Thus, St. Paul says, "having the desire to be dissolved," not simply speaking, "but to be with Christ."[108]

God's lover, as a lover, wishes to enjoy God's presence precisely on account of God's own goodness. God becomes present to man through the intellectual operations of faith and vision. The beatific vision is the most perfect operation available to a man by which he can have God present to himself. Charity itself drives a man to this perfect operation, not primarily because it brings him beatitude but primarily because God Himself is all good and the object of charity's love.[109] No more banal reading of charity is possible than that which prizes it as "disinterested."

Conclusion

Charity is a supernatural friendship of man for God, a gift beyond human nature yet infused into the soul as a further actualization thereof, both healing human weaknesses and elevating human goodness, especially the natural love of beatitude and the natural love of God. Since it is a true friendship, love of friendship for God is included therein. This love includes the note of benevolence but is not reducible thereto, since it is a real *love* and issues in a tending towards union with God. As the proper act of friendship is to be with, live with, and act together with one's friends, charity draws the human person towards the very vision of God. Since this drawing is ecstatic, it is not the drawing of the beloved into the lover but rather the going out of the lover to the beloved, to rest therein. Being with God is ultimate happiness. Thus, charity is not only developmentally rooted in the natural love of beatitude. It also augments love of beatitude and orders the acts of various licit human loves towards the ultimate end

---

[107] *DC* 11, ad 8.
[108] *Ad Phil.* 1.3, par. 35.
[109] See *ST* 1-2.4.2, ad 3 and Ramírez, *La esencia*, 282–86 and 364.

of supernatural beatitude. The relationship between charity and love of beatitude can be considered in two phases of charity, its pilgrim phase and its glorious phase. To this twofold consideration we now turn.

CHAPTER 6

Charity in Faith

EARTHLY LIFE, the realm for decision and action, prepares the way for heavenly life. As much as a man abounds in divine love in this sojourn, so much does he take with him to his paradisal rest, wherein he dwells within his beloved. Charity, together with faith and hope, guide and inspire him towards ever-deeper communion with the Trinity. Although faith and hope, which connote darkness and absence respectively, pass away at the advent of perfect knowledge and intimacy, charity never passes away. Charity reaches its bloom in the heavenly vision of the Holy Trinity. Of course, delving into matters so profound as eternal life risks presumption and error. Nevertheless, we can, with Thomas as guide, glean something of heavenly charity from the signs legible on earth. The smallest knowledge of the greatest truths is more worthy of pursuit than extensive research of mundane things.[1]

The transition from what St. Thomas calls the charity of the way (*in via*) to that of the fatherland (*in patria*) pivots upon the shift from faith to vision. Thorough discussion of faith and vision is not possible in this monograph; it is sufficient to note the chief characteristics and differences between the two in order to identify significant differences between earthly and heavenly charity. The pilgrim who labors in faith attains to knowledge of God under the veils of symbolic and propositional expressions. He endures trials of conversion, suffering, and toil and *cannot* experience the immediate union with God that would quell his longing. Consequently, his charity is affected in three ways. First, it can be lost. Second, pilgrimage is the time for growth and merit. Not knowing God's will in all its material detail, he can happen to desire for himself and for his friends a greater share in God than shall be realized. His very concentration on

---

[1] See *Sent.* 4.49.3.5.1 and *ST* 1.1.5, ad 1.

growth involves an element of legitimate self-concern that will nonetheless be transformed in heaven, wherein he will rest content in the concrete details of God's will. Third, human need, suffering, and sin distract him from explicit and constant devotion to God. So his love of God can be interrupted and is therefore less delightful. When the veil of faith is replaced by the vision of God, the various defects of earthly charity will be healed and perfected. The present chapter treats the conditions of pilgrim charity as it relates to love of beatitude.

Knowledge as Cause of Love

Knowledge is prior to love in the order of generation, for nothing can be loved save what is known. So, the intellect specifies the object of the will by presenting possible objects of affection. Knowledge is in this way a necessary, albeit not sufficient, condition for love. The object of love is the good:

> Something is a cause of dilection in two ways. In one way, it causes love as being the aspect on account of which something is loved (*ratio diligendi*). In this way good is a cause of love because each thing is loved insofar as it has the nature of good. In another way, something causes love as a kind of way towards the acquisition of love. In this way, vision is a cause of love. This is not as though a thing is lovable by reason of its being visible but because through vision we are led to dilection. Therefore, it is not necessary that that which is more visible be more lovable, but that it occurs to us sooner to love what is more visible.[2]

Aquinas uses the term "vision" in this passage to stand for any type of apprehension as a cause of love.[3]

Though knowledge is not a sufficient cause of love, the more a good thing is known, the more it can be loved: "The more a man knows the causes for love, the more reasonable it is that he love more."[4] A wonderful cycle can develop, for love also leads towards greater knowledge of the beloved precisely because the lover is impelled to converse with and contem-

---

[2] *ST* 2-2.26.2, ad 1 (my translation).
[3] The context of the discussion is whether or not a man can love God as much as he can love his neighbor, even though God is less "visible."
[4] *Eth.* 8.12, par. 1707.

plate his beloved. The pilgrim's friendship with God thus grows in intimacy. Thomas compares this deepening penetration to a circular motion: knowledge begets desire (and its cause, love), while desire strives for greater knowledge. It is as though the lover spirals into his beloved:

> Being tasted, spiritual things arouse desire, although before they were known they were held of little account. After the first reception of light, the things already being tasted by the knowledge of the light of truth, the light is more desired. And into those who desire more, more of it is infused, for the effects of grace are multiplied according to the increase in desire and love. . . . Thus a certain circulation can be perceived, since from the light, desire for the light increases, and from an increase in desire, the light increases.[5]

Of course, the rule that greater knowledge leads to greater desire applies only insofar as it is greater knowledge of good aspects of the beloved. On earth, greater knowledge can sometimes lead to disappointment, as when the romance of new love wears thin and must either fathom the truth of the other person or wither. Better, greater knowledge of what one mistakenly *thought* to be a worthy end can occasion conversion to a truer way of life. God, however, is Infinite Goodness, and in Him there is nothing undesirable. Thus, for one who loves God, greater knowledge should only increase love in the one who already loves God.[6] So "as much as a good thing is known more fully, so much is it more lovable, especially that good which is the end and in which there is not found anything by which the appetite might be offended. And thus, since God will be more fully known in heaven than now, so also will He be more fully loved."[7] Consequently, for one who would become proficient in the love of God, preparing in himself a more abundant dwelling for God, meditation about God's goodness is indispensable. In true devotion, one reaches the totality of love for God, subjecting oneself entirely to God.[8] Meditation leads to this devotion, for,

---

[5] There may be a typo in the Marietti edition, which reads "et ex desiderio aucto crescit lumen."*DDN* 4.4, par. 330.

[6] Perhaps, however, greater knowledge can raise a difficulty before unknown. If one has an errant understanding of Divine Mercy, a correction in terms of Divine Justice might occasion doubt about God's lovability. Doubt would of course only be the fault of the human person, for true knowledge of God discloses only what is objectively lovable.

[7] *Sent.* 3.27.3.1, ad 3.

[8] *ST* 2-2.82.1.

"[i]*n my meditation a fire shall flame out*. But spiritual fire causes devotion. Therefore meditation is the cause of devotion."[9]

God calls men to love Him as a friend, but no man can know this by nature. Therefore, in order for someone to love God as beatific friend, he needs to have faith. Faith is the source of knowledge of God upon which charity depends.

Faith's Knowledge

Necessity of Faith

Faith is necessary for two reasons, according to St. Thomas. First, it presents the final end of life to the intellect so that the will can tend thereto. Experience proves how difficult it is for men to identify that in which true human flourishing consists. The goods of the higher powers are despised, while base goods are frequently sought. The distinction between our bodily and spiritual powers is partly responsible. The weight of sin and the height of our supernatural calling are additional factors. More significantly, God calls all men to beatific union with Himself, an end that completely surpasses the natural power. Not only can man not attain it by natural power; he cannot even desire beatific union under that formality. Desire follows love, and human nature as such has principles for the love of God only as source and end of nature.[10] Man is an embodied spirit, and his mind, although it can perceive the natures common to different individuals, is always conditioned by its origin in sense perception. The human intellect has as its connatural objects the essences of material things. From knowledge of these, it can rise to knowledge of immaterial things by discursive and analogical reasoning.[11] God, however, wills that created persons attain an end that surpasses even this analogical knowledge, that is, the face-to-face or intuitive vision of Himself. Rather than simply bestowing this great good on His children, God wills them to journey towards Him through pilgrimage of commitment. They are to journey towards Him as towards supernatural beatitude. In order to intend it, they must know of this end. Thus, they must be given the gift of faith in order to commence the journey:

---

[9] *ST* 2-2.82.3, sed contra.
[10] See *Ad 1 Corin.* 13.4, par. 806; and *ST* 1-2.109.3, ad 1.
[11] See *ST* 1.12.2; *ST* 1.13.5; and *ST* 1.13.12.

The last end must of necessity be present to the intellect before it is present to the will, since the will has no inclination for anything except in so far as it is apprehended by the intellect. Hence, as the last end is present in the will by hope and charity, and in the intellect, by faith, the first of all the virtues must, of necessity, be faith, because natural knowledge cannot reach God as the object of heavenly bliss, which is the aspect under which hope and charity tend towards Him."[12]

Faith presents a foretaste of the final end of human life, realizing a necessary condition for tending to that end by the love of charity.[13] This is the chief sense in which faith is necessary, but there is another sense as well.

Man is a finite pilgrim on the way towards perfection. In order to reach the final end, he must submit to the wisdom of God, who teaches him gradually. To learn the way, he must "first of all believe God, as a disciple believes the master who is teaching him."[14] The student arrives at perfection only by taking his master's word as true, even though he does not understand it initially.[15] Aquinas writes:

> The final perfection toward which man is ordained consists in the perfect knowledge of God, which, indeed, man can reach only if God, who knows Himself perfectly, undertakes to teach him. Early in his life, however, man is not capable of receiving perfect knowledge. So, he has to accept certain things on faith and by means of these he is led on till he arrives at perfect knowledge.[16]

Frail man must submit to God's discipline in order that he might increasingly partake of the divine wisdom until at last he arrives at beatific knowledge of God. God's pedagogy not only involves gradual disclosure

---

[12] *ST* 2-2.4.7.
[13] See *SCG* 4.54, par. 4.
[14] *ST* 2-2.2.3.
[15] The believer accepts the word of his Teacher because it is divine. In teaching, God does not simply communicate things about Himself that could well be conveyed by someone else. The tutee is led into the very knowledge that God has of Himself so that through faith he partakes ever more in the divine knowledge itself. So, the journey of faith is not merely a period of waiting; it is a pilgrimage of growth into the divine mysteries, flowering into the vision itself of God. See *ST* 1.1.2.
[16] *DV* 14.10, corp. Unless otherwise stated, the English is taken from Thomas Aquinas, *Truth: X–XX*, trans. James V. McGlynn, SJ, vol. 2 (Chicago: Henry Regnery Company, 1954).

of truths but also the manifold display of His power and love. The Son of God not only expiated our sins and offered right worship, but also took flesh to teach sinners the intimate truths of God in understandable ways and to manifest the depths of divine love through human suffering.[17]

The Act and Habit of Faith

Through the gift of faith, the mind attains to knowledge of God Himself, the principal material object of faith.[18] However, an act, together with its habit, is specified not by material objects but by its formal object, the aspect under which the act touches the material objects it touches. The formal object of faith is also God; more precisely, the formal object is God as First Truth or God as revealer. The believer assents to various truths because God reveals them.[19] The divine trustworthy authority as the formal aspect of faith is of central importance. It specifies the object precisely. Further, it enables us to identify the infallible character of the virtue. As a gift of God, faith is not subject to error. On the other hand, a believer may entertain an erroneous interpretation of an article of faith. Not grasping the meaning correctly, he might understand, for instance, "creation" to be "making something from something." He may also be mistaken about whether or not some claim is revealed. Not knowing that some claim is revealed, he might judge it to be false. For instance, he might believe that Mary was not immaculately conceived as a result of mistaken human judgment about the material content of faith. If he readily believes true whatever he judges that God is revealing, he displays the mark of a believer, since he clings to all that falls under the formal object of faith.[20] In this regard, his faith hits the mark unerringly. Catholics have the clear and unambiguous duty to af-

---

[17] See *SCG* 4.54, par. 4 and *SCG* 4.54, par. 5.

[18] See *ST* 2-2.1.1.

[19] See *ST* 2-2.6.2. There is a fascinating interconnection between the intellect and will in faith and charity. Charity, residing in the will, depends upon faith's presentation of the last end to the intellect. But the believer cannot see the end with his mind. So, he cannot make an assent in faith except at the command of the will. This command can take place without charity, enabled by the natural love of the good as touched inwardly by God's illuminating and inspiring assistance. When faith is informed by charity, the very act of faith is commanded out of the love of charity. For an excellent account of this interconnection, see 279–84 of D. Bourgeois, "'Inchoatio vitae eternae.' La dimension eschatologique de la vertu théologale de foi chez saint Thomas d'Aquin," *Sapienza* 27 (1974): 272–314.

[20] Nor is the formal object merely a matter of subjective conditions. One ought to seek the locus of the true revelation.

firm as revealed by God everything of faith that is taught infallibly by the Magisterium. In this way, the above errors are greatly limited. Now, by assenting to God as revealer, a man believes God as an infinitely trustworthy teacher, One who knows all truth and who deceives not. The ultimate end of this assent is God Himself. Thomas articulates the distinction between the material and formal objects with the phrases "believing that God exists"[21] and "believing *God*."[22] The former involves the material element of faith, and the latter involves the formal aspect.[23]

Having treated faith in its formal and material objects, we can turn to the act of faith, which Thomas defines as "to think with assent."[24] On the one hand, faith resembles the act of thinking (*cogitare*) as a process towards certain knowledge. In this sense, to think is not yet a perfect operation but a motion towards a perfect operation. When we are struggling to understand the calculus, we are thinking in this sense. Faith in this way contrasts with certain knowledge (*scientia*), which is a perfect operation since the operation itself is what is sought as an end. Faith also diverges from *scientia* in that its act is free. The intellect cannot but assent to self-evident principles and to the truths demonstrated from these.[25] By contrast, the believer holds what he holds at the command of the will, which is moved by grace. This free act differentiates faith from *scientia* and makes it resemble opinion. At the same time, the believer does not waver in suspense but firmly inclines towards one side of a contradiction: this is truth, and its contradiction is false. In this respect, faith again resembles opinion but differs from doubt. In cases of doubt one vacillates between two contradictory judgments as though in suspense: should I ask her to marry me or not? Such doubt presents an obstacle to love. When we opine, we incline to one judgment rather than its opposite. Faith is, therefore, in this respect midway between fluctuating doubt and accomplished certainty. Faith also transcends both, since the formal object of faith is God as First Truth, whose knowledge is infinite and who deceives not. In this respect, faith shares in the certainty that *scientia* enjoys. One who opines inclines to one side of a contradiction, perhaps firmly, but fears that the opposite opinion may be true. By contrast, the believer assents with certainty to what God reveals.

Putting the foregoing pieces together, Thomas identifies the distinc-

---

[21] *Credere Deum*.
[22] *Credere Deo*.
[23] See *ST* 2-2.2.2.
[24] See *ST* 2-2.2.1.
[25] The term "demonstrated" implies a sound argument that is clearly understood.

tive act of faith as follows: "This act *to believe*, cleaves firmly to one side, in which respect belief has something in common with *scientia* and understanding; yet its knowledge does not attain the perfection of clear sight, wherein it agrees with doubt, suspicion and opinion."[26] Since the truth to which one assents is not self-evident to man or known as demonstrated from self-evident truths, the assent remains free.

By way of this assent, a believer attains to some knowledge of God. This knowledge is mediated through propositions because to know by way of propositions accords with the human manner of knowing and claiming.[27] In faith a man assents to the truths about God by way of propositions signifying divine truths.[28] Although God in His nature is utterly simple, mortal man arrives at knowledge of Him only through various judgments, some of which are expressible in propositions.[29] God's excelling goodness in the face of our impoverished knowing requires that we extoll Him with many names for diverse perfections, remembering all the while that His Excellence is Simple. Through the many, we arrive at the One:

> The object of faith can be considered in two ways. In one way, on the part of the very thing believed. In this way the object of faith is something simple, namely, the thing itself about which one has faith. In another way, on the part of the believer. In this way, the object of faith is something complex, in the manner of a statement.[30]

These two considerations, the complexity of the many judgments and the simple object that is the goal, are ordered, for faith is the act of the believer terminating in the believed. Hence, through propositions, the believer comes to knowledge of God Himself, since "the act of the believer does not

---

[26] *ST* 2-2.2.1.
[27] See *ST* 2-2.1.2.
[28] See Bourgeois, "Inchoatio," 302–03 on the comparison of immediate vision and medium.
[29] Finding the right word is often quite important. When we cannot find the right word, we often find we do not quite know. The vocal or written word expresses the concept, and the concept is what is really at issue here. If I know, I have a concept. If I have a concept, I might carve out a word with the tools of language at hand. Thus, not having the right vocal sound often indicates failure to have the concept. Of course, we should not think that the concept is that which is known. The *thing* is what is known. However, a completed act of knowledge, however sleight in comparison to the thing known, suffices for issuing in a concept expressive of the knowledge of the thing.
[30] *ST* 2-2.1.2 (my translation).

terminate in a proposition, but in a thing."³¹

We can gloss a further significant point. In our acts of knowing, we have recourse to images and phantasms. Similarly, our faith rises to God also through the symbols and images that God bestows upon us unto this end. God's symbolic vocabulary includes also the mighty deeds of the two great Covenants. We can think of the Exodus, the prophetic miracles, the Temple actions, and above all the gestures, the words, the looks, the glory in the face of Christ.³² In fact, the Scriptures are not simply lists of propositions. Rather, they narrate these divinely wrought deeds and relate the divinely wrought images experienced by the prophets.³³ The creeds also point to these things we strive to picture with our imagination. Now, the propositional aspect alights upon these with a precision indispensable for mature grasp of the real and for communal life.

It remains to treat Thomas's linking of faith and eternal life. In another significant definition of faith, Thomas links faith's character as habit with the goal of faith, eternal life. Faith attains knowledge of God Himself as the Beatific End of human life. Thus, through faith the mind already begins to taste inchoately, under the veils of figures, the end God has promised to those who love Him. St. Thomas reads the following Pauline description of faith in this light: "Faith is the assurance of things hoped for, the conviction of things not seen."³⁴ St. Thomas observes three elements of faith in this description. Faith is the "assurance of things hoped for" insofar as it consists in a foretaste of eternity. Faith is "conviction" as being certain knowledge. Finally, faith regards "things not seen" because the object it presents to the believer is, by definition, not yet attained. The Angelic Doctor then rephrases the Pauline description as a definition: *"Faith is a habit of the mind, whereby eternal life is begun in us, making the intellect assent to what is non-apparent."*³⁵ Faith is necessary for the act of charity and the attainment of supernatural beatitude, for no one loves what he does not know. Nevertheless, faith falls short of vision, and the life of faith therefore suffers various imperfections. How do the imperfections of faith, and of the pilgrim state generally, impact charity?

---

³¹ *ST* 2-2.1.2, ad 2.
³² These points follow from close inspection of the implications of *ST* 1.12.13.
³³ *DDN* 1.2, pars. 64–69.
³⁴ Hebrews 11:1 (RSV).
³⁵ *ST* 2-2.4.1.

Imperfections of the Charity of the Wayfarer

Faith implies certain imperfections: the lack of vision and the state of potentiality with regard to one's final state of holiness. All believers also experience the many pressing needs of their physical nature and the excesses of concupiscence. Unless specially graced, even the justified commit at least venial sins.

These difficulties notwithstanding, faith's knowledge suffices for believers genuinely to love God as Beatifying, Triune Friend. Although natural knowledge of God begins in sense perception and although faith's knowledge goes through symbol and proposition, the love of charity begins with God. Charity does not arrive at God through a medium because the inclination of love is that of lover to beloved itself. Attaining God immediately and principally, charity extends to other things on His account.[36] Even so, the charity of pilgrims bears the marks of the imperfections due to faith and the pilgrim state of fallen human nature. To these imperfections of faith's knowledge we now turn.

Lack of Vision

Faith unites man to God as to one who remains quidditatively unknown. The articles of faith give us knowledge about God, but do not amount to knowledge of His essence, which cannot be known except by being "seen" without medium. Still, through faith God discloses Himself to man more intimately than through natural reason:

> Although by the revelation of grace in this life we cannot know of God *what He is*, and thus are united to Him as to one unknown; still we know Him more fully according as many and more excellent of His effects are demonstrated to us, and according as we attribute to Him some things known by divine revelation, to which natural reason cannot reach, as, for instance, that God is Three and One.[37]

This lack of the vision of God entails two chief imperfections for earthly charity: the intrinsic possibility of sin and the lingering attention of mind to one's own spiritual growth.

First, those who walk by faith have the capacity to turn away from

---

[36] See *ST* 2-2.27.4.
[37] *ST* 1.12.13, ad 1.

God. This "freedom" to reject God is more properly described as incapacity to love God perfectly. Why is there this incapacity to love God perfectly? Why is it possible for the wayfarer to make shipwreck of his salvation?

In Chapter Two, we considered Thomas's understanding of the scope of freedom. There is the freedom of specification and the freedom of exercise. Freedom of specification regards the freedom to determine what appetitive stance to take towards some known object. This determination requires, of course, that one have an appetitive act towards said object. Thus, freedom of specification is the freedom to determine whether one loves or hates an object towards which one has an appetitive act. (Whether this hatred or love issues in desire, sadness, hope, etc., involves further determinations, some of which would be free and some of which would not be free.) The will has freedom of specification for all objects that are not known to be good in every respect and without drawback or which are not known to be necessarily connected with such an object. Freedom of exercise regards the freedom whether or not to have any appetitive act towards some object. As we saw in Chapter Two, Aquinas contends that we have freedom of exercise even regarding an object that is known as good in every respect and without drawback. Nonetheless, Aquinas also argues that the will has no freedom to opt out of the beatific vision of God.

Consequently, only God as seen in the beatific vision so meets the will's range of appetite as to render it impossible to choose the contrary or to choose not to remain in the vision. (We shall take up this point in the next chapter.) By contrast, the pilgrim can consider even the Triune God proposed to faith in a negative light. The pilgrim can consider the Triune God as a particular good that either lacks some alternative attractive good or presents an obstacle to such an alternative or is in some way unpleasant. With true faith and sound reasoning, one can know theoretically that God lacks nothing of attractive perfection, cannot be an obstacle to happiness, and is in no way unpleasant. Knowledge of this universal premise does not prevent, in the practical order, one from failing to call it to mind when acting. So, concrete attractive goods present themselves to the pilgrim's attention, and enjoyment of some of them might be contrary to the love of God. Hence, the pilgrim may consider illicit goods—another's property or spouse—in opposition to his commitment to the Divine. When such consideration leads to a judgment that the illicit good is to be pursued and an acceptance of that judgment, one commits to it and acts with culpable neglect of what one knows theoretically. This partial ignorance can be magnified by an unwillingness to trust the divine reasons for the adversities of life. Such unwillingness comes ultimately from disordered loves. The ravages of these and of original sin itself, though surmountable by grace, weigh down the mind. Thus, Aquinas writes, "Now our mind does not see that essence of divine goodness; it sees some of its effects which can seem either good or not-good, according to different considerations. For, the spiritual good appears as not-good to some insofar as it is contrary to their carnal delight, which concupiscence desires."[38] Hence, the believer can err by thinking that "God" or "this god" gives cause for sorrow. Insofar as one more firmly develops virtue, of course, one approximates to the solidity of the beatified state.

This possibility of errantly judging is not a neutral one; it is the possibility of losing genuine happiness. Charity transforms this situation by inclining and equipping the pilgrim to judge matters correctly. One with charity inclines to the act of faith not simply by an act of natural love touched by grace; charity draws the pilgrim to the act of faith precisely out of love for God. Thus, charity orders the acts of faith, as well as those of all other virtues, towards the last end, God. So, for Thomas charity gives birth to a life well-lived:

> Charity is called the end of the other virtues because it ordains all the other virtues to its end. Since a mother is one who conceives in herself from another, for this reason charity is called mother of the other virtues, because from an appetite for the ultimate end she conceives the acts of the other virtues by commanding them.[39]

Directing and commanding these acts, charity is the form of faith and of the other virtues.[40] In short, one with charity assents to God's truth out of love for that truth, believing *unto* or *into* God (*credere in Deum*).[41]

This disposition of charity is crucial for genuine self-love, because beatitude is not simply the external presence of a wonderful object. Rather, it is a person's "touching" of the object through properly attuned powers. Charity directs all human acts to God as end, thus enlarging the heart and preparing it for beatitude.[42] Charity's chief intention is to love God and rejoice in His good, but precisely in doing this it renders the lover fit

---

[38] *DC* 12.
[39] *ST* 2-2.23.8 (my translation).
[40] See *ST* 2-2.23.4, ad 2.
[41] See *ST* 2-2.1.9.
[42] See *ST* 1-2.4.4 and 1-2.5.7. For a discussion of the necessity for moral rectitude in contemplation, see David Gallagher, "Moral Virtue and Contemplation: A Note on the Unity of the Moral Life," *Sapientia* 51 (1996): 385–92.

for and zealously desirous of beatitude. So, he who loves God for His own sake perfectly loves himself. The wicked, on the other hand, seek some end other than God. Ultimately, each wicked man pursues himself as his own end. In doing so, he fails to love himself properly because (a) even in the order of nature God alone is the last end and (b) in the concrete order of sin and grace, God actively invites each person to beatific union with Him.

Thomas highlights the difference between the self-love of the righteous and that of sinners by considering how each treats himself with respect to the following five elements of friendship: wishing the friend to be and to live; willing good things for him; doing good things for him; living with delight in the company of his friend; and being of one mind with him, delighting in the same things and lamenting in the same things. With respect to each of these points, just men love themselves as to the interior good:

> They will [their interior life] to be preserved in its integrity. They desire goods, namely spiritual goods for it. They also devote labor to attain these things. With delight they enter into their own hearts because therein they find good thoughts in the present, and the memory of good things in the past, and the hope of good things in the future. From these considerations delight is aroused. Similarly, they do not suffer within themselves dissension of will because their whole soul tends to one thing.[43]

The wicked stand in stark contrast. They do not will the preservation of their interior life. They do not desire its spiritual goods and devote work unto this end. They do not find it pleasant to return to their hearts, for there they find wicked things, which they detest, such as regrettable deeds in the past, loathsome deeds in the present, and dreaded deeds to come. Finally, the wicked man is at odds with himself, on account of the biting sting of conscience. In short, God's friends love themselves truly according to the inner man, but those who seek base goods find only sadness. So, the first effect of the lack of vision of God is the imperfect way in which man has charity, leaving open the possibility that he can lose charity tragically.

As its second effect upon charity, non-possession of the beloved entails a state of potentiality of the lover vis-à-vis the possession of the good he wishes to attain. The pilgrim's status as *not yet* beatified relates to the character of his similitude with God. Recall that there are two types of

---

[43] *ST* 2-2.25.7, corp. (my translation).

similitude: potential and actual.⁴⁴ As Thomas notes in *ST* 1-2.27.3, the former serves as basis for love of concupiscence while the latter serves as basis for love of friendship. Of course, we should not forget that Thomas in his most precise treatment recognizes that love of concupiscence can (a) be grounded in love of friendship for someone else and (b) be present even when the "desired" good is present, taking the form of joy that the loved one has his good. Notwithstanding, we have Thomas's (and the tradition's) frequent use of love of concupiscence as (a) grounded in love of friendship for oneself and (b) targeting an absent good (since *concupitum* refers to what is desired). Relevant to the case we are investigating, those eager to meet their friends have a love of concupiscence for the friend's presence, since this presence pertains to their good. Pilgrims labor for union with God. Though their primary aim is to love God for His own sake and thus ecstatically seek beatitude, they also strive for beatitude because they love themselves. Dedication to spiritual progress is for them necessary and laudable. The fittingness of such dedication notwithstanding, since they are busy about many things pertaining to progress, they cannot achieve simple, continual, and explicit devotion to God.⁴⁵ We shall return to distractions below.

Possibility of Merit and the Order of Love

The wayfaring state is also one of meriting and demeriting.⁴⁶ Such a state affects the order of love. This order is twofold. It regards the excellence of the objective good one wills for the beloved and it involves the intensity of love. The objective good that charity wills for another regards the beloved's nearness to God, either actual or potential. The intensity of charity is determined by the closeness of the beloved to the lover himself. As Thomas writes,

> Every act should be proportionate both to its object and to the agent. But from its object it takes its species, while, from the power of the agent it takes the mode of its intensity. . . . Accordingly love

---

⁴⁴ See *ST* 1-2.27.3.

⁴⁵ See *ST* 1.62.2, ad 3. Those who enjoy God's presence still bear a natural love for this presence based upon their self-love, yet their attention is no longer occupied by the acts necessary to achieve this presence. They rest therein.

⁴⁶ There is not space to discuss merit in itself. The focus of this section is the implication of merit for the order of love. For a fine work on the topic, see Wawrykow, *God's Grace and Human Action*.

takes its species from its object, but its intensity is due to the lover. Now the object of charity's love is God, and man is the lover.[47]

We will treat each of these in turn.

With regard to the objective good, one loves "more" the person to whom one wills a greater good. Of course, there must be a proportion between the beloved and the good willed for him. We can wish our pets to be healthy and perky, but we cannot wish the goods of musicality or literacy for poodles or goldfish. This proportion can be actual or potential. If the proportion is actual, if our beloved has what we will him to have, joy emerges. If the proportion is only potential, desire and possibly sadness emerge. The possibility of development in life can make it reasonable to will a great good for one who does not have it actually. Parents, for instance, can will their children to surpass them in wisdom and virtue, while children can wish their parents to be both kinder and stronger.

The good that in charity we will for ourselves and for our neighbors is being in communion with God as Supernatural Friend. A significant question arises. Should someone with charity simply love more a person who is holier? Should a less holy person love a holier person more than himself? Pious thoughts might make it seem so, but Thomas's principles allow us to judge the matter more subtly. On the one hand, the actual state of things is what God has willed or permitted, and so the person with charity should surrender to God's wisdom regarding what is. Such surrender should make him will (rejoice in) the holier person's being holier. On the other hand, pilgrim existence is not completed but under way; one can grow in virtue or fall from it.[48] There is possibility that sinners may convert and that a spiritual beginner may become proficient. So, one can justly will for oneself a greater spiritual good than that of which one is presently worthy. One can likewise will for one's closer neighbors a greater spiritual good than one wills for the holier person down the road.[49] One can imagine a sort of fraternal rivalry of striving for holiness, provided this is devoid of pride and moderated by a greater love of God for His own sake, a universal benevolence, and a prudent contentment. A father who begrudged his son's increasing sanctity would utterly fail in his vocation. Regarding one's

---

[47] *ST* 2-2.26.7.
[48] See *ST* 2-2.26.7.
[49] See *ST* 2-2.26.7. Although certain prayers deemed pious (perhaps not wrongly) urge one to pray that others may be holier than oneself, nothing in divine law mandates such prayers.

own spiritual good, paying due attention to a diligent reading of the signs of divine providence, one's will, petitions, and labor can express hope for greater good from God than one might in the end actually achieve. In the pilgrim state, therefore, the order in which one loves others, as to the good willed, can vary according to one's hopes for oneself and others. A good mentor will hope for the best.

With regard to the intensity of love, it is another matter. Aquinas argues that each person loves himself more intensely than any other created person but God more intensely than himself. His argument is as follows. The intensity of love is determined with respect to the closeness of the beloved to the lover. God is closer to the lover than the lover is to himself because God is the entire source of one's own good: "God is loved as the principle of the good upon which the love of charity is founded, but a man loves himself according as he is a participant in this good."[50] Therefore, a holy person loves God more intensely than himself.

Further, fellowship with others is consequent upon one's own participation in God: one has fellowship with others because, just as one participates the divine good oneself, so they participate that same good. Thus, love extends to self and to neighbor "by reason of a fellowship in this good."[51] That is, both self and neighbor are each ordered to the divine good first; in consequence, each child of God has fellowship with every other child of God by reason of a common sharing in the divine good. Therefore, "as unity is greater than union, so, that a man himself participates the divine good is a greater reason of being loved than that another is associated with him in this participation."[52] As an indication of the priority of love of self, no one who has charity would, by the gift of charity itself, will to act against his share in beatitude by sinning in order to save his neighbor from sin.[53] Aquinas thus unequivocally maintains that one loves oneself more than one's neighbor in terms of the intensity of love.[54]

---

[50] *ST* 2-2.26.4 (my translation).
[51] *ST* 2-2.26.4.
[52] *ST* 2-2.26.4.
[53] *ST* 2-2.26.4.
[54] De Koninck argues that love of the common good of the heavenly Jerusalem, a created common good, exceeds the love of self. Although he does not to my knowledge explicitly address the question of the intensity of love, his thought seems to me to incline to the thesis that love for the common good is also more intense than love for self. If De Koninck is correct, how should one interpret the passages just cited? Perhaps they regard individuals taken individually. So, for example, I will love myself more intensely than I love St. Catherine, but perhaps I love the common good of the communion of saints

Of course, this primacy of the intensity of self-love regards spiritual goods of virtue, grace, and beatitude. One can, and at times ought, to sacrifice goods of intellectual knowledge, play, health, and life itself out of love for one's neighbor. If this is the case especially for one's dependents, it extends, given the proper circumstances, to all, especially to those in dire need.[55] Aquinas follows Augustine in ranking the goods one should will as follows: God, one's own soul, one's neighbor, and one's body.[56] The choice to care for neighbor before one's own health even pertains to self-love, since it is a nobler thing to suffer for a friend than to abandon him in his need.

We should consider the order of the intensity of love with regard to neighbor. Aquinas observes that pilgrim man spontaneously loves with greater affection those who are closer to him by ties of blood, marriage, and companionship. Charity, while ordering the acts of these friendships to itself and thus to God as Supernatural Friend, even commands the acts of these virtues, so that the pilgrim saint labors *more* for those closer to himself, especially if they are in need, than for distant strangers. Someone might object that such an ordering of love seems too subjectively grounded or insufficiently supernatural. Aquinas finds nothing untoward in this kind of order. His eye is towards what is proper and fitting for a given state of life. Grace does not destroy but perfects nature, and the natural order demands that one take greater care of those closer to home. Indeed, justice calls one first to meet the needs of those closer to home, without pursuing extravagant goods to the neglect of helpless neighbors. The life of charity hardly bypasses the mundane needs of nature; indeed, it consists significantly in meeting these needs through sincere acts of love. In short, justice demands that one devote primary attention in exterior acts to those closer to home. A Marxist reading of nature might find something with which to object here, as might a Christianity gutted of common sense and groundless, but Thomas and Augustine and the classical tradition are not at odds on these points.

Thomas and Augustine both converge and diverge on the ordering of interior affection as regards the neighbor.[57] Augustine proposes that the

---

more intensely than I love myself.
[55] See *ST* 2-2.26.5 and *Eth.* 9.9.
[56] See *ST* 2-2.26.3, 4, and 5. See also Augustine, *De Doctrina Christiana*, I.27.
[57] Mansini shows that Thomas's integration of "intensity" and "objective order" is actually an attempt to reconcile the apparently contradictory theses from authority. On the one hand, there is Augustine's insistence that love be ordered simply by objective standards. *De Doctrina Christiana*, chap. 28, n. 29 (PL 34, 30). Accordingly, all men as potential

interior affections ought to be ordered in a neutral or disinterested way, whereas, all things being equal, one ought to devote greater attention in exterior acts to those closer to home, to those with whom one has greater ties of affinity. Aquinas agrees with Augustine about exterior acts and for that reason differs from him about the ordering of interior affection. The voluntary character of exterior actions, Aquinas reasons, requires that interior inclinations be ordered in a manner corresponding to the proper order of exterior actions. Interior dispositions, as inclinations to exterior actions, must have an order that allows the exterior actions to be voluntary and connatural. Consequently, all things being equal, one ought also to have greater *interior affection* for those who are closer to oneself. Aquinas's point makes sense. Imagine a father who felt more intensely about caring for an anonymous person down the street suffering some real but only moderate sorrow than for his own daughter saddened by an obnoxious boy. The virtue of prudence calls for such correspondence between interior and exterior actions as well. As Michael Sherwin has shown, for Aquinas, prudence regulates both the interior and the exterior acts of charity as these regard one's neighbors.[58] Generally, then, prudence moderates interior charity to be more intense with regard to those closer to oneself according to the variety of these ties. Notwithstanding, prudence can and should also recognize cases of extreme or urgent need, and one's interior affection ought to be moderated in accordance with such cases. The following passage exhibits the general ordering of loves from the broadest perspective, treating first the love of God, second the love of self, and third the love of neighbors:

> [T]he love of charity is a certain inclination infused in rational nature for the purpose of tending toward God. Therefore, ac-

---

sharers of eternal life should be loved equally by the interior act of charity. Augustine, *In Galat.* 6, 10, n. 61 (PL 35, 2146).

On the other hand, there is a claim in the *Glossa ordinaria*, attributed to Ambrose (on Cant. 2:4), that love must be ordered in accordance with the "proximity" of the beloved to us. Lombard noted the contrast between these authorities and suggested reasonable ways to read Augustine in harmony with Ambrose (see Peter Lombard, *Liber III, Sentences*, d. 28, chap. 2). See also Mansini, "*Similitudo*," 6. For Thomas's examinations of this issue, see *DC* 9 and *ST* 2-2.26.6–8.

It might also be noted that Thomas is attentive to the natural aspect of things. The principle that like loves like is embedded in nature, and grace does not subvert this in a revolutionary manner. The needy child wants his father to love him with great affection.

[58] See Sherwin, *By Knowledge*, 178ff, and *ST* 2-2.32, arts. 2–3.

cording as it is necessary for one to tend toward God, thus is he inclined out of charity.

However, for those who will tend toward God as to an end, what is [maximally] needed is that there be divine help; secondly, that there be [help from oneself]; and thirdly, that there be cooperation with fellow-men. And in this we see a gradation, for some cooperate only in a general way, while others who are more closely united cooperate in a special way. Not all are able to cooperate in a special way. Our body and those things which are necessary for the body also help us tend toward God, but only instrumentally.

Thus it is necessary that the affection of man be so inclined through charity that, first and foremost, each one loves God; secondly, that he love himself; and thirdly, that he love his neighbor. And among the fellow-men, he ought to give mutual help to those who are more closely united to him or who are more closely related to him.[59]

We see, in this hierarchical order of the inclination of love or of its intensity, the logic of the *bonum suum*: the closer something is to one's good, the more intensely is it loved. God is loved most intensely, then the self according to the spiritual nature, then the neighbor according to the spiritual nature. Among neighbors, those are loved more intensely who are closer to oneself by the various lawful human bonds. All such bonds ought to be ordered to charity as to an end, but every licit love may and, given the proper circumstances, ought to be approved and nurtured. In short, charity does not flatten the topography of nature. As Thomas writes:

> We love more those who are more nearly connected with us, since we love them in more ways. For, towards those who are not connected with us we have no other friendship than charity, whereas for those who are connected with us, we have certain other friendships, according to the way in which they are connected [to us]. Now since the good on which every other friendship of the virtuous is based, is directed, as to its end, to the good on which charity is based, it follows that charity commands each act of another friendship, even as the art which is about the end commands the

---

[59] *DC* 9.

art which is about the means. Consequently this very act of loving someone because he is akin or connected with us, or because he is a fellow-countryman or for any like reason that is referable to the end of charity, can be commanded by charity, so that, out of charity both eliciting and commanding, we love in more ways those who are more nearly connected with us.[60]

As we have more reasons for loving someone, our love for them is more intense.

Distractions

The demands of life make complete, continual, and explicit devotion to God impossible. A pilgrim cannot understand many things, as many, at the same time. The reason for this is that the mind understands according as the intelligible form of the thing known is in the knower. But diverse forms cannot inform the same potency, except when they are united together under some single higher form. Therefore, "[i]t is impossible for one and the same intellect to be perfected at the same time by different intelligible species so as actually to understand different things."[61] Of course, various things can be gathered together under something common; they can in this way be considered simultaneously. Similarly, by one act of will, one can intend the end and things that are for the end.[62] Thus, it is possible for a pilgrim to deal with various things related to God without being divided in heart, even advancing towards the goal. Further, in Aquinas's opinion, whoever has charity orders himself and all that is his to God at least habitually; that is, even if one with charity is not actually thinking of God in some given act, he orders this act to God at least habitually.[63]

In making this claim, Thomas is simply borrowing from the distinction utilized by his contemporaries and predecessors, yet Thomas adds greater precision to the analysis, as Thomas Osborne shows.[64] An act is ac-

---

[60] *ST* 2-2.26.7.
[61] *ST* 1.85.4.
[62] See *ST* 1-2.12.3.
[63] See *ST* 1-2.88.1, ad 2.
[64] See the following fine articles on this topic: Thomas Osborne, Jr., "The Threefold Referral of Acts to the Ultimate End in Thomas Aquinas and His Commentators," *Angelicum* 85 (2008): 715–736 and "Thomas Aquinas and John Duns Scotus on Individual Acts and the Ultimate End," in Kent Emery, Jr., Russell L. Friedman, and Andreas Speer, ed., *Philosophy and Theology in the Long Middle Ages* (Brill: Boston, 2011), 351–74.

tually ordered to God if God is the end one has in mind when committing the act.⁶⁵ For example, one actually orders a recitation of the *Ave Maria* to God if one has God in mind as end while saying the prayer. Of course, the limitations of the human mind are such that it is impossible to refer every good act to God in this way. While praying the Rosary, one's mind may drift. Thomas contends, however, that every act that is (a) intrinsically orderable to God and (b) committed by one who has charity is more than merely "habitually" ordered to God. Every such act is "virtually" ordered to God. The term "virtually" leans on the notion of power or cause (*virtus*). The power of the intention of the end is present in the act being performed. It is possible for the power of charity to be in some act provided (a) that there be an act and (b) that this act be good in itself.⁶⁶ As Thomas uses the term, an act is "virtually" ordered to God as supernatural end in that it really is ordered to God (the end of the love of charity) although the mind of the one performing the act is actually occupied with some secondary end. Thomas gives the example of a doctor, who goes out to find the requisite herbs for a medicinal concoction. The doctor is fulfilling his duty of providing health, and so his act really is ordered to the health of the patient even though at the time he is busy identifying the proper herbs.⁶⁷ It is obvious that the limitations of the human condition make a virtual intention not only tolerable but even necessary.⁶⁸ Were the doctor not focused on identifying herbs when appropriate, he would fail to heal. Thus, virtual intention of the end conduces to acts of virtue.

Thomas's contribution is in the distinction between virtual referral of an act and merely habitual referral of an act. An act is merely habitually referred to God as supernatural end if (a) it is performed by one who has charity and (b) it is not an act actually referable to God. Thomas offers as example the "act" of sleeping. Since the will is not engaged while one is sleeping, there is no volitional act while sleeping. Hence, sleeping is not an "act" that is referable to God. Thus, intention of the primary end cannot be present with its power in the act of sleeping, at least not in the same way that it is in a good act. However, since the person sleeping has the

---

⁶⁵ See, e.g., *De perf.* 6 and *DC* 11, ad 2. It should go without saying that the act must itself be good. However, many complications immediately come to mind, which are properly addressed in moral theology.

⁶⁶ For Thomas, every deliberate act is either good or evil in itself. An act is good in itself if its object, circumstances, and end are good. Further treatment of this highly complex matter must be left to moral theology.

⁶⁷ See *DC* 11, ad 2.

⁶⁸ See Osborne, "Threefold," 718.

habit of charity, he and all he has are ordered to God habitually.[69] More controversially, Thomas contends that every venial sin committed by one who has charity is "habitually" ordered to the end of charity, with God as supernatural end. As Osborne writes, "[Venial sins] by their nature cannot be actually referred to God and yet they can be committed by someone who has God as his supernatural end."[70] Despite the impossibility of actually ordering a venial sin to God, one refers it to God "habitually" simply because (a) the sin is not of such kind as to expunge or exclude the habit of charity and thus (b) is caught up in the holy person's habitual orientation to God.[71]

As Osborne demonstrates, Thomas's contribution enables him to address a difficulty presented by some uses of the merely twofold distinction in the prior tradition.[72] If one held that an act can be meritorious if it has God as end merely in habit, would not the act of sleeping, which is habitually ordered to God as end, also be meritorious? However, sleeping is not a volitional act and so cannot be meritorious. According to Thomas's distinction, neither sleeping nor venial sins have that by which the intention of the end can actually order them to God. Sleeping is not a volitional act, and a venial sin is evil; neither is a good free act. Acts that are not free and good can be only habitually ordered to God in one who has charity. Thomas holds that acts that are not both free and good are nonetheless habitually ordered to God because of the transformative effect of the very habit of charity on the person.[73] By contrast with both venial sins and sleep, all good acts are intrinsically referable to God as end. That is, they are free acts and are intrinsically referable to God as end. Because of the power of charity in the holy person, all such acts do receive the power of the intention of the end and so are really meritorious.[74] Of course, acts actually ordered to God as supernatural end are also meritorious. Thus, only acts that are virtually or actually ordered to God as supernatural end are meritorious; acts habitually ordered to God as supernatural end are not meritorious.

The habitual order to God ranks lower than the virtual order to God. Further, all things being equal, the virtual order to God order ranks lower

---

[69] See *DC* 11, ad 3.
[70] Osborne, "Threefold," 719.
[71] See *DM* 7.1, ad 4, 9; *ST* 2-2.24.10, ad 2; and Osborne, "Threefold," 719–24.
[72] See Osborne, "Aquinas and Scotus," 359ff.
[73] To be more precise, this transformative effect is a matter of charity *as* operative grace. Neither sleep nor venial sins engage charity *as* cooperative.
[74] See Osborne, "Threefold," 721–22.

than the actual order to God. The reason is that the goal of life, and the end of the precept to love God's glory in all things, is the actual love of God in heavenly life. So, if one undertakes deliberate actions out of love of charity while actually retaining the divine good in mind, one's actions are even more firmly rooted in charity.

These considerations help us evaluate the perfection of charity. Aquinas notes that charity is called perfect in various ways. With respect to its object, perfect charity loves God as much as He is lovable. God being infinite, only the divine love loves God as much as He is lovable. Thus, only God's own love is perfect with respect to the proportion of the act to its object. However, charity can also be considered perfect with respect to the lover's capacity, when the lover loves according to his capacity. For Thomas, there are three degrees of perfection:

> First, so that a man's whole heart is always actually borne towards God: this is the perfection of the charity of heaven, and is not possible in this life, wherein, by reason of the weakness of human life, it is impossible to think always actually of God, and to be moved by love towards Him. Secondly, so that man makes an earnest endeavor to give his time to God and Divine things, while scorning other things except in so far as the needs of the present life demand. This is the perfection of charity that is possible to a wayfarer; but it is not common to all who have charity. Thirdly, so that a man gives his whole heart to God habitually, viz., by neither thinking nor desiring anything contrary to the love of God; and this perfection is common to all who have charity.[75]

The more actual the charity, the more perfect. The charity of the blessed is always actual, while that of the religious way of life is as actual as possible on earth. Finally, there is the perfect charity of those who at least habitually love God in all their deliberate actions, avoiding all mortal sin.[76] We may interpolate a fourth state between the third and second degrees of charity: all are called to perfection, albeit in different expressions. The distracted mother of three can, by following a path less trod, order the sundry duties of motherhood to her union with Christ.

The greater the perfection in charity, the less the possibility of sin. While actually loving God out of charity, one cannot sin mortally. For in-

---

[75] *ST* 2-2.24.8.
[76] See *ST* 2-2.24.8 and *DC* 10.

stance, when praying with true devotion or explicitly ordering a good work to God, one cannot sin mortally. However, when not actually engaged in an act of charity, one can intend something other than God as the final end and thus lose charity.[77] As great a transformation as charity works in the pilgrim, enlivening him and formally justifying him, conforming him to God, it does not render sin impossible. Experience shows quite the opposite to be the case.

Charity is a form perfective of the Christian, while the Christian considered in his own nature is compared as matter to this form of charity. Some forms perfectly actualize their matter so that the composite cannot be corrupted. Other forms do not actualize their matter perfectly. Such is the case with earthly charity, for no pilgrim can always actually love God in this life. There are many times when a man loves God only habitually. When not actually considering and loving God, one can lose charity:

> It is natural for a form to be in its subject in such a way that it can be lost, when it does not entirely fill the potentiality of matter: this is evident in the forms of things generated and corrupted, because the matter of such things receives one form in such a way, that it retains the potentiality to another form, as though its potentiality were not completely satisfied with the one form. Hence the one form may be lost by the other being received. . . . [So] the charity of the wayfarer does not so fill the potentiality of its subject, because the latter is not always actually directed to God: so that when it is not actually directed to God, something may occur whereby charity is lost.[78]

In addition to simple distractions which affect all pilgrims and to worldly concerns which still affect some holy pilgrims, venial sins can interrupt the act of charity, even though they do not remove it as an infused habit: "A man can live in this life without mortal sin, but not without venial sin; this is not contrary to the perfection of this life but to the perfection of the life in heaven which consists in being always actually directed toward God. Venial sin does not take away the habit of charity, but it impedes its act."[79] The constant danger of temptation and sin threaten the fluid continuity of the life in charity.[80]

---

[77] See *ST* 2-2.24.11, ad 4.
[78] *ST* 2-2.24.11.
[79] *DC* 10, ad sed contra 1.
[80] See *DC* 10.

Conclusion

The relationship between self-love and love of God for His own sake in earthly charity is complex. In some senses, self-love can be greater with earthly charity than with heavenly charity, but in other respects self-love is lesser. The possibility of falling away from charity correlates with a self-love that is less perfect than that in glory. However, the possibility of gaining merit allows one legitimately to desire a greater degree of holiness and beatitude than one might achieve. Further, the believer's state of potency and neediness requires that one act out of self-love. Paradoxically, however, the heightened play of the act of self-love regards the bodily or lower nature, whereas perfect self-love regards chiefly the spiritual or higher nature. Indeed, the difficulties of distractions and sin correlate with less perfect self-love because those love themselves best who love the highest part of themselves. If self-love targets the good of the lover, he loves himself best who is swept up in the love of God. Having treated the imperfections of earthly charity, we proceed in the next chapter to discuss the correlative perfections of heavenly charity, which are rooted in the state of perfection and the glorious vision.

CHAPTER 7

Charity in Glory

WE ARE IN POSITION TO INFER some aspects of heavenly charity, which transcends even the experience of grace. The advent of glory perfects earthly charity, leaving only those imperfections due to the creaturely status and finite measure of the saint's love. Because knowledge is a necessary cause of love and because pilgrim imperfections of charity are dispelled by beatific knowledge and the consequent state of perfection, we must first treat of Thomas's understanding of the vision of God. Then, we will treat the consequent conditions of heavenly charity as these converge with or diverge from those of earthly charity.

GLORY'S KNOWLEDGE

Thomas suggests an intelligible account of the mystery of the beatific vision by comparison with human intellection generally. In any act of apprehension, the thing known is in a way taken into the knower, so that the apprehensive power becomes as though one with the intelligible form of the known.[1] In a less perfect way, something of the sort happens in sense knowledge. A distinction between the thing as existent and the thing as known remains, of course, because an organ of sense cannot actually become one with its object. The organ retains its identity as part of a man, and the object retains its identity as a substance. Nevertheless, the sensitive organ receives into itself the character of the object under which the animal knows it.[2] Sight receives a likeness of the "redness" of the apple. On a higher level, the intellect receives the formal intelligibility of that which it knows. This intelligibility is termed the "intelligible species." The mind,

---

[1] See *DA* 2.12 and *ST* 1.85.2 and 3.
[2] See *ST* 1.84.1.

which is capable of knowing that which is, receives into itself the intelligible species of the known. The intelligible species informs or actualizes the intellect in its act of intellection so that what exists comes to be known. Crucial to note, the intelligible species is not what is known, but that by which what is known is known.[3] For Thomas, the human person understands things as they really are through the intelligible species.

The intelligible species is obtained by way of an act of abstraction.[4] Through many acts of sensation, one develops memories. Through many memories, one comes to experience, and from many similar experiences, one can rise to knowledge of an essence.[5] The many similar experiences help one to form in one's imagination a rarefied image of the kind of thing to be known, an image of its common essential features. This image is called a phantasm.[6] We have every reason to think that there is for each intelligible thing in the corporeal world a *set* of phantasms with which one can play, which collectively enable one to abstract one intelligible species that is the intelligible structure of what one is aiming to know. For example, it would seem useful to have a set of triangular images constituting a collective phantasm, as it were, from which one abstracts the one intelligible structure of triangularity, which is not determinately acute, right, or obtuse.[7]

---

[3] See *ST* 1.85.2.
[4] See *ST* 1.85.1 and 2.
[5] Aristotle, *Metaphysics* I, 980b-981a.
[6] See *ST* 1.85.1, ad 3.
[7] One frequently hears the Thomistic expression "phantasm," as though there is one best image for any given concept. Thomas employs the term in the plural in *ST* 1.84.7, even in the context in which it seems a single act of understanding, a single formal intelligibility, is under discussion. Thomas more clearly teaches the abstraction of one intelligible species from a plethora of phantasms in *ST* 1.76.2. Following Berkeley, David Hume famously indicates that no one image can represent all things defined as a triangle. He concludes that there are no universals. A proper response must of course distinguish image from concept. However, it would also be to the point to acknowledge the veracity of an aspect of Hume's narrative: there is a certain free imaginative play with a set of images.

Whereas Hume excludes the concept and bluntly asserts that one can come to utilize some name to stand for a certain range of images, attaining functionally as it were a universal, we should insist on the possibility of genuine abstraction yielding a concept. Hume cannot account for the fact that we very strictly judge between a triangle and every four sided figure. We have a definite judgment concerning the limits of the use of the word "triangle." This is inexplicable without a universal concept. Still, we always depict the concept, as Hume recognized. The capacity to understand requires a certain dexterity and facility in the imaginative play to which Hume points, even though the

Because it is sensitive, the phantasm has a material element. Knowledge at the level of imagination and phantasm remains animal-like. Striking the surface only, it does not attain to the nature of that which is known.[8] Rather, it attains to the individual characteristics of individual things. However, the phantasm does not share the (designated) matter of the external thing it images. Our imagination gains the color red, albeit not the individual materiality of this apple, actualized by the apple's substantial form. So, although the imagination is not the apple, it is stuck in the "thisness" of the apple seen or imagined. In order to have an intellectual grasp of the nature of the thing, the mind must cast a higher light upon the phantasm and abstract from it the intelligibility of the form represented. This act of abstraction occurs through the power of the intellectual light called the agent intellect.[9] This formal intelligibility of the thing to be known is received into or produced within the "possible" intellect so that understanding can occur.[10] The possible intellect is the intellectual power that can receive into itself, intentionally, the intelligible formalities of things in the world. Understanding consists in the "information" of the possible intellect—of the possible intellect's being actualized by some intelligible form—as this actualization enables the thinker to target the real. Despite the immateriality of the intellect's act, one must always, in the present state of life, return to phantasms in order actually to understand.

Judgment of the truth of things presupposes understanding. I can judge, abstractly, that all red things are colored and that all simple things are intrinsically immutable. Even such abstract judgments require advertence to phantasms, since the acts of understanding presupposed to them require this as well. I can also judge concretely: this is a man. The judgment requires not only recourse to phantasms for the abstract understanding of "man" but also recourse to present sense knowledge regarding the

---

"intellectual" might lack the imaginative skill of an artist. Nonetheless, the act of understanding yielding the concept "triangle" digs deeper than anything in the field of imaginative play.

[8] The nature of something is universal in that it is common to all the individuals of the species.

[9] See *ST* 1.85.1 and 2.

[10] See *ST* 1.79.2. The intellect is called "possible" as being capable of (in potency to) intelligible forms. Thomas utilizes two images to capture the abstraction process. On the one hand, the intelligible content is "abstracted" from the phantasm; on the other hand, the intelligible content is "wrought" in the possible intellect by the agent intellect as it studies the phantasms. Each image has its strength. I leave it to the experts to wrestle with these as they pertain to important discussions concerning realism.

signs of the quiddity of what stands before me.

This dependence upon sense knowledge and imagination remains in place both in the philosophical study of God and also in the knowledge of faith.[11] The philosopher rises to knowledge of God through knowledge of the visible world. The conclusion that there exists a prime mover, not moved by anything, involves advertence to images, despite the analogical reach of the proposition beyond all things material. Although by God's grace the believer's assent truly reaches the one and triune God, this assent requires recourse to symbols and images, and it rises to God by way of propositions.[12] Thus, when a religious thinker considers the divine "oneness" or mercy, he adverts in part to his experiences of these qualities so as to ground his articulated apprehension of the mysteries in something to which he more naturally relates. True, the believer's awareness and apprehension of revelation is assisted by a new, intellectual light called the light of faith.[13] Still, as exalted as the light of faith is, it does not provide a unified, simple knowledge of God Himself. It illuminates the truths of God only in a mediated way, through the complexity of propositions expressive of diverse judgments.

By contrast, when the souls of the righteous are taken into heaven, they enjoy the vision of God. To be seen, God must become present to the seer's power of knowing; rather, the seer must be opened to God's presence. The knowing power intends things as known (it can have knowable things present to itself, so to speak) *through* being informed by the intelligible species. What, then, is the intelligible species whereby the human intellect is informed so as to see God? Does any created species accomplish this? Can any created intelligible species mediate knowledge of God's essence? Aquinas is unequivocal: no created species can serve as an adequate medium of beatific knowledge of the infinite God. There are three reasons for this:

> First, because, as Dionysius says (*Div. Nom.* 1), *by the similitudes of the inferior order of things, the superior can in no way be known*; as by the likeness of a body the essence of an incorporeal thing cannot be known. Much less therefore can the essence of God be

---

[11] See *DT* 6.2.
[12] See *DV* 2.1, ad 9 and *DT* 1.2. See also John F. Wippel, "Quidditative Knowledge of God," in *Metaphysical Themes in Thomas Aquinas*, Studies in Philosophy and the History of Philosophy, vol. 10, ed. John K. Ryan and Jude P. Dougherty (Washington DC: The Catholic University of America Press, 1984), 219.
[13] See *ST* 2-2.1.4, ad 3.

seen by any created likeness whatever. Secondly, because the essence of God is His own very existence, as was shown above (Q. 3. A. 4), which cannot be said of any created form; and so no created form can be the similitude representing the essence of God to the seer. Thirdly, because the divine essence is uncircumscribed, and contains in itself [in a supreme way] whatever can be signified or understood by the created intellect. Now this cannot in any way be represented by any created likeness; for every created form is determined according to some aspect of wisdom, or of power, or of being itself, or of some like thing. Hence to say that God is seen by some similitude is to say that the divine essence is not seen at all; which is false.[14]

As a result, nothing created, whether earthly or angelic, can adequately represent God. No one who knows God simply through such a representation sees God in His essence.

If created species are involved in wayfaring man's acts of understanding, what is the intelligible species in the beatific vision? Aquinas argues by analogy that in the beatific vision God Himself must accomplish for the saint what the intelligible species accomplishes in a wayfarer's acts of understanding. We should not so much think that God becomes an "intelligible species" as that God unites the intellect to Himself immediately, making the intellect to be in act just as the intelligible species makes the intellect to be in act in the wayfaring state:

> The divine essence is existence itself. Hence as other intelligible forms which are not their own existence are united to the intellect by means of some entity, whereby the intellect itself is informed, and made in act; so the divine essence is united to the created intellect, as the object actually understood, making the intellect in act by and of itself.[15]

We witness here truly the profoundest sense of "deification" conceivable, apart from the qualitatively distinct hypostatic union. There remains a distinction between the knower and the known. Man remains a created

---

[14] *ST* 1.12.2.

[15] *ST* 1.12.2, ad 3. This use of Aristotelian epistemology beckons one to think of spousal imagery, for God Himself is taken into the believer. Such an image should then be complemented with Aquinas's analysis of ecstasy and mutual inhesion.

being, while God is uncreated. Moreover, man's vision of God is finite and therefore created.[16] This distinction notwithstanding, through his beatific vision of God, the saint is united to God as though being one with Him.

In order for this beatific union to take place, the human intellect must be properly disposed. No creature has the capacity to dispose itself or others to the vision of God because the disposition to a form is proper only to the natural subject of that form.[17] Every created being has a creaturely mode of knowing. Thus, no one but God is capable of enjoying the divine vision "unless God by His grace unites Himself to the created intellect."[18] God prepares the human intellect by raising the light of faith to the light of glory, making the intellect participate in the divine capacity to see His own essence:

> Since the natural power of the created intellect does not avail to enable it to see the essence of God, as was shown in the preceding article, it is necessary that the power of understanding should be added by divine grace. Now this increase of the intellectual powers is called the illumination of the intellect.... By this light the blessed are made *deiform*—that is, like to God, according to the saying: *When He shall appear we shall be like to Him, and ... we shall see Him as He is* (1 John ii. 2).[19]

What is the light of glory? The expression "light of glory" (*lumen gloriae*) resembles the expressions "light of faith" (*lumen fidei*) and "light of the intellect (*lumen intellectus*)."[20] The light of the intellect is the agent intellect, an efficient cause, that casts light upon the phantasms in order to abstract the intelligible species therefrom.[21] Does the *lumen gloriae* perform the same function as the agent intellect, rendering intelligible the thing actually to be known? To answer yes would be absurd, since God

---

[16] We must then qualify the words of William Hoye: "[T]he beatific vision demands not just that man become the divine essence intentionally (as would be the case in regard to knowledge per essentiam of a pure intelligence, that is, of an angel) but that he become the divine essence really." Hoye, *Actualitas*, 274. It is true that the possible intellect is totally actualized and that this actualization, the intelligible species, is God Himself. Nevertheless, the divine nature and human nature remain distinct.

[17] See *ST* 1.12.5, ad 3.

[18] *ST* 1.12.4.

[19] *ST* 1.12.5.

[20] See, for example, *ST* 1.12, arts. 2, 5, 6, 7; *SCG* 3.45.9; and *ST* 1.84.6, ad 1.

[21] See *ST* 1.79.3 and 4.

is already actually intelligible.²² Christian Trottmann notes that the early opponents of Thomas mistakenly thought that he depicted the *lumen gloriae* as the efficient cause of vision. The light of glory is, instead, more akin to a perfecting disposition than an efficient cause. The light of glory enables the passive intellect to be actualized by the Divine Essence in a manner analogous to the way it is actualized by the intelligible species.²³

This light of glory is a *created* perfection, a further actualization of the intellect, likening it to the divine nature and enabling it to be united beatifically to God.²⁴ Thus, the blessed are deified in the object seen and also in their interior principles, since the light of glory, although (ever) infused from above, becomes a stable interior disposition never to be lost.²⁵ According as one receives a greater illumination of divine light, so much the more perfectly can one see God. Each saint sees God face to face, without reasoning and mediation. Still, the act itself of vision is in each case limited.²⁶ One person's vision can be greater or lesser than another's, in accordance with diverse participations in the uncreated light and entailing diversity in degrees of heavenly beatitude. Diverse participations of the *lumen gloriae* are proportionate to diverse participations in charity.²⁷ The greater the charity by which one loves God, the greater the participation in the light of glory.

Now that we have discussed the perfections of the knowledge of God in glory, we can investigate the correlative perfections of heavenly charity.

Perfections of Charity in Glory

Unlike faith and hope, charity remains in heaven: "Charity is love, the definition of which does not include any imperfection, since it can be for what is possessed or not possessed, of what is seen or not seen. Thus, charity is not taken away by the perfection of glory, but remains the same in number."²⁸ By this phrase "remains the same in number," Aquinas indi-

---

²² See *SCG* 3.53 and *Quodl.* 7.1.1.
²³ See *SCG* 3.35. See also Christian Trottmann, *La vision béatifique des disputes scolastiques à sa définition par Benoît XII* (Rome: École française, 1995), 349.
²⁴ See *ST* 1.12.5
²⁵ See Hoye, *Actualitas*, 275–76.
²⁶ The whole God is seen, but not wholly. See *ST* 1.12.7, ad 5.
²⁷ See *ST* 1.12.6.
²⁸ *ST* 1-2.67.6 (my translation). It is worth noting that in the *Sent.*, wherein Aquinas struggles to identify the order of the passions, Aquinas arrives at the same conclusion but perhaps more forcefully, since therein he holds that love "rather implies perfection,

cates that the very virtue of charity the pilgrim has is the same that he has in heaven. Not the same only in kind but the very same ontological habit, infused at the moment he was last justified from ungodliness. By contrast, the habit of charity that one receives at Baptism is not the same in number as that one receives through Confession after having committed a mortal sin. "The same in number" indicates identity of some given form, not only an identity of species.

Heavenly charity differs from pilgrim charity in three respects. First, the quality of charity is purified and enhanced because God is known in Himself and no longer through symbolic and propositional veils. Still, because pilgrim charity and heavenly charity are the same in number, there remains a proportion between the degree to which a person partakes of pilgrim charity and the degree to which he partakes of heavenly charity. Second, heavenly charity involves the total and final conformity to God's will, so that the order of one's love, as regards the good willed, conforms to the objective order of the degree of holiness of each saint. One also rests content with the actual order of holiness, for there remains no potentiality for further achievement of greater or lesser holiness. Third, the human mind and heart shall continually and actually be devoted to God, without distraction or hindrance.

The Vision of God

The vision of God entails two chief perfections of charity.[29] (1) First, those who enjoy the beatific vision cannot but love God above all things and intimately. The capacity for sin is changed into the incapacity to sin or, rather, into the capacity to love perfectly.

Aquinas offers three grounds for this claim. First, one who actually possesses some good does not wish to be without it unless either (a) it is

---

insofar as it implies the completion of the appetite" (*Sent.* 3.31.2.2). In the *Summa*, he affirms that love becomes more perfect but does not define love by this inclusion of perfection.

[29] The vision of God can also be described as the presence of God to the saint. God is not made present "physically" since He has no body. Furthermore, God is not made present by a change in Himself. Rather, God becomes present to the saint through a change in the saint. The saint changes by having a new relation to God through his intellect and will. This new relation is set up by acts of knowledge and love. See *ST* 1.43.1 and *ST* 1.43.2. It is outside the scope of this monograph to investigate the various senses in which God is present to the justified and to the saved. Javier Prades argues that there are several senses of this presence. He contends that Aquinas does not reduce God's presence to that of an object's presence as a term of an operation. See Prades, *Deus specialiter*, 375.

lacking in some respect what another good promises, or (b) it is somehow unfitting or burdensome. The beatific vision has neither aspect. In God one finds unrestrictedly that which is of perfection in any other desirable good, so that nothing can draw the beatified away from God, the fountain of all good. Neither God nor the sight of God has anything wearying about it:

> The vision of the Divine Essence fills the soul with all good things, since it unites it to the source of all goodness. . . . In like manner neither has it any inconvenience attached to it; because it is written of the contemplation of wisdom (Wisd. viii. 16): *Her conversation hath no bitterness, nor her company any tediousness.*[30]

God is all good and contains no evil. Every good besides God that a saint can consider is only a limited, created good. All created goods derive their limited being and excellence from the creative hand of the unlimited God, having nothing positive in them that is not from God. Hence, there is nothing of perfection in the created thing that the saint does not know exists in a more excellent way, without imperfection, in God. For this reason, no one who sees God can love anything more than God. Thus, Aquinas concludes, "It is impossible that anyone seeing the divine essence wish not to see it."[31]

Such impossibility of turning away, and *a fortiori* of sinning,[32] shores up a necessary quality of true beatitude, namely, security in the continual possession of the good. This security must exist and be true. Insecurity is opposed to happiness, and so is the evil of falsehood.[33] So, the beatific vision excludes the freedom of exercise regarding the same, and this exclusion is eminently fitting.

Does this line of thought contradict Aquinas's contention, in *DM*, q. 6, that no object moves the will necessarily to exercise its act? I argue that there is no chronological argument in favor of change. Gilles Emery dates *DM*, q. 6, very close to the Condemnations of 1270. The *Prima secundae*, wherein the argumentation about the impossibility of leaving the vision of God occurs, dates from 1271. Either these texts are contemporaneous or the *Prima secundae* comes later. Hence, the *Prima secundae* represents

---

[30] *ST* 1-2.5.4.
[31] *ST* 1-2.5.4.
[32] See *ST* 1.94.1.
[33] See *ST* 1-2.5.4.

Thomas's mature position. Moreover, even in the *Prima secundae*, Thomas also teaches that no object at all moves the will to its act necessarily: "No object moves the will necessarily, for no matter what the object be, it is in man's power not to think of it, and consequently not to will it actually"?[34] If there is no argument in favor of definite and consistent change, how can we explain the apparent discrepancy?

I suggest that when Aquinas affirms freedom of exercise with regard to any object, he is considering the perfect good *in particular* or *as realized in the particular*. He is not considering God as seen in the vision. The object of vision cannot be "particular" in the aforesaid sense. That which is particular is finite and something reaches beyond it. Notably, when Thomas refers in *DM* to the object that is good "in every conceivable particular," he mentions Boethius's definition of happiness as the combination of all goods. Now, a happiness that is a symphony of goods is a natural happiness, not the supernatural good of immediate union with the infinite good. Such a collection of goods cannot exhaust the will's vector towards the good in general; at most, it can present itself as the best candidate meeting the will's range of appetite. The supernatural good differs from any "best available instantiation" in that it alone truly meets and surpasses the will's range. However, there remains that range itself, in light of which the best candidate appeared to pilgrim man as best candidate. Hence, that the will has its range is not subject to free choice. That the will rests in the beatific vision is not subject to free choice. That the pilgrim chooses not to consider the "best candidate" is subject to his self-determination *in light of* his appetite for what falls within the range of the will. Furthermore, arguably, even such choice can only be made because of a greater attractiveness in some other option, even if that option is the non-exercise of an act.[35]

Since the "perfect object" considered by a pilgrim is not God as supernaturally attained, it is an object of consideration for free choice. Such an object is, therefore, one of the items in *ea quae sunt ad finem*, although the first among them, that which the pilgrim judges to instantiate the will's range of appetite. By contrast, God seen in the vision is not volitionally targeted as among *ea quae sunt ad finem*. An objection argues that even the beatified can choose no longer to see God, since the will is a power for opposites. Aquinas responds that the will's power over opposites regards only "those things that are ordered to the end."[36] The necessity of love of the blessed loving the vi-

---

[34] *ST* 1-2.10.2.
[35] See *ST* 1-2.5.4.
[36] *ST* 1-2.5.4, ad 2 (my translation).

sion is analogous to the natural desire for the end in general.[37]

This reflection leads to the second reason for Aquinas's claim that the beatified are impeccable. The transition from faith to glory is correlated with a fundamental shift in the reason for loving (*ratio diligendi*). The innate and ineradicable love in a pilgrim is for beatitude, not as a determinate concrete good but as the aspect of the good in universal as it relates to the *bonum suum*. The pilgrim chooses as ultimate end some object that he judges to manifest or instantiate the universal and fitting good. By contrast, the saint clearly recognizes that God Himself *is* the Ultimate Good and thus loves everything he loves insofar as it is related to God. On earth, the scope of the general tendency to good measures that of the appetite's tendency to this or that good. Even the justified pilgrim chooses God as "this good," judged adequate to the appetite for the universal good. In heaven, there is no such split: God who is Good Itself Subsisting is also seen. For those in heaven, *God* is the reason for the lovability of anything: "The will of the one who sees the essence of God of necessity loves whatever it loves with respect to God (*sub ordine ad Deum*), just as the will of one who does not see the essence of God of necessity loves whatever it loves under the common notion of the good which he knows."[38] Again,

> Since the divine essence is beatitude itself, in this way the intellect of the person seeing the divine essence bears itself to God as every man bears himself toward beatitude. Now, it is obvious that no man is able by his will to be averted from beatitude, for it is natural for man to will beatitude, and he wills it of necessity, and flees misery. Thus, no one seeing God by his essence can by his will be averted from God, which is to sin. On account of this, all those who see God by his essence are thus made firm in the love of God, so that they cannot sin, even unto eternity.[39]

The epiphany of the Godhead reveals that God alone suffices, and more than suffices, to quell the human appetite. If God is the reason for loving anything in heaven, nothing can be loved in heaven except in view of God. Further, the vision of God brings about full clarity concerning the order of goods. Thus, one loves only for the right reasons and one knows rightly what to love. Sin is impossible.

---

[37] See *ST* 1-2.5.4, ad 2.
[38] *ST* 1-2.4.4. See also *SCG* 4.95, par. 7 and *Comp.* 166.
[39] *ST* 1.94.1.

A third foundation is that no sin can be committed where there is no ignorance of the pertinent good. Every sin requires some ignorance of the pertinent good. Those who enjoy the vision of God are ignorant of nothing pertinent to their good. Therefore, it is impossible that they sin. Now, it would be sin to choose not to remain in the vision of God.[40] Hence, leaving the vision of God is not presentable as an option.

As a result of the aforementioned foundations, every beatified person enjoys rectitude of the will, intimately loving God above all things and all other things with respect to God.[41] The advent of beatitude confirms the pilgrim's choice to love God above all things out of charity. The saints cannot lose this rectitude of will:

> It is proper to a habit to incline a power to act, and this belongs to a habit, in so far as it makes whatever is suitable to it, to seem good, and whatever is unsuitable, to seem evil. For as the taste judges of savors according to its disposition, even so does the human mind judge of things to be done, according to its habitual disposition. Hence the Philosopher says (*Ethic.* iii. 5) that *such as a man is, so does the end appear to him*. Accordingly charity is inseparable from its possessor, where that which pertains to charity cannot appear otherwise than good, and that is in heaven, where God is seen in His Essence, which is the very essence of goodness. Therefore the charity of heaven cannot be lost.[42]

The saints cannot but love everything in subordination to Him. They know with certitude that God alone is the supreme good for which their hearts are made. Thus, they cannot fall from the vision of God because they cannot fail to see God as the ultimate end of their lives. They are forever confirmed in their rectitude of will.

This perfect and immutable rectitude of will provides sure grounds for authentic self-love. Pilgrims love themselves according to the inner man in a manner that is true but imperfect and subject to fragility, whereas the beatified love themselves perfectly. Let us consider the difference in light of the five points of friendship with respect to which a justified pilgrim is

---

[40] See *SCG* 4.92, par. 6.
[41] "Charity, in which the divine object is loved, not only forms faith, but also is active in vision." James A. Mohler, *The Beginning of Eternal Life: The Dynamic Faith of Thomas Aquinas, Origins and Interpretation* (New York: Philosophical Library, 1968), 79. See his discussion on 58–83.
[42] *ST* 2-2.24.11.

a friend to himself. First, as the justified wills himself to exist and to live as to the inner man, all the more does the saint rejoice to exist and live in beatific union with God. Indeed, the object in this volition is not simply substantial existence but the composite good of substantial existence *in* the fruitional state.[43] The saints truly will such a good for themselves, which is at once most active and most achieved. In beatitude, life and joy are complete. The second and third elements of friendship are willing and doing good for one's friend. As described, the second and third elements of friendship are tied to the mode of pilgrims, who do not have their various goods. Hence, the second and third elements as described regard things ordered towards the end as useful on the way. One not only *wills* but also *labors* so that one's friend may have these necessary goods. The beatific life admits no such needs, since the end is already attained. Are the second and third elements therefore irrelevant? To the contrary, the beatific life does admit a manifold variety of goods that do not contradict the state of perfection. Glory does not destroy what is perfect in grace, and grace does not destroy what is perfect in nature. Granted, goods willed and done for another are indeed *ea quae sunt ad finem*. Their way of being "*ad finem*," however, differs in beatitude, wherein such goods are not willed not as instrumental towards but as expressive of beatific life. The saint's every inward volition and act of intellection expresses in manifold ways the simple glory of beatitude. The resurrected life constitutes the bodily dimension of this overflowing of glory. The saints not only will good things for themselves but also achieve these good things. Fourth, the blessed man dwells with himself delightfully, in recollection of his victorious pilgrimage and in restful anticipation of the beatitude whose unending character is one with its present, delightful participation. Fifth, the blessed is entirely at peace with himself, since all his activities begin in beatitude and tumble out from it as variegated expressions thereof. Truly, he is no longer "of the world" but only "of God."

(2) As its second effect upon charity, the divine vision so actualizes man's faculties that it entirely removes the state of potentiality.[44] Beatitude precludes potentiality, the capacity to attain some further end, for beatitude is the perfect attainment of the final end: "[beatitude] is man's

---

[43] On this point, see also Aquinas's thoughtful *Eth.* 9.4, par. 1807.

[44] We are speaking of the proportion of the substance to its achievement: This proportion is perfectly met, or rather the substance is entirely reduced to its proper operation. It goes without saying that the substance is in potency to the act of existence. Some substances are loftier than others.

supreme perfection. Now each thing is perfect in so far as it is actual; since potentiality without act is imperfect."[45] Carl Peter puts it pithily: "The intrinsic reason for the inability to progress in the Vision of God—a particular aspect of beatific immobilization—is that the complete capability of the creature *in this order* has been actuated."[46] Participating in the eternal life of God Himself, the blessed enjoy an operation without motion or change. That is, the vision of God does not consist in a succession of parts by which there is a disjunction between past and future elements.[47] Eternity does not stretch out unendingly; it consists in the "at once entire possession of unending life."[48] God is unparticipated eternity, for His beatific operation is not other than His divine substance. The beatified participate in this eternity, for they are not their beatific operation, although that operation, by which they are further actualized towards God, is without any succession on the part of the object. For the saints, all succession and temporality flow expressively from this eternity of beatitude.

Excluding the state of potentiality, beatitude renders the love of charity to be expressed not as desire but simply as joy. The appetitive rest of charity's joy affects the love of concupiscence for the vision of God. The saint does love the vision of God with a love of concupiscence for himself; still, he has no reason for acting upon this love in order to progress from potentiality to actuality. For the pilgrim, it is otherwise, because "the love of concupiscence will not rest in any external or superficial possession or enjoyment of the beloved but seeks to possess the beloved [completely], as though penetrating into his inmost being."[49] For the saint, the habit of this love of concupiscence remains, but it is not always engaged as an explicit act of love. Charity itself is always in act in heaven, and any other love that one has in heaven is commanded by ever-actual charity. Since, however, it is possible for the minds of the blessed to consider various finite objects, one after the other, in heaven, it is possible for them actually to engage in various acts of various loves essentially distinct from charity. When a certain love is not engaged in act, it can be described as habitual. In heaven, the acts of love of concupiscence for one's own beatitude cause no desire

---

[45] *ST* 1-2.3.2.

[46] Carl J. Peter, *Participated Eternity in the Vision of God: A Study of the Opinion of Thomas Aquinas and His Commentators on the Duration of the Acts of Glory* (Rome: Gregorian University Press, 1964), 38. See also P. Glorieux, "Saint Thomas et l'accroissement de la béatitude," *Recherches de théologie ancienne et médiévale* 17 (1950): 121–25.

[47] See *Sent.* 2.11.2.1; *Sent.* 4.49.1.2.3; and *ST* 1-2.67.4, ad 2.

[48] *ST* 1.10.1.

[49] *ST* 1-2.28.2 (my translation).

but only delight, since the saint rests from his labors. The life of spiritual progress is complete: saints neither worry about avoiding sin nor concern themselves with growth in holiness. They simply take joy in God for His sake. So the manifold expressions of beatitude are chiefly expressions of the love of friendship for God.

In sum, the vision of God ratifies charity by making it firm and always actualized. In this respect, the vision also increases the saint's self-love because those perfectly love themselves who submit themselves perfectly to God. The vision also removes the state of potentiality and thus allows the saint all the more to act towards God by a love of friendship for Him.

Cessation of Merit and the Order of Love

Charity is also affected by the impossibility of a man attaining a further degree of holiness through merit. One can no longer wish for a greater share in the good than one has because there is total rest and no room for an increase or decrease in merit: "In the state of future happiness man has arrived at perfection, wherefore there is no room for advancement by merit."[50] Merit and enjoyment of beatitude cannot coexist, "for merit has the character of a way towards the end. It is not, however, fitting for the one who has already arrived at the end to be moved towards it. So, no one merits what he already has."[51] The impossibility of merit correlates with the total rest implied in heavenly life. At the end of history, all indetermination shall cease, and each saint shall rest in the divine (consequent) will for himself and for every other person. The saint is in total conformity with God's will. Part of this conformity consists in the order of loves one has for self, neighbors, and God.

Heavenly conformity is greater than earthly conformity with the divine will; the transition to glory entails a transformation of the order of loves. Let us consider this difference. Whatever a man loves, he ought ultimately to order it towards the love of God. Formally speaking, the right ordering of love constitutes conformity to God's will. Yet, it may happen on earth that someone judges a thing differently than God judges it, loving something that is not in itself evil, but which God would not have him love then and there. Because of his ignorance of all the concrete implications of the divine will, a pilgrim who is justified can love a material object that God does not will him to love. He might, for instance, not will his brother

---

[50] *ST* 2-2.182.2, ad 2.
[51] *ST* 1.62.4 (my translation).

to die this year whereas God in His wisdom has determined otherwise. So long as the loved object is not in itself evil, such material divergence with the divine will does not impede formal acceptance of the divine will:

> [I]n order that a man will some particular good with a right will, he must will that particular good materially, and the Divine and universal good, formally. Therefore the human will is bound to be conformed to the Divine will, as to that which is willed formally, for it is bound to will the Divine and universal good; but not as to that which is willed materially.[52]

By contrast, beatific union comes with knowledge of God's will regarding salvific matters past and actual. Although no creature can know all that God can or does do, the blessed know God's will with regard to the sanctity of both other saints and themselves.[53] The uncertainty of one's ultimate holiness being removed, God's beatified friend adjusts to God's will in concrete matters, so that there may be perfect concord between his will and God's: "in the state of glory, everyone will see in each thing that he wills, the relation of that thing to what God wills in that particular matter. Consequently he will conform his will to God in all things not only formally, but also materially."[54] The result of such material concord with the divine will is also deeper peace. As Thomas writes, "Dissension about very slight matters and about opinions is inconsistent with a state of perfect peace, wherein the truth will be known fully, and every desire fulfilled."[55]

How does heavenly conformity with the divine will affect the order of loves? Whereas on earth it is possible for someone to wish a greater degree of holiness and beatitude for himself or a beloved one than for a holier saint, in heaven every person wills for himself and for all others exactly that which is proportionate to their accomplished merits, exactly that which God wills.[56] The saint loves holier persons "more" in terms of the order of the goods willed for heavenly friends. Why does a saint's love for

---

[52] *ST* 1-2.19.10.
[53] See *ST* 1.12.8.
[54] *ST* 1-2.19.10, ad 1.
[55] *ST* 2-2.29.3, ad 2.
[56] We are speaking of the divine will considered consequently, that is, with regard to the conditions and circumstances of individuals in the concrete. The issue of the relation of this "consequent will" to predestination cannot be treated here. Further, we are not excluding the pious and right tradition, to which Aquinas subscribes, that the divine

a fellow saint follow a strictly objective order in terms of the good willed? The reason resides in the combination of (a) the impossibility of merit or sin, increase or decrease of holiness, for any of these beloved persons, (b) the knowledge of the actual state of holiness each has achieved, and (c) the transition whereby the saint wills whatever he wills under the specific character (*ratione*) of reference to God. Charity thus (c) directs the acts of all loves to God as to their ultimate end. God wisely ordains that the reward of beatitude (b) corresponds proportionately to holiness, which (a) is immovably established. So, in terms of the good willed, the saint will better men a greater participation in God. They love better men more:

> [A] man will love better men more than himself, and those who are less good, less than himself: because, by reason of the perfect conformity of the human to the Divine will, each of the blessed will desire everyone to have what is due to him according to Divine justice. Nor will that be a time for advancing by means of merit to a yet greater reward, as happens now while it is possible for a man to desire both the virtue and the reward of a better man, whereas then the will of each will rest within the limits determined by God.[57]

Saints rest in the divine will, embracing it perfectly rather than desiring greater perfection for themselves, if such increase were even possible.[58] Since such greater perfection is not possible, they do not desire it.

With regard to the order of charity's intensity, matters are somewhat different. According to Aquinas, a saint loves himself more intensely than he does any other created person. Why? First, intensity of love derives from its relation to the lover. That love is an operation of the lover necessarily entails that it regards its subject more intensely than any other created object. Only the ultimate transcendent principle of the operation, God, whose reach is more interior to the will than the will is to itself, can be loved with greater intensity.[59] Second, the structure of the act of charity indicates this order. The first "movement" of charity is to direct its possessor's mind to God and, in consequence, to will others to share this order to God. Now, to direct one's mind to God pertains to one's ultimate good

---

generosity exceeds the merits of each, but proportionately so.
[57] *ST* 2-2.26.13.
[58] See *Sent.* 4.49.1.4.2, ad 3.
[59] On the causal reach of God concerning the will, see *ST* 1.105.4 and *ST* 1-2.9.6.

and thus to self-love. As Thomas argues, love of neighbor follows:

> [A] man will love himself more than even his better neighbors, because the intensity of the act of love arises on the part of the person who loves, as stated above (AA. 7, 9). Moreover it is for this that the gift of charity is bestowed by God on each one, namely, that he may first of all direct his mind to God, and this pertains to a man's love for himself, and that, in the second place, he may wish other things to be directed to God, and even work for that end according to his capacity.[60]

Third, similarly, the structure of participation in the friendship of charity indicates this order. The friendship of charity is founded on the divine gift to man. This participated foundation in the saint, the created charity and created beatitude formally actualizing him, is found in its plenitude in God from whom it comes. Hence, just as the part tends primarily and more intensely to its whole than to its own limited good, so the holy person tends more intensely to the divine good than to his own. That another also partakes in the divine beatitude presents a reason for lovability, namely, a common sharing in deification. That two or more share in deification depends, as upon its root, on the participation each has in divine beatitude. Hence, the act of love for oneself is more intense than the acts of love for this other and that other person, since the love of a fellow participant is based on a common sharing in the fellowship one has immediately with God.[61] Accordingly, there is a direct correlation between an increase in charity and an increase in authentic self-love: "As regards man himself, he ought to love himself so much the more than others, as his charity is more perfect, since perfect charity directs man to God perfectly, and this belongs to love of oneself."[62]

While the blessed love themselves with greater intensity than they do other created persons, the order of the intensity of their love for others follows a strictly objective pattern. Here, there is a remarkable difference from the order of intensity on the way of pilgrimage. Earthly pilgrimage requires charity to incline one more intensely to the needs of those closer

---

[60] See *ST* 2-2.26.13.

[61] Once again, whether there is a more intense love for the created common good of the communion of saints is another question to be pursued by those competent in the study of the common good.

[62] *ST* 2-2.26.13, ad 1. For other references see *Ad Rom.* 9.1, par. 740, and *Ioan.* 15.2, par. 2009.

to home, not of course to the exclusion of any affection for others, especially for those within reach who are in dire need. The heavenly life is not a pilgrimage but an achievement or completion; hence, the order of loves has no reference to pilgrim neediness. Rather, all the variety of loves and goods besides communion with God tumble out as expressive of this higher and loftier good. All is centered on God. Hence, Thomas concludes, holier neighbors will be loved more intensely than less holy neighbors:

> As to the order to be observed among our neighbors, a man will simply love [more] those who are better, according to the love of charity. Because the entire life of the blessed consists in directing their minds to God, wherefore the entire ordering of their love will be ruled with respect to God, so that each one will love more and reckon to be nearer to himself those who are nearer to God. For then one man will no longer succor another, as he needs to in the present life, wherein each man has to succor those who are closely connected with him rather than those who are not, no matter what be the nature of their distress: hence it is that in this life, a man, by the inclination of charity, loves more those who are more closely united to him, for he is under a greater obligation to bestow on them the effect of charity.[63]

Once again, we see the notable difference between the pilgrim state and the state of beatitude. As regards intensity, what primarily determines the order of charity any beatified person has for all neighbors is likeness to God. Rather than willing what he wills under the aspect of the "good in general," the saint wills what he wills "with respect to God." So, saints love holier neighbors more intensely than less holy neighbors because holiness is closeness to God and God is the chief object of charity.

It would be erroneous, however, to conclude that beatific charity is "disinterested," that is, that such love relates purely to "goodness" as such without reference to the lover's *bonum suum*. Heavenly charity still has reference to the *bonum suum* and its analogical extensions. Saints love God because their *bonum suum* most truly rests in Him. Heavenly charity is most "interested," although never "selfish." Love of another is not selfish, because it involves not the subjection of another's good to one's own but the *expansion* of one's good to include that of the other. It involves a welling up of concern, so that what is at stake for another becomes significant,

---

[63] *ST* 2-2.26.13.

just as what is at stake for oneself is significant. Charity, being love of the heavenly Other, whose good is not only infinite but also the very source of one's own good and of the very bond between beatified friends, draws one to be more concerned for the things of God than the things of earth. Heavenly charity accomplishes this prioritization perfectly but is never "disinterested." We must recall the following significant passage: "If we make the impossible supposition that God were not man's good, He would not be man's reason for loving."[64] We could, perhaps, will infinite good to an infinite God that is unrelated to us, as though by a sort of wishful and remote benevolence, but we could not love such a God more intensely than we love ourselves. The order of loves follows not simply a hierarchical but, more precisely, a participatively hierarchical pattern.

On earth, men love more those who are closer to themselves in regard to ties of blood or human companionship. The order of love becomes more "objective" in heaven not because disinterested love more truly reflects divine charity. Rather, the situations of life are radically different. There are no conditions of need and correlative responsibility in heaven. Earthly conditions of mutual dependence necessitate a certain domestically centered structure in the order of love. The removal of these conditions allows the principal ties of heaven to be rooted simply in closeness to God. Further, this change does not reflect a movement towards disinterest. Better men are loved more intensely than those with whom one was bound more closely on earth precisely because the former are deemed closer to oneself than the latter. The unity is unity of fellowship in the uncreated good. Just as at all times God is the measure of one's similitude with God, and not conversely, so in heaven the neighbor who is closer to God will be regarded as closer to oneself.

Finally, natural human friendships that are virtuous continue to exist in heaven. The *ratio diligendi* of virtuous self-love remains in heaven, even though its act falls perfectly under the commanding power of charity. Bonds of affection rooted in spousal union, blood ties, and earthly companionship extend in various respects into the beatific life, perfectly directed to the love of God. These friendships provide additional reasons for loving those with whom one was especially close on earth. Nevertheless, the love of God for His own sake so transcends the other concerns that, as stated above, men will deem holier persons to be closer to themselves than even friends and family. Thomas writes: "It will however be possible in heaven for a man to love in several ways one who is connected with him,

---

[64] *ST* 2-2.26.13, ad 3.

since the causes of virtuous love will not be banished from the mind of the blessed. Yet all these reasons are incomparably surpassed by that which is taken from [nearness] to God."[65] In short, we will love holier persons more, but we will also love in more ways those with whom we have more bonds. The former principle transcends but does not obliterate the latter.

We can bring the considerations in this section to a summary formulation. The order of love can be considered in two respects, with respect to the objective good willed and with respect to the intensity of the love. According to the order of the objective good willed, heavenly charity perfectly conforms to the divine will both formally and materially. Saints wish for themselves and for all others the exact degree of beatitude that God wills for each person. Thus, saints love best those whom God loves best. According to the order of intensity, saints love themselves most intensely after God. After themselves, saints love holier persons more than less holy persons, precisely because the former are closer to them in the society of beatific friendship. There is another consideration: a saint loves more the person with whom he had greater ties on earth than someone of equal holiness with whom he had no ties on earth. In short, nature's concerns are not obliterated, though they are transformed. Nature, too, minds the times. In respect of both orders of love, the objective good and love's intensity, heavenly charity purifies the imperfections of earthly charity due to the indeterminacy of one's degree of holiness and the believer's ignorance of many aspects of the material objects willed by God.

Cessation of Distractions and Disordered Passions

The cessation of distractions in heavenly life renders man's participation in charity all the more fervent and continual. In their earthly state, human concerns are dispersed over many matters. The dispersal of concern causes a certain diffusion of energy in charity. Insofar as the concerns are not frivolous but instrumental to charity's proper responsibility, this is not regrettable. Still, however much the active life is praiseworthy, its acts are ordered to those of the contemplative life. So, whereas a certain diffusion of energy may be at the service of charity's ultimate aim with respect to present demands, the undividedness of heavenly life allows charity to reach the intensity and fervor for which it was given. The saint's mind is not preoccupied with interests rooted in lowly needs but is turned towards God continually, allowing a perpetually actual love. Being devoted entire-

---

[65] *ST* 2-2.26.13.

ly to the contemplation of God's goodness, the saint loves God as perfectly as he is able. Perhaps in a redounding manner, the saint's mind tumbles musically towards song or thrills in the refracted beauty of God's light, but never in such a way as to be preoccupied unto distraction. Such additional loves would be fruits of charity and contemplation.

Perfect attention to and love of God makes the loss of charity impossible, since the habit of love so totally fills the power of the will that it is always reduced to its act. In heavenly life, no human activity can occur in such a way as to distract from the continual love of God. Charity is totally reduced to act, leaving no potentiality in the will for something contrary by which it would be possible for someone to sin mortally and lose charity. Thomas writes,

> [T]here is a consideration of charity from the side of the will insofar as the will is subjected to charity, as matter is to form. It must be noted that when form completes the entire potentiality of matter, the potency cannot remain in matter as potency to another form. Whence, it possesses that form in a manner such that it cannot be lost, as is evident with celestial matter.... But charity completes the potentiality of its subject according as it reduces its subject to the act of love. [Thus, in heaven, where the rational creature loves God in act by his whole heart and where it loves nothing else except by actually referring it to God, charity will be possessed in such a way that it cannot be lost].[66]

Not only are the spiritual powers free from distraction, but there are also no disordered bodily movements or appetites in the heavenly life. There is complete purification from sin and what is associated with it.[67] Were there any disordered movements of the appetites or of the bodily powers, were there any bodily aggravation, the saint would not enjoy communion with God *as* perfectly as he could. Why not? Thomas writes, "Although the body does not add anything to the operation of the intellect whereby the divine essence is seen, it is able however to impede this act. Therefore, the perfection of the body is required [for beatitude] so that it might not impede the lifting up of the mind."[68] Man is a substantial unity; so, if he is disturbed in a bodily power, *he* is disturbed. Since heaven excludes dis-

---

[66] *DC* 12. See also *ST* 2-2.24.11.
[67] See *Sent.* 4.21.1.1.1, ad 2.
[68] *ST* 1-2.4.6, ad 2. See also *Sent* 4.47.2.1.1.

turbance, it excludes bodily aggravation and disordered movements of the passions.

End of the Pilgrim State: Perfect Actualization

There is another aspect to consider. Does the distinction between love of friendship and love of concupiscence have any operative place in the heavenly life? We can ask this question in two respects, as regards love of neighbor and as regards love of God. In this inquiry, let us recall that the rationale for the distinction is (a) the distinction between substance and perfection in creatures whom we love and who constitute our connatural objects of knowing, and (b) the mode of knowing and loving proper to the intellectual creature.

Now, whereas the distinction between substance and perfection always obtains in any creature, attainment of the final supernatural end is a permanent state. It cannot be lost on the part of the lover, who would never turn away from God. Nor would it be taken away on the part of the giver, who is infinitely just and would not strip His lover of his reward except on account of fault. Nor could any created power interrupt the immediate spiritual union of a creature with God.[69] So, do the saints continue to love their beatitude with a love of concupiscence, rejoicing in it? On the one hand, the distinction seems to lose its traction. The reduction of potency to actuality in the saint as it were indelibly marks the hypostasis of the saint by beatitude. So, the *desire* normally associated with love of concupiscence is certainly irrelevant with respect to eternal beatitude. On the other hand, love retains its primordial role as foundation of all volitional operations. Further, the saint remains substantially non-identical with his beatitude. So, the distinction has permanent relevance. Its modality, however, must be simply that of joy; the "indelible mark" of beatitude enables one to rest in the fulfilled neighbor-person.

With regard to love of God, the saint sees that God is His goodness. The saint still knows and loves with finite acts. However, the act of knowing attains God without any medium. The intellect is brought to simplicity of understanding, indeed, to a share in eternal beatitude. It would seem that an analogous simplicity would be realized in love. The horizon of this movement towards simplicity, while not erasing the infinite distinction between creature and Creator, would seem to render the divinized person's love for the Holy Trinity to be more and more a simple affirmation "of

---

[69] See *ST* 1-2.5.4.

God's existence and goodness," charged with the fervor of divine love.[70] If God is seen face-to-face, one knows God as He is. Since love always attains God Himself as He is even when cognition of Him is imperfect, the distinction would seem to lose any role with regard to God as object.

Conclusion

In contrast to the life of faith, heavenly life includes the intuitive vision of God, the impossibility of merit, and the cessation of distractions and sin. The implications of these perfections for the relationship between charity and love of beatitude differ in each case. The manifest vision of God increases self-love in that saints securely and eternally behold the object of beatitude so that they can never cease to love God or to be blessed. Still, the reduction of the pilgrim's potency to the saint's actuality entails that saints cease to act out of love of concupiscence to possess their ultimate end. Saints retain the self-love by which they love this end, but such love is not "in act" except as commanded by charity, just as all *ea quae sunt ad finem* are ordered to the end by intention. Hence, self-love and all other loves are ordered to charity's chief act, the intimate love God above all things. The impossibility of further merit can, in a sense, decrease self-love in that no saint can wish himself greater good than he presently enjoys. Nevertheless, love is greater which is truer, and truth is ultimately measured by the accordance of things to God's Mind.[71] So, heavenly self-love is greater. Further, the cessation of distractions also renders one's hold on charity secure, so that saints love themselves more certainly, as the virtuous love themselves more than sinners and the damned.

---

[70] Sherwin, *By Knowledge*, 157.
[71] See *ST* 1.16.1.

CHAPTER 8

An Aporia?

THUS FAR, we have followed Thomas's variegated depiction of the distinction and relation of love of beatitude and love of God for His own sake. Thomas's portrait is subtle, metaphysically grounded, and consonant with a Christian outlook, even if not all will agree with him. Despite our labor in depicting his appreciation of the harmonious character of these loves, there remains a difficulty to be considered. In a nutshell, the difficulty is whether Thomas's opinions regarding love of the divine Other can be harmonized with his opinions regarding beatific vision as the ultimate end, love of which grounds all free choice. We will tour this difficulty in several stages. First, we take stock of the way in which Aquinas qualifies the priority of the intellect over the will. Second, we will examine the grounds of one of his major arguments that vision rather than joy is the ultimate human operation. We will do so in light of his hierarchical ordering of two joys: joy in happiness and joy in God for His own sake. Third, we will consider texts in which he speaks of sacrificing beatitude for love of God.

PRIORITY OF INTELLECT OR OF WILL?

Thomas's inquiry concerning the priority of the intellect over the will is subtle and differentiated. We can note several of his observations. First, in union with nearly all others, he notes a priority of the intellect in the order of generation, which presents the will with possible objects for consideration. The will can love only that which the intellect somehow understands.[1] Put better, we can love something only if we know something about it. (The powers are not the man.) Of course, God can incline

---

[1] See *Sent.* 3.14.1.2, qla. 2; *DC* 4, ad 4; *ST* 1-2.27.2; *ST* 2-2.26.2, ad 1; and *DM* 16.3, ad sc 4.

non-cognizant beings to goods that He wills for them. However, such inclinations are appetites. They serve as grounds for the "fifth way" to argue for God's existence.

Second, in the order of "moving" to the end, the will ranks higher than the intellect in some ways. The reason is that the will moves the intellect and other powers under its control to their particular acts.[2] The freedom of exercise is at play here. Of course, this priority depends, in turn, upon the genetic priority of the intellect. It also depends upon the absolute priority of the intellect, the next item to be mentioned. Further, the reader will recall that some objects necessarily evoke love in the will, *if* the will elicits an act concerning such objects. Such objects need to be in every conceivable way good and in no way repugnant. In such cases, the intellect specifies the act of the will. The will ranks higher with regard to the exercise of the act.

Third, Thomas argues that the intellect is, simply or absolutely speaking, a higher faculty than the will. His argument regards the very character of the objects of the respective powers. The object of the intellect includes the "very character (intelligibility) of the good that is appetible," whereas the object of the will is the "good thing itself that is appetible."[3] The object of the intellect is something as universal; the object of the will is an individual thing as good.[4] Thus, there is greater simplicity in the object of the intellect than in the object of the will. Simplicity entails a certain kind of priority of universality.[5] Since the order of powers is determined by their relations to their objects, the intellect is, simply considered, a higher or more primary power than the will.

Fourth, Thomas finds that the intellect more foundationally specifies the human species than does the will. His argument is that everything has an inclination to its proper end. An order or inclination to an end requires cognition. So, differences in inclination are specified by different kinds of cognition. Some things lack cognition entirely and thus have merely a natural inclination received from the author of nature. Some things have sense knowledge and thus have sensitive appetite. Finally, some things have intellectual cognition and thus have rational appetite or will. In this respect, intellect is more primordial than will. This analysis seems to add a

---

[2] See *ST* 1.82.4 and *ST* 1-2.3.4, ad 4.
[3] *ST* 1.82.3.
[4] See *ST* 1-2.66.3.
[5] Of course, the good and the true are coextensive *in re*.

deeper causal priority to the mere appreciation of genetic priority.[6]

Fifth, the intellect and will can be compared with respect to their relations to various ranks of objects. Here, we find a remarkable difference of consideration. Simply speaking, the intellect ranks higher. However, with respect to a certain rank of objects relative to the knower and lover, the order is the reverse. The will ranks higher than the intellect with respect to those objects that are "higher" than man. The reason for the reversal is that "knowledge is perfected according as the known thing is in the knower, whereas love is perfected according as the lover is drawn towards the beloved."[7] When an intellectual being knows things lower than itself, it raises them, as it were, to a higher level of being: the flower understood is in a way nobler than the real flower. Put better, *that* a real flower is understood is greater than *that* a real flower exists without being known. When a lover loves things lower than itself as an end to which it submits itself, it brings itself down and debases itself. Similarly, when an intellectual being knows something higher than itself, it constricts the known, as it were, to what it can conceive about it. The higher thing, as known by the lower thing, is less than it is in itself. When, however, a lover loves something higher than itself as an end to which it submits itself, it raises itself up towards this lofty good. Consequently, with regard to a man's relation to God, "The love of God is better than knowledge (*cognitio*) of him."[8] Recently pursuing this line of thought, Daniel Shields concludes that the most excellent human act is that of love of God for His own sake. Shields does not, however, contend that this act should be considered an end: "God is the end, and love is the human being's best act simply because it puts him in the proper relation to this end."[9] I suggest that Shields is arguing that such love is the *finis quo*.

Sixth, the way Thomas connects the "psychological analogy" for the Trinity with the supreme rank of angels offers a concrete case of this inverted priority of intellect and will with respect to objects above the self. As is well known, Thomas holds that when two hierarchically ordered

---

[6] See *SCG* 3.26, par. 8.
[7] *ST* 1-2.66.6, ad 1.
[8] See *ST* 1.82.3. The imperfection of knowledge of God indeed affects one's love of Him, but it does not render that love impossible; indeed, love of something not perfectly known can even be "perfect" with respect to the lover's capacity (see *ST* 1-2.27.2, ad 2). In "Ultimate Ends," 585–93, Shields has studied the various texts in which Aquinas treats this matter.
[9] Shields, "Ultimate Ends," 584. Less careful, Wohlman appears to identify love and beatitude. See Wohlman, "Amour du bien," 233–34 and "L'élaboration," 267.

realms touch each other, the highest thing of the lower order resembles most closely the lowest thing of the superior order. For instance, a Venus flytrap approaches a cognitive mode of existence. Now, in the Trinity, Love Proceeding is the "ultimate thing" completing the Trinitarian cycle of processions.[10] This point can be considered in a technical manner and in a more profound manner. Technically, the Father is first because He is from no one. The Son is second because He is from the Father and there is one who is from Him. The Holy Spirit is third because He is from the Father and Son but no one is from Him. Thus, The Holy Spirit completes the cycle of processions considered technically, showing the balance of all three. If we couple this technical account with the widespread practice, fully endorsed by Aquinas, of appropriating "love" to the Holy Spirit, we see that the procession by way of intellect is prior to that by way of will in Trinitarian order.

More profoundly, this appropriation is based on Thomas's honed and refined portrait of the (pejoratively so-called) "psychological analogy."[11] The Father is God in the manner of speaking one perfect, immanent Word expressing His Wisdom. The Son is God in the manner of a spoken, immanent Word, by way of reflection or likeness of God as known. In knowing, one bears within oneself a likeness of the known. In speaking inwardly what one knows, one "reflects" that likeness (of the known) to oneself, as it were. So, the Word is God in the manner of subsistent reflection. By contrast, the Holy Spirit is God in the manner of an impulse towards the beloved. The Spirit is God as impulse towards God-as-loved. In love we embrace the known good by way of an appetitive act; we bear ourselves towards this known good. Thus, the Spirit is God in the following way: He is God-from-God-as-turned-towards-God. This admittedly awkward phrase houses an ordered development of concepts. The Spirit is God, for He is divine. He is God-from-God because He is from Father and Son, spirated by both equally and conjointly as one. Finally, the spirative act is unto Him (the Spirit) existing *as* towards Father-and-Son. Hence, His unique mode of existence is *as* turned towards God in the mode of love. This is but a dim analogy, yet marvelous to ponder in this weary land. On the foregoing bases, one may say that "love" marks the ultimate or final note in God. The Holy Spirit is as it were the "Flower" of God's uncreated beatitude.[12]

---

[10] See *SCG* 4.19 and 26. See also *ST* 1.27.

[11] I first pursued this argument in my manuscript developed during my sabbatical in 2007–2008.

[12] We can suggest this if we weave together *ST* 1.26 with *ST* 1-2.4.2.

Does Thomas's general principle apply here? Does the highest thing of a lower order touch the final thing of a higher order? Of course, there is no order of superiority and inferiority in God, but there is processional order of first, second, and third. Remarkably, Thomas bears witness that his principle applies in this case. He contends that love marks the property of the highest rank of angels, the Seraphim, whereas knowledge marks the property of the second highest rank, the Cherubim.[13] Thomas writes,

> The highest in an inferior order always has affinity to the lowest in the higher order; as the lowest animals are near to the plants. Now the first order is that of the Divine Persons, which terminates in the Holy Ghost, Who is Love proceeding, with Whom the highest order of the first hierarchy has affinity, denominated as it is from the fire of love.[14]

This passage is a surprising Thomistic witness to the supremacy of love in created persons.[15]

Seventh, it may be that Thomas qualifies the claim noted above in the fifth remark. In the *Prima secundae*, he writes, "love is preeminent to knowledge in moving, but knowledge ranks above love in attaining."[16] Could it be that the primacy of love of God regards the pilgrimage of the way? In beatific union with God, does the intellect come to have priority over the will? Then again, perhaps Thomas forestalls such an implication in the following passage: "The love of God is something greater than the knowledge of him, *especially* according to the state of pilgrimage."[17] Does the word "especially" leave room for an ongoing primacy of the will in the afterlife?[18]

Given the foregoing considerations, one may ask whether Thomas's principles call for reconsideration of what the ultimate operation of man is, the *finis quo*. Could it be that an act of "elicited joy over God" is man's

---

[13] See *ST* 1.108.5.
[14] *ST* 1.108.6. See also *Ad Eph.* 1.7, par. 62, and *Ad Col.* 1.4, pars. 41f.
[15] Shields also refers to these passages in "Ultimate Ends," 591ff. Some contend that this passage of Aquinas applies only in the order of nature, short of the beatific vision of God. See Jacques Maritain, *The Sin of the Angel: A Re-Interpretation of Some Thomistic Positions*, trans. William Rossner (Westminster, MD: The Newman Press, 1959), 17.
[16] See *ST* 1-2.3.4, ad 4.
[17] "Dilectio Dei est maius aliquid quam eius cognitio, maxime secundum statum viae." (*ST* 2-2.27.4, ad 2, my translation).
[18] Shields contends so (see Shields, "Ultimate Ends," 589n15).

ultimate operation? Or does Thomas's thesis that the ultimate operation is that of the speculative intellect still obtain? There are yet further reasons for raising these questions, to which we now turn.

Twofold Joy vs. Happiness as Intellectual Operation

Thomas is well known for holding that beatitude, man's ultimate end *quo* (end in the sense of attainment), consists essentially in an act of the intellect, not in an act of the will. Hence, the ultimate operation of man is intellectual. This is not, of course, to say that eternal life is simply intellectual and that volitional activity, especially joy, is inconsequential.[19] Indeed, Thomas's loose manner of expressing man's ultimate end as "vision" or "happiness" or "fruition," etc., attests to the inclusive character of his notion of eternal life. He can signify the ultimate end by the terms "vision" or "fruition," the former identifying the end according to its principal act and the latter identifying the end in its consummating crown.[20] Thomas argues in a number of ways that happiness as attainment is in its essence the act of beatific vision.[21] One of his favored arguments, enshrined especially in his *Prima secundae*, touches directly upon our theme. We encountered this argument in Chapter Three.

Beatitude, or the ultimate end, is both object and attainment. As attainment, beatitude is a perfecting operation by which the created person is reduced to second act.[22] Thomas argues in *ST* 1-2.3.4 that the operation cannot be an act of the will. The will's fundamental act is to love, which regards the good whether the good is possessed or not. Hence, love cannot be the *attainment* of the good. The will's second fundamental act is desire, which arises in the absence of the loved good. Hence, desire is not attainment of the good. The will's third fundamental act is joy, which arises in

---

[19] See the fine remarks in Toner, "Egoist?," 589–91.
[20] See Ramírez, *De hominis beatitudo*, pt. 4, 89–91. Ramírez's treatment of Thomas's "inconsistency" of language is thorough and lucid. See also 89–127.
[21] One argument depends on the foregoing: Beatitude must consist in the highest operation of man touching the highest object; whereas the latter is God Himself, the former is the act of the speculative intellect (see *ST* 1.12.1).
[22] In his thorough articulation of this argument, Ramírez first discards the possibility of beatitude consisting in an act of the will regarding the means. Formal beatitude he defines as the "attainment of objective beatitude." Now objective beatitude is, as Pope Benedict XII teaches, attained immediately, not mediately. Therefore, if formal beatitude is to consist in an act of the will, it must be an act of will regarding the end. See Ramírez, *De hominis beatitudo*, pt. 3, bk. 1, 186.

the attainment of the good. Since joy presupposes attainment, it cannot itself be attainment. Therefore, none of the three fundamental volitional acts regarding the good constitutes the union of real presence at which love for a good aims. Since happiness is attainment of the ultimate good, happiness cannot consist essentially in an act of will.[23] Therefore, the operation by which one attains the ultimate good is an act of the intellect.

The foregoing argument is convincing on its own terms, but it is based upon love of self, not upon love of the uncreated good for its own sake.[24] That the question seeks to identify the operation by which the end is *attained* shows this. One loves the attainment of the end and the object targeted by this attainment by the love of concupiscence. By the love of friendship, one wills this attainment for the person one loves. If the beloved attains his good, the lover rejoices; if not, the lover desires its attainment for his beloved.[25] This is true for both love of self and love of another. In love of another, desire or joy emerge with respect to the *friend's* having or not having *his* good. This joy and this desire do not, of themselves, emerge with respect to the lover being or not being with his beloved. Of course, in order to rejoice for the beloved, the lover must know him and know about his welfare. Cognitive awareness of my friend's happiness is a *sine qua non* cause of joy; however, neither cognition nor real union with the beloved is that "about which" the lover is primarily joyful in this love. The beloved's operational union with his good is the essential factor of joy in this love.

If the beloved is another, one's love becomes joy or desire with respect

---

[23] See *ST* 1-2.3.4; *ST* 1-2.4.2; and *SCG* 3.26, par. 16; and *Quodl.* 8.9.1

[24] I first developed my argument in my dissertation. See Christopher Malloy, "Love of God for His own Sake and Love of Beatitude: Heavenly Charity According to Thomas Aquinas" (PhD diss., The Catholic University of America, 2001) 344–55 and elsewhere.

[25] The question we are pursuing is not the relation between love of God and joy. Shields, pursuing the same question, puts the matter in that way (see Shields, "Ultimate Ends," 590 and n. 19). The love of God flowers in joy, just as the love of one's own happiness flowers in joy. Love emerges into joy through the mediation of the presence of the good to the one loved, whether this be oneself or another. Because love in this way is cause of joy, it outranks joy.

On the other hand, because joy is the flowering of love it signals love as come to consummation and in this respect outranks love. Properly speaking, we should compare the love of self to the love of God. This involves examination of love of one's own happiness as integral to the act of self-love. Strictly speaking, then, we should compare the two loves (love of self which involves love of the vision and love of God for His own sake) with each other, as well as the relation of the two joys (joy in having the vision and joy in God's being God) based on these two loves. See Malloy, "Love of God," 345–348.

to the beloved's having or not having his ultimate end. If the beloved is oneself, one's love becomes joy or desire with respect to one's own having or not having the ultimate end. Attainment must then be an act of the intellect, not of the will. Aquinas's argument rests on the love by which I love my good (the ultimate object and its attainment), not on the love by which I love the ultimate good *for its own sake*. Employing scholastic precisions, we could say: this love of happiness is a love of formal or subjective happiness; it is not a love of the ultimate end to whom (*cui*) I will the good.[26]

Love of beatitude is thus a love of concupiscence based on a love of friendship for oneself. Further, Aquinas holds that love of beatitude is the fundamental human love on the basis of which one chooses to love any other good.[27] If these two assertions were correct, would it be possible to love God for His own sake? Scotus, answers in the negative. He is far from alone in criticizing the eudaimonism espoused by such figures as Aquinas. Apparently, Thomas recognizes that his treatise on beatitude raises a question about this issue and proposes to treat it in his questions on charity.[28]

In those later questions, Aquinas claims that charity, as an honest friendship, is premised upon love of friendship for God; charity includes the benevolence of love of God for His own sake. God is loved absolutely for His own sake in three respects: as the ultimate end of all things, not referred to another; as He who is identical with His goodness; and as the

---

[26] I pursued this line of inquiry in my dissertation (2001) and again in an unpublished manuscript developed during my first sabbatical (2007–08). Ramírez, with whose thought I was insufficiently familiar at the time, laid out the principles for advancing these precisions. More recently, Daniel Shields has pursued this line of thought. He and I have alighted upon many of the same issues and remarkable passages. He draws a definitional distinction between the end *cui* and the end *cuius*, appealing to *SCG* 3.18 (see Shields, "Ultimate Ends," 601n51). Whereas the material end would be the same, God, it would be under notably different aspects that God would be end.

This distinction is meaningful in light of Shields's distinction between the essence of love (of friendship) as an affective union and the act of love as willing the good for someone. Somewhat in contrast, my judgment is that for the pilgrim wayfarer, love of friendship always has reference to love of concupiscence, which is always part of the structure of love. Thus, when I describe the end *cui*, I am indicating what Shields indicates by the end loved for its own sake as object.

[27] Consider, especially, the argument of *SCG* 3.26, par. 10. It is clear that what is at stake is the question of the ultimate operation, *beatitudo quo*. Thomas answers that it must be an act of intellect. Then he states: "Now the first thing willed by a thing of an intellectual nature is beatitude itself or happiness, for on account of this we will whatever we will" (my translation).

[28] See *ST* 1-2.2.7, ad 2.

cause of all other good things.[29] So, one must love God more than one loves oneself. Aquinas then countenances the fact that God is object of our affection in two ways, as the end we seek to attain and as the one to whom we will the good: "[O]ur end is God towards Whom our affections tend in two ways: first, [as we will the glory of God], secondly, [as we will] to enjoy His glory. The first belongs to the love whereby we love God in Himself, while the second belongs to the love whereby we love ourselves in God."[30] It is the former love that ranks supreme: "We love God more by a love of friendship than we love him by a love of concupiscence, because the good of God is greater in itself than that which we are able to participate by enjoying him."[31] If the love whereby we seek to attain God ought to rank beneath the love whereby we will God's own good, is not the love of God for His own sake a higher love than the love of beatitude?

At this point, some readers may understandably object that this question involves a misreading of the previous citation. Aquinas grounds his evaluation in the following reason: God's good is greater in itself than we are able to partake by enjoying Him. The objection to my use of this citation would be that Aquinas relates love of friendship to God and love of concupiscence to the participated good of our union with God. Thus, the objector might continue, there is simply one ultimate love, love of God as uncreated beatitude, while concomitantly there is love of concupiscence for the vision itself.

I am not satisfied with such a reading. First, is the objector proposing that love of concupiscence is ordered to love of friendship? If so, it is love of friendship for whom? If for God, then the love of concupiscence should regard God's "attainment" of His good. However, the love of concupiscence clearly is for the lover's *vision* of God. Thus, this reading does not work. Second, love of concupiscence for the vision has God as its target object, just as love of concupiscence for beholding a marvelous sunset has the sunset as its target. Love of concupiscence does not target simply an interior act of "seeing." In short, the accidental good that is willed, seeing, is an *intentional* act. We cannot isolate an intentional act as though it were itself a non-referential quality of man. It has its object—God. Now, this object is loved as object of the act, which is an accidental perfection. So, in each case (in the case of love of beatitude and love of the sunset) the lover is not in this precise act willing good to the object but to himself. The

---

[29] See *ST* 2-2.27.3.
[30] *ST* 2-2.83.9.
[31] *ST* 2-2.26.3, ad 3 (my translation).

"terminal" object of this love is the self.

The question thus returns: if the love whereby we seek to attain God ought to rank beneath the love whereby we will God's own good, is not the love of God for His own sake a higher love than the love of beatitude? Let us explore this question in light of charity's two "joys." By charity, God's friend wills God to have His good. Since God *is* His own goodness and happiness, the object of the love of friendship and the object of the love of concupiscence are identical in reality. Consequently, whoever loves God *must* be joyful. It is impossible to love God without being joyful. This principle joy of charity, Thomas argues, is incompatible with sadness.[32] There is another, secondary joy of charity that is compatible with sadness. The latter regards the lover's participation in or real union with God. Insofar as sin and temptation present obstacles to this participation and insofar as God's lovers yearn, as wayfarers, for the running streams of God, they are to some extent saddened. Still, for God's friends the greatest joy comes not "on account of the presence [to the lover] of the loved good," but rather because "the proper good is present and preserved in the loved good."[33]

In sum, we have discovered the following two theses. In the *Prima secundae*, Thomas argues that one seeks the ultimate good (*finis cuius*) and does not take joy until it is attained (*finis quo*). In the *Secunda secundae*, he contends that God's friend loves God not simply as a good to be obtained but more chiefly as the one for whom (*finis cui*) he wills the good or as the beloved Friend loved for His own sake. God's friend requires a cognitive act in order to rejoice in God's having His own good, and the more perfect that cognitive act the more perfect the joy can be. Yet, this cognitive act is not that "about which" God's friend has his chief joy. The precise "operation" that is the reason for the chief joy is God's own uncreated beatitude, dimly discerned by reason, believed firmly by faith, and to be seen clearly in glory.[34] This chief joy emerges because of charity's love of God for His own sake.

So, is the love of God for His own sake a higher love than the love of beatitude? An affirmative answer raises another question. If love of God for His own sake ranks above love of God as object beatitude, can Aquinas's argument that the ultimate operation is that of the intellect still stand? Is it not the case that, as Daniel Shields has recently argued, "loving

---

[32] See *ST* 2-2.28.2.
[33] *ST* 2-2.28.1 (my translation). See Ramírez, *De hominis beatitudo*, pt. 2, 303.
[34] See *ST* 1.26.1.

God is better than knowing him" in every situation whatsoever?[35] Might one even opine that the very love of God is itself our beatitude?[36] Further, if we ought to order our love of God as beatitude to our love of God for His own sake, can it still be the case that love of beatitude is the root of all our loves? If we were in a circumstance that required surrender of one of the two loves, would we not be required to surrender love of beatitude for the love of God? So, is not love of God the root of all our loves? These questions are put in starker relief by consideration of certain texts in which Aquinas discusses sacrifice of beatific joy and even of beatitude itself.

Love of God Unto Sacrifice of Beatitude

Three related lines of thought set the foregoing aporia in starker relief. By drawing attention to these lines of thought, I hope not only to indicate the presence of a difficulty in Thomas's corpus but also to respond to facile criticisms of Thomas as subordinating ethics and interpersonal love to the love of "one's own happiness." Thomas's thought is subtler.

First, throughout his corpus, Thomas meditates on the virtue of sacrificing, under the right conditions, the contemplative act, the ultimate happiness achievable on earth. The contemplative act involves "real" union with the ultimate good insofar as such union is possible on earth. As such, it is a climactic operation that God's friend seeks. The one who does not love God does not seek this act, while every lover of God seeks this act. Notwithstanding, one who truly loves God would be willing for a time to forego prayerful contemplation in order to work for God's glory. Similarly, he would be willing to delay beatific consummation of his love. The implication of this teaching is clear: love of "being with" the beloved is subordinated to love of the beloved for His own sake.[37] The following texts, among others, illustrate this thesis.

In his commentary on Philippians, Thomas refers to the powerful saying of Paul, "My desire is to depart and be with Christ, for that is far better. But to remain in the flesh is more necessary on your account" (Phil 1:23–24, RSV). Thomas remarks,

---

[35] See Shields, "Ultimate Ends," 606.
[36] See Geiger, 98ff.
[37] It goes without saying that this important teaching of Aquinas also had practical implication, namely, defense of the mendicants against monastic opponents. See esp. *ST* 2-2.182.

An Aporia?

> The love of God is twofold: namely, the love of concupiscence by which a man wants to enjoy God and to take delight in Him. This is man's good. There is also the love of friendship by which a man places the honor of God even above the delight by which he enjoys God. This is perfect charity.... And the Apostle says this in order to show that he has a more perfect charity, as though he were prepared, on account of the love of God and His glory, to be cut off from the enjoyment of the vision of God; and so, he chose this, and he chose well, as something more perfect.[38]

The interpretation is remarkable: Paul was willing to forego enjoyment of the beatific vision for the sake of God. Does this willingness not indicate that love of God as beatitude ought to be ordered to love of God for His own sake?

We find other iterations of this line of thought. In *On the Perfection of the Spiritual Life*, Thomas praises the willingness of God's lover to forego contemplation for a while, in service of God. Such willingness "attests to the perfection of divine love. For he is proven to love someone more who, on account of love of the beloved, desires for a while to be without the enjoyment of his presence in order to be occupied in his service, than if he were to wish always to enjoy (*frui*) his presence."[39] In this and the previous citation, Thomas speaks of sacrificing the "enjoyment of his presence." Although remarkable, the point might seem to regard sacrifice merely of joy and not of "real union." To the contrary, real union with the beloved produces joy; so, sacrifice of joy implies sacrifice of real union. This implication is expressly brought forth in the *De caritate*: "According to this friendship, therefore, a man who on account of his friend absents himself from this friend, loves him more than one who does not want to depart from his friend's presence, even for his friend's sake."[40]

One of the more remarkable Scriptural passages that elicit reflections such as these is the following line from St. Paul: "I could wish that I myself were accursed and cut off from Christ for the sake of my brethren, my kinsmen by race" (Rom 9:3). The text is puzzling. What good Christian would wish to be cut off from Christ? A gloss attempted to solve the puzzle by attributing Paul's sentiment to his life before justification, as though it

---

[38] *Ad Phil.* 1.4, par. 36. This lecture may come from 1265–68 (Torrell, 340). See, similarly, *Sent.* 3.35.1.4.2.
[39] *De perf.* 18.
[40] *DC* 11, ad 6.

were the wish of a sinner. The gloss was concerned that the wish indicated that St. Paul loved his neighbor more than God, since to sin is to offend God and to wish to sin in order to free one's neighbor is to love the latter more than God. Thomas recommends another solution, that of John Chrysostom:

> Or it may be said, as Chrysostom says in his book *On Compunction*, that by this it is not shown that the Apostle loved his brothers more than he loved God [as the gloss worries] but that he loved God more than himself. For he was willing to be deprived of the divine fruition for a time, a fruition which pertains to love of self, in order that he might procure the honor of God in his brothers. The latter pertains to the love of God.[41]

Thomas approves the willingness to forego contemplative union with God for a time. Such willingness can even be meritorious, provided it is done out of love. Although simply speaking the contemplative life is superior to the active life,

> [I]t can happen, however, that someone may merit more in the works of the active life than another person does in the works of the contemplative life, as may happen if on account of an abundance of divine love, one may now and then undertake to be separated from the sweetness of divine contemplation for a time in order that, for the glory of God, the divine will may be fulfilled.[42]

As evidence, Thomas cites Rom 9:3 and Chrysostom's exegesis. Of course, this willingness to sacrifice must be measured. The motive of the contemplative taking time for practical action must be "abundance of divine love." The ecclesiastic who calls a contemplative to practical action ought not compel him to forsake contemplation entirely. Further, the contemplative ought to retain his orientation to contemplation, which in itself is superior to practical action. Thus, the mixed life *adds* practical action, for the sake of necessities in this state of life, to what is in itself superior.[43] We could say that the contemplative life is objectively more heavenly but that the active life (still grounded in contemplation) is better *as more suited* to pilgrim man.

---

[41] *ST* 2-2.27.8, ad 1.
[42] *ST* 2-2.182.2.
[43] *ST* 2-2.182.1, ad 3.

An Aporia?

Thomas sometimes presses the spirit of sacrifice even further. God's friend would prefer to be in hell without sin (i.e., in hell *with* the love of charity towards God) rather than in heaven with sin (i.e., in paradise without the love of charity). In a Quodlibetal question, Thomas remarks,

> On the contrary, there is what Anselm says in his book "On Similitudes": That someone ought to prefer to be in hell without fault rather than to be in paradise with fault. For the innocent man in hell would not sense punishment and the sinner in paradise would not rejoice over glory.
>
> I respond: It must be said that the penitent ought, in general, to will to suffer any pain whatsoever rather than to sin. And this is indeed because contrition cannot exist without charity, through which all sins are absolved. Now, out of charity, a man loves God more than he loves himself. But to sin is to do something against God. To be punished is to suffer something against oneself. Therefore, charity requires this: That a contrite man prefers any pain to fault.[44]

If we should love God for His own sake more than we love Him as beatitude, we should be willing not only to delay union with Him, but even to suffer the pain of hell. Hell, a punishment, is contrary to the human person's good, whereas moral fault is contrary to God's goodness. Charity inclines God's friend to the divine good chiefly as it is in itself and secondarily as it is the good of man. Hence, better to suffer hell and not sin than to sin and "enjoy" heaven.[45]

The above passages run contrary to readings of Aquinas, such as Rousselot's, that reduce love of God for His own sake to love of God as beatitude. Rousselot interprets such passages as indicating willingness for a merely temporary sacrifice: "St. Thomas appears to prefer to understand this, not as a complete renouncement (through an 'impossible supposition') but as a temporary sacrifice."[46] Thomas explicitly contradicts Rousselot's limitation in his *Commentary* on Rom 9:3. For Thomas, Paul was

---

[44] *Quodl.* 1.5.

[45] Given Thomas's insistence on a natural love of God above all things, Thomas would clearly hold, *mutatis mutandis*, that a man in the state of integral nature would choose innocence in a state of punishment over guilt in a state of bliss. See *DM* 1.5, esp. ad 3, 10, and 11.

[46] Rousselot, *The Problem of Love*, 103.

willing to sacrifice not merely his *joy* in union with God, but his very glory itself. More startlingly, Thomas suggests that Paul was willing to do this everlastingly. Of course, Paul was not willing to sin, since sin is never justified (see Rom 3:8; 8:35; and John 14:15); rather, he was willing to forego beatific union with God:

> In another way, one can be separated from Christ, that is, from the enjoyment of Christ which is had in glory. It was thus that the Apostle wished to be separated from Christ for the salvation of the Gentiles, not to mention the Jews, as he relates in Phil 1:23f.... And in this way he said "I could wish," that is, were it possible, "to be anathema," that is, separated from glory, either simply or for a time, on account of the honor of Christ which shall come from the conversion of the Jews.... Thus, Chrysostom says in his book *On the Compunction of the Heart*: "Love so totally ruled his mind that although being with Christ was more lovable than anything, he would yet renounce it, and, though the kingdom of heaven seems to be the reward of labor for Christ, he would nevertheless suffer loss of it, should it please Christ."[47]

Thomas writes, "simply or for a time." Simply means everlastingly. Because of an exceeding love of God, someone could will everlasting separation from the vision of God if, *per impossibile*, God willed it. The one thing that no lover, *qua* lover, could ever will is to be turned away from *loving* his beloved.

Clearly, Thomas rejects the subordination of love of God for His own sake to love of God as beatitude. Moreover, Thomas's opinion on the primacy of love of God is not so easily harmonized with self-love, *pace* Rousselot and Egenter. Egenter pauses before Thomas's analogy of part and whole. The part sacrifices itself for the good of the whole, but a human being does not make and is not called to make an absolute sacrifice of himself to God. Although the good citizen sacrifices his body for the good of the nation, yet he earns thereby a great reward for his soul. Egenter points out that the extremes of quietism were condemned by the Church. All this is true. Yet, Thomas so esteems love of God and so recognizes the priority of love of God over love of self, that he is willing to say that a soul aflame

---

[47] *Ad Rom*. 9.1, par. 740. Thomas's lecture on Romans is in his hand through the Eighth Chapter. Thus, this text is not corrected. It dates from 1272–73, from his time in Naples (Torrell, 340).

with love of God would, if God willed it, accept being in hell without sin, accept the loss of eternal glory, which is perdition, but without sin, without the loss of charity. Still, for Aquinas, God would never demand a love so "perfect" that it must totally exclude love of self. The question remains: how does the primacy of love of God comport with Thomas's teaching in the *Prima secundae*? Are his teachings insolubly discordant?

CHAPTER 9

Towards a Resolution

Several considerations converge towards resolution of the difficulty expounded in the previous chapter. First, Thomas offers a distinct argument that beatitude is an intellectual operation, one that does not subject love of God for His own sake to love of God as beatitude. According to this argument, precisely love of God for His own sake points towards beatific union with God as the locus of its final rest or culminating act. Second, the character of the beatific vision as *immediate* knowledge of God calls for reconsideration of the relative priority of love of God over knowledge of God. Third, Thomas's doctrine of participation exposes the mistaken character of any evaluation of the relationship between love of God and love of beatitude premised upon a natively non-relational or alienational metaphysical structure.

The Ultimate Operation Cannot be Volitional

In *SCG*, Thomas presents another argument for beatitude as an intellectual operation, more tenacious than the one just critiqued for its privileging love of self:

> In the case of all powers that are moved by their objects the objects are naturally prior to the acts of these powers, just as a mover is naturally prior to the moving of its passive object. Now, the will is such a power, for the object of appetition moves the appetite. So, the will's object is naturally prior to its act. Hence, its first object precedes every one of its acts. Therefore, no act of the will can be the first thing that is willed. But that is what the ultimate

end is, in the sense of happiness. So, it is impossible for happiness, or felicity, to be the very act of the will.[1]

The argument is dense. The backdrop to the analysis is the poverty of the creature. The creature's existence as substance is not identical with its perfection, its flowering, its achievement. Only existence in the state of flowering is desirable in itself; sheer existence as substance is *for* existence in this flourishing state. The poverty of the creature entails, further, that the powers by which this achievement takes place are passive with respect to their objects. The good understood moves the will and intelligible truth moves the intellect. Consequently, the will begins in a state of potency. Now, that which is in a state of potency is not brought to actuality except by something already in act. In this case, the will is brought to actuality by an actually understood good. Hence, the first object of the will cannot be the act itself of the will. Once the will is actualized or brought to an act, then this act can itself constitute an object to be willed. Once one loves, one can love to love. The starting point, however, the first object willed, is something other than the will's own act. Now, the ultimate end is twofold, external object and act of attainment. The will loves this twofold end as its object. The attainment of the ultimate end, therefore, is an element in the primary object of the will. Since the will's first object includes attainment and since its first object is not its own act, the attainment is not an act of will.

In the *Prima secundae*, Aquinas presents a similar argument with some additional distinctions. The context is the inquiry whether man acts "on account of an end." An objection maintains that since the last end itself (as contact with the end) is a human action, not everything a man does is "on account of the end." Thomas concedes the objection but contends that at least some other human act is for or "on account of" an end. His argument is as follows. If there is some human act that is the ultimate end, it must be voluntary, for all human acts are voluntary. Now, voluntary acts are either commanded or elicited. The will elicits its own act "to will" and commands the acts of other powers, such as "to know" or "to move the hand."[2]

---

[1] *SCG* 3.26, par. 9.
[2] In this article, Thomas does not investigate the will commanding its own act in virtue of two different habits or objects. Recall that the will, by one act targeting some object (under some formal aspect), can also command its own act regarding another object (or the same object under another formal aspect). In this case, however, the commanded act falls under the commanding act as the means falls under what directs the means to the end. That is, the object of the commanding act is as end to the object of the commanded

Can the ultimate end (as contact) be an act elicited by the will? It cannot. The object of the will is the end in its twofold structure, external object and operational contact. That is, the will is the faculty of inclining *towards* that act of contact. Inclining towards contact, however, cannot constitute contact itself. So, if the ultimate end (as contact of the last end) is a human operation, it must be imperated by the will, and thus, there will be at least one act that is "on account of" the end, namely, the volitional act.[3]

In both of the forgoing arguments, Thomas draws an analogy. The will is to the first appetible as the eye is to the first visible. Now, the first visible is not the act itself of sight but an exterior visible thing. So, the first appetible is not the act itself of willing but an exterior understood good thing.[4] The analogy itself serves as ostensive demonstration of the claim that the operational contact with the external end cannot be an operation of the will. As seeing targets something other than seeing, so willing targets something other than willing. So, insofar as the will targets an operational act as something ultimate, this operation must be of another power, namely, that of the intellect. The will targets this act of the intellect. In turn, the intellect itself targets an actual intelligible—the infinite God. We witness here a strong dose of relationality, of other-centeredness, of objectivity. The will attends to the *good* understood, and the intellect to the *understood*.

This other-centeredness may surprise some; critics often reject Thomas's intellectualism as eudaimonistic and self-centered. By contrast, the Franciscan school is usually considered better apt to protect the other-centeredness of our beatific end. For instance, Scotus famously contends that the operation of beatitude is love itself: "The beatitude of an intellectual nature consists simply in the act of fruition alone."[5] Similarly, Peter Au-

---

act. Since the human act that is the ultimate end is not a means, this possibility is irrelevant here.

[3] See *ST* 1-2.1.1, ad 2 and *ST* 1-2.3.4, ad 2.

[4] If the exterior thing is to be made, it does not exist. How, then, can it cause or move? It moves as a final end already actually *understood*. The ultimate end itself is not constructed but encountered.

[5] Scotus, *Ord.* IV, d. 49, q. 5, in *Opera omnia* (Vivès, 1894), 171b–72a. The early Bonaventure, similarly, offers what could be a response to the standard Thomistic line of argument. He distinguishes three ways in which something is the "end." Something can be an end (a) as that in which one rests, (b) as that by which one rests now, or (c) as that by which one rests simply. God, obviously, is that "in which" we rest as in our last end. But God is charity (1 John 4:16). Also, charity is that "by which" we rest, both now and simply.

Bonaventure's argument for charity being the end "by which" we rest in God is

reol (1280–1322) teaches: "Beatitude is formally a delight, so that the joy in God or the complacency in Him is formally the act of beatitude."[6] For these medieval proponents of the primacy of love, such fruition is by no means subordinated to a love of self. They speak of a fruition by which one takes delight that one's ultimate beloved is infinitely good. Peter Aureol makes this point more clearly:

> Beatific enjoyment is not the delight which the blessed take in the divine vision, since such delight has for its object something created and changeable, but enjoyment regards nothing but the unchangeable good. Therefore, delight is the complacent love (*complacentia*) by which the blessed delight in the Lord and are pleased and rest finally in him, as the prophet says, "to delight in the Lord." But this complacent love by which God is delightful and pleasing to the blessed is, in the end, nothing other than beatific love; consequently, "enjoyment" indicates one simple act, namely, the love of complacence and delight in God.[7]

The arguments of Thomas just treated contain principles by which one can question this Franciscan line of thought.

It is by an act of will, an act of love, that one wills one's ultimate operation, whatever this may be. Now, on the Franciscan line of thought, the human person would "love" his ultimate "to love." Evaluated with respect to Thomas's principles, the Franciscan thesis presents several problems. First, were the will directed in this fashion, it could never come to rest but would endlessly seek to seek. Why? For Thomas, every agent intends an end in every deliberate act. Distinct acts involve distinct proximate

---

virtually the same for the charity of the pilgrim as it is for the charity of the saint. We would not rest in God except through the medium of love (*Sent.* 2.3.81.2 in *Opera omnia*, vol. 2 [Quaracchi, 1938], 917b–19a). Later, Bonaventure appears to place love, vision, and retention on the same level (*Breviloquium* 7.7). See Peter Aureoli, *Scriptum Primum super Librum Sententiarum*, no. 3, Franciscan Institute Text Series (St. Bonaventure, NY: Franciscan Institute, 1952–56), 1.7.1.5, 3rd prop., vol. 1, 399–400. See also, Aureol, *Sent.* 3.15.1.3.

[6] Peter Aureol, *Sent.* 3.15.1.3 (Rome, 1605), 444, cited in Ramírez, *De beatitudine*, 3:176. This third book of the Aureol's commentary is a *reportatio*, only part of which he actually edited. Ramírez's citation, however, accurately reflects the author's views, as can be discerned in the citation that follows.

[7] Peter Aureoli, *Sent.* 1.7.1.5, 3rd prop., *Scriptum Primum super Librum Sententiarum*, Franciscan Institute text series, no. 3 (St. Bonaventure, NY: Franciscan Institute, 1952–56), vol. 1, 399–400.

intentions yielding different moral objects. The child intends to pick up her plate, and the cashier intends to receive the payment. However, such discreet acts can be ordered to one remote end or good taken as ultimate.[8] The free agent intends this ultimate good and can order his discreet actions towards it. This act of intention generates an act of love, love of the end.[9] Now, the ultimate good is twofold, external object and act of contact with this object (*finis quo*). So, if the ultimate act of contact (*finis quo*) were "to love," one would ever love (intention of the end) to love (act of contact). This sounds lovely. The early Bonaventure suggests something of this sort in arguing that the ultimate operation by which we attain the end in which we rest is love. For that reason, "Everyone acts well who acts so that love of God and charity might be increased in him."[10]

But let us consider the ramifications. One's primordial act of will, one's ultimate act of intention, is to love. What one targets in this primordial act is yet another "to love," with God as object. Indeed, the goal of the target seems to be maximal *loving* of God. Is there, in this picture, any identifiable basis for appetitive rest in a terminal operation (*finis quo*)? Would one not, rather, ever target one's targeting? Would not one ever incline to incline? Indeed. One would not live dramatically towards a consummating end, real union with God. Rather, one would live towards further increasing one's love for God. One would incline to incline. It would be a drama without end. However, once a determinate ultimate end is removed, there remains no ground for any choice at all.[11] Rousselot's description of what he styles the "ecstatic theory of love" in the middle ages captures the difficulty:

> Here love is both extremely violent and extremely free. It is free because no reason can be found for it other than itself, independent as it is from the natural appetites. It is violent because it runs counter to these appetites and tyrannizes them. Indeed it seems it could only be satisfied by the destruction of the loving subject, by its absorption in the object loved. Being such, love has no other aim than itself and everything in the human being is sacrificed for its sake, including happiness and reason.[12]

---

[8] See *ST* 1-2.1.7.
[9] Sherwin, *By Knowledge*, 91.
[10] Bonaventure, *Sent.* 2.38.1.2, ad 6 (Quaracchi, 1938), 918b.
[11] See *ST* 1-2.1.4.
[12] Rousselot, *The Problem of Love*, 79.

Towards a Resolution

In short, if we take out the thesis that the human operation that constitutes the ultimate end is an act of the intellect, we seem to leave the will itself without an ultimate end. Rousselot's description echoes Thomas's analysis of this situation: "If there were no ultimate end, nothing would be desired, nor would any action reach a terminus, nor would the intention of the agent ever rest."[13] Such a situation, at first seemingly marvelous, describes an unrest ever searching but never finding. Simultaneously, Thomas also indicates an opposite problem, a paralysis of the will, which could not begin to act were there no end in sight. Both aspects of the problem indicate nihilism.

Second, conversely, would not the thesis of love as the ultimate operation lead to a situation of *no* drama? The object targeted admits of no dramatic development, for God already has His infinite goodness. So, if to love God were the ultimate human operation, would one not be already at rest in the goodness that God is?[14] Consequently, there would be little room for desire but only for joy. Simply by willing, one would be content. But is this the case? Thomas argues that it is not, having recourse to an argument by way of analogy from sense experience. Love of sensible goods shows that attainment does not occur by volitional operation. If attainment were by volitional operation, the very love of money would already constitute its possession. So, if loving God in charity constituted the beatific attainment of Him, one would immediately be beatified simply by loving God. Individual experience and knowledge of world history refute both consequents. In this argument, I employ the word "attainment," whereas, the reader will note, I evaded it in the previous argument. This argument itself is the defense of the choice of words. Attainment is union with or dynamical contact with the ultimate end. That we do not have this from the beginning or even from the beginning of willing our end is obvious. Achieving attainment draws us forwards in life. Hence, the *finis quo* is precisely attainment.

Third, the portrait of life with "love" as the *finis quo* would, paradoxically, focus a man's concern on himself. I say "paradoxically" because those arguing for "love" or "joy" as the ultimate act no doubt wish to free

---

[13] *ST* 1-2.1.4.
[14] Scotus wrestles with this question. See Scotus, *Ord.* IV, d. 49, q. 5, in *Opera omnia*, vol. 21 (Vivès, 1894), 175ff. Bonaventure simply appeals to charity as distinguishable into inchoate and consummate charity (*Sent.* 2.38.1.2, ad 5 [Quaracchi, 1938], 918b). Ramírez notes the problem of uprooting the "telos" of life if one identifies the supernatural act of charity with beatitude (see Ramírez, *De hominis beatitudine*, pt. 3, bk. 1, 189–90).

man from self-referentialism. They fear the Thomistic principles fall prey to this error. Such an intention, much more than any desire for "radical autonomy," appears to be the key motive behind the theory of freedom as "freedom of indifference."[15] To recognize such an intention behind defenders of "freedom of indifference" allows one to appreciate the noble sentiment while rejecting its banal interpretation and the nihilism to which such misconceptions lead. Indeed, we might say that the sickness Nietzsche found in Kant, in Luther, and in Christianity generally (as he understood it) is rooted in this aberration. Paradoxically, however, the thesis that love is the ultimate operation turns man's focus inward. One makes it one's ultimate aim to love all the more. Hence, one's willing is all about willing. One wills to will, loves to love. The reader will recall that to focus on improving in virtue and love constitutes the chief goal of only the *second* stage of perfection. According to Thomas, there are three stages in the life of the justified. During the first stage, one's chief preoccupation is to avoid sin. During the second stage, that of proficients, one chiefly seeks to grow in charity. If "to love" were man's ultimate operation, this stage would be the final and crowning stage of the true lover. Indeed, it would be a stage "without end," a stage of endless growth, unless God were arbitrarily to impose a limit to growth.[16] However, this second stage is not final; by definition it is oriented towards the next stage. Indeed, love points to the *beloved*; focus on the beloved is the essence of the third stage.

In the third stage of perfection, one melts into God, as it were. In this *unitive* stage one's attention is on the beloved. One is so swept up in this concern that one simply yearns to be with Him.[17] Persons in this stage are no longer focused on becoming better lovers. They are awash in concern

---

[15] Servais Pinckaers does not attend to this intention in his otherwise excellent *The Sources of Christian Ethics*.

[16] Bonaventure appears to avoid the difficulty of this situation by simply saying that one "has" God by charity, which is now imperfect but will be perfect in heaven: "When God shall be had in heaven, nothing further will be sought, because in heaven the uncreated good will be had, in which consists the end and rest of all our desires" (*Sent*. 2.38.1.2, ad 4 [Quaracchi, 1938], 918b).

[17] Being with the beloved, an intentional act, is an ingredient to true happiness. Charity makes certain that one is with and wants to be with one's friend properly. That said, being with one's friend is the climactic act itself. Thus, I find the following similar statement misconstrues the fabric of love and friendship both as Aquinas understands them and as they are: "The friend himself, who is the object of the love of friendship, is more important than being in the friend's presence, that is, than the attainment of the object of the love of friendship" (Shields, "Ultimate Ends," 599; see also Shields, "Will," 121n28).

about the beloved himself; they wish to "depart and be with Christ" (Phil 1:23). This explosive utterance of Paul sums up the whole pathos of love in the Song of Songs. The lover is drawn ecstatically towards his beloved. There is no other consideration. There is only ecstatic attraction: one is drawn completely outside of oneself and must see God.[18] Hence, *especially* for perfect souls, for whom there can be no sadness with respect to God being the one and only beatific God, life on earth under the veil of faith is but a "vale of tears" or "loud cries and tears" (Heb 5:7). The perfect lover does not aim at continually loving the more but wishes only "the beloved" and so "to be with" the beloved. The perfect lover aches until this wish is consummated. The imperfect condition of the "perfect" wayfarer illustrates, for Aquinas, the non-achievement of the end. Since the wayfarer's charity is perfectly in order (according to the measure of his state) while the wayfarer has not yet achieved the end, the operation of attainment is not essentially volitional but rather intellectual.

The foregoing argument from the *SCG* and the *Prima secundae* stands the test of the love of God for His own sake. In charity, one loves God *not* "in order" to see God, as though "to see" God were the end for the sake of which one loves God. One loves God *and so* is restless to see Him. The attraction is ecstatic. The Scotist objects that an intellectual appetite without an *affectio iustitiae* (appetite for what is right in itself) is not free. Scotus insists that one whose intellectual appetite has no *affectio iustitiae* but only an *affectio commodi* (an inclination to beatitude) necessarily wills the greatest beatitude, and maximally. However, unwittingly for the Scotist, the search for beatitude does not really achieve its high mark in the search for *objective beatitude*, for the Uncreated, Thrice Holy Trinity. Rather, its high mark is in the search for "my (volitional) share" in that Uncreated Trinity. For Aquinas, although things may begin in this manner—"Master, what good must I do to obtain happiness?"—they should not end in this manner.[19]

---

[18] See *ST* 1-2.28.2 and 3.

[19] Consideration of the entire discussion in Scotus *Ord*. II, dist. 6, q. 2, shows that Scotus does not believe that the drive towards beatitude can, from roots in a quest for what is fitting, blossom into a love for what is best, for the Only One who is Good. Of course, for Scotus, natural love is not sinful. However, a Thomist reading Scotus could say this: There is, for Scotus, a possible (counterfactual) world in which the natural inclination would ultimately center on the self and not on God. How can this reading be established?

For Scotus, it is possible for God to create an angel without the *affectio iustitiae*. Such an angel could not but love *its* beatitude, and maximally. Thus, it would not be

Thomas's depiction of "ecstatic attraction" serves at the same time to ward off both critics and misguided proponents of eudaimonism. As a love, albeit the most perfect, charity shares all the aspects of love that are pure perfections.[20] One pure perfection associated with any love is appetitive proportion to union with the beloved. A pure perfection is a perfection the concept of which does not include defect or limit. Now, affective proportioning does not indicate or require limit or defect. Love itself can be of what is either had or not had; love has no necessary reference to non-possession or non-union. Further, love can be either sensitive or immaterial (intellectual). Now, such proportion does imply desire in the absence of the beloved and joy in the presence of the beloved. Thus, Aquinas writes, "In every person who loves, there is caused a desire to be united with his beloved, insofar as this is possible; for this reason, holding converse with friends is most delightful."[21] Insofar as love of friendship for X is also love, and not sheer benevolence, it inclines one towards real union with X. Now, the most proper act of friends is being and living with one another so as to hold converse: "Nothing is so characteristic of friends as living together. . . . [T]he principal act of friendship is to live with one's friends."[22] As we have seen, there are many reasons for this. Above all, it is simply climactic for friends to live with one another, for life is act, and acting together is proper to friendship. Nor does just any joint action constitute this proper good. Action concerning the common good of union or relation is proper to friendship. In short, friendship in act is its proper good. Second, insofar as friendship consists in a mutual sharing of selves, being with one another

---

able to moderate its only natural inclination, its desire to have God present to itself; it would desire this presence more than it would love God's good for God. Precisely such an inversion of love is the sin of the actual demons, "for they loved God to be present to themselves more than they loved God in himself." Scotus, *Lectura II In Sent.*, dist. 6, q. 2, n. 37, in *Opera omnia*, vol. 18 (Vatican City), 381: 21–22. This sin of excessive love of beatitude is rooted, Scotus claims, in a kind of spiritual luxury, an inordinate love of self (see *Lectura II In Sent.*, dist. 6, q. 2, n. 37, 384). Hence, there is for Scotus a possible world that is naturally narcissistic. For Thomas, such a naturally narcissistic world is not possible.

[20] A pure perfection is a perfection the concept of which implies no defect or limitation. Whereas the concept is applicable to realizations that include defect or limit (e.g., love of sin or love of ice cream), the concept itself does not imply the defect.

[21] *SCG* 3.153, par. 3. I render the text "in every person" because by employing "*diligens*" Thomas indicates rational love.

[22] *Eth.* 8.5, par. 1600. See also *Sent.* 3.27.2.1; *Sent.* 3.32.1.2; *SCG* 4.22, par. 2; *SCG* 4.54, par. 5; *ST* 2-2.23.1; *ST* 2-2.24.9; *ST* 2-2.25.3; *ST* 2-2.180.7; *ST* 3.75.1. See also Egenter, 15.

enables this sharing.²³ Third, in the presence of a friend, one can appreciate all the more his goodness and beauty, thereby rejoicing the more in the friend.²⁴ Fourth, mutual presence enables common pursuit of good activities.²⁵ In the case of the divine friendship, the common pursuit is the very Life that is God.²⁶ So, "[i]f by grace a man is made a lover of God, there will necessarily be aroused a desire for union with God, insofar as this is possible."²⁷ God's friend is not disinterestedly benevolent. "The love of God spurs one on to the vision of the first principle, namely, God."²⁸

Without subordinating God to anything else, Thomas preserves the priority of knowledge over love. Obviously, he upholds the priority of knowledge in the genetic order; in that respect, he is not unique, for the whole tradition follows Augustine on this point. Thomas differs from the later Franciscan tradition in that he *also* preserves the priority of knowledge in the order of finality. What is fascinating is that his securing this priority is defensible precisely on grounds of love. What is it charity does to the lover? "For this reason is the gift of charity given by God to each person: Primarily, that he might turn his mind to God, which turning pertains to the love of self."²⁹ Hence, because of his charity for God, "The lover ardently pines to gaze upon His beauty."³⁰

Uncreated Aspect of Beatific Vision

We can recall here Thomas's assessment of the diverse ways in which priority and posteriority are found in intellect and will. With respect to an object greater than oneself, Aquinas teaches, love ranks above knowledge. In knowing the truth about something, I take the intelligible structure into myself. Thus, that structure exists in the measure possible for me. If the object is above me, a certain diminishment takes place. Conversely, since love of another draws me to the thing itself, if the object is above me, love draws me outside myself to the beloved. Love does so, that is, *if* it truly is focused on the beloved more than on its own act.

The foregoing analysis regards ordinary knowledge of a superior ob-

---

²³ See *Eth*. 9.14, par. 1946.
²⁴ *Eth*. 9.14, par. 1947.
²⁵ *Eth*. 9.14, par. 1948.
²⁶ See *ST* 1.18.3 and *ST* 1.26.1.
²⁷ *SCG* 3.153, par. 3.
²⁸ *ST* 2-2.180.1, ad 2.
²⁹ *ST* 2-2.26.13.
³⁰ *ST* 2-2.180.1.

ject. The beatific vision is no ordinary knowledge. Thus, we should reconsider the foregoing analysis with respect to vision. In the knowledge of faith, the media of propositions are limited to the capacities of the human knower. By contrast, there is no created intelligible species by which the mind sees God. The *lumen gloriae* is not an intelligible species but a created light disposing the saint for the vision. In the vision, God Himself is both object seen *and*, insofar as there may be need for a distinct intelligible species, the intelligible species by which the mind sees. Although the act itself of seeing remains finite and created, the known is not reduced to the finite capacity of the knower. Rather, the known is known immediately, albeit in the measure of the intensity of the seer's act. Hence, in the beatific vision, it is not that God's truth enters the mind within its limits, but that the mind is brought to God Himself without medium. Hence, the basis for noting an inverted priority of will over intellect with respect to a superior object may well not apply. If so, love's priority over knowledge when the object is above the self would be a priority for the wayfarer but not for the blessed. Knowledge would be chief in attaining, whereas love is chief in aiming.[31]

Metaphysical Participation

There is a final consideration. Aquinas's metaphysics of participation also underpins his analysis of the issues at stake in the "problem of love."[32] The part loves the whole more intensely than itself precisely because its good is related to the good of the whole. The consideration is not abstract, as though God's supremacy were the sufficient reason that He must be loved more intensely than self. The reason that the creature naturally inclines to love God more intensely than it loves itself is that (a) its being and good is partial, whereas God's is complete or perfect, and (b) its being and good derive entirely from God, in whom what is perfect in it is found without limit. These two notes constitute the pitch of participation. So, the reason that the creature naturally inclines to love God more intensely than itself is that it participates in God.

As scholars have been indicating in the recent literature, this participation involves also the interconnection of creatures with one another. The universe is an ordered tapestry of parts, whose main parts attain God directly. The good of the whole universe is twofold. On the one hand,

---

[31] See *ST* 1-2.3.4, ad 4.
[32] See Osborne, *Love of Self,* 98ff.

there is the order of the parts together, the intrinsic good of order in the universe. This is the good of which God said, concerning all that He had made, it is "very good." This good of the whole universe is a greater good than the good of any part.[33] On the other hand, there is the extrinsic good of the universe, that to which even the whole universe as a great good is ordered. This extrinsic good is, of course, The Holy Trinity, of whom our Lord said, "One there is who is Good" (Matt 19:17).

Both kinds of good are common goods.[34] The intrinsic good is a common good because it can be shared by many. Each creature can enter into the order of the whole in its own way. The rational creature can enter into the order of the whole by willing that good of order. Following Oliva Blanchette, Ezra Sullivan portrays Thomas's lovely vision concerning this manifold reality.[35] Each rational creature, willing the common intrinsic good of the universe, thereby participates in friendship with every other such rational creature. The reason is that this common good is the good of each rational creature; it involves ultimately a net community of friendships. Of course, its pilgrim and bodily realization are confined by practical limitations of realized friendship. I can befriend only so many. However, in befriending these, I indirectly befriend their friends. Thus, a virtual network arises. The heavenly realization of this network in the communion of saints constitutes the supreme created common good. We have been made citizens of the Heavenly Jerusalem.

Transcending even this created good of the bond among the saints, whether pilgrim or heavenly, and indeed underlying it, is the good that is God Himself. If the symphony of the many that is the universe is *for* (*propter*) God, then each of the parts, which is for the whole symphony, is also for the good that is God; the good of the part as the good of the created whole is to represent or magnify or illustrate the infinite goodness of God.[36] The very good of the creature is *for* the good of God. Consequently, the right way to *be* towards this good of God, the right way to be towards beatitude, is to love this good, which is God, ultimately for its own sake,

---

[33] See *SCG* 2.44.

[34] That is, they are both truly common goods. As Sullivan notes, a truly common good is common not just in predication but "in causation," being "the formal cause of the good of all who share in it." See Sullivan, "Self-Transcending," 927 in the context of his discussion on 925–28. Sullivan is following De Koninck, *Primacy* and *Defense*.

[35] See Sullivan, "Self-Transcending," 930–38 and Oliva Blanchette, *The Perfection of the Universe According to Aquinas: A Teleological Cosmology* (University Park, PA: The Pennsylvania State University Press, 1992).

[36] This is Olver's reading of *ST* 1-2.109.3. See Olver, "Love of God," 126–29.

that is, for God's sake. This is the way a citizen loves the good of the society of which he is part. The saint loves the good of God for His sake more than for the saint's own sake.[37]

Indeed, things cannot but be this way. Created being is but an imitation of the divine goodness. Each creature imitates the divine goodness in a unique, irreplaceable way. Insofar as creatures are bound together in various ways, their various communities of goodness also imitate the divine goodness. Finally, the symphony itself of all creatures imitates the divine goodness in a manner that surpasses the goodness of the sum of the parts. Communion in the good is not a matter of mere addition, but of order and integration. In creating the universe, God wills that His own infinite goodness be participated or imitated. This participation can be directly appreciated by rational creatures who can know this order as it is and will it as such. Hence, with virtuous rational creatures, the order intended by the chief parts of the universe is the very order willed by the Creator. If in the order of generation, these parts journey from elected self-love to elected love of God, the order of excellence and maturity matches the intention of God. Thus, in the final state of things, there is concord between the intention of rational agents and the divine intention.

By definition able to be shared, the common good is a relational good. Thus, God's good *is* the good of the rational creature. This identification does not mean that God is an instrument of the creature's ends, but it does mean that the connection of man with God as common good is the reason that God is more loved. Let us recall the following significant passage: "God will be to everyone the whole reason for loving for this reason: God is the whole good of man. For given that, *per impossibile*, God were not the good of man, he would not be for him the reason of loving. Thus, in the order of love, it is necessary that after God man most loves himself."[38] God is loved more intensely than self not because He is simply the greatest being but precisely because He is the infinite good *in whom* one participates.[39]

---

[37] See *DC* 2.
[38] *ST* 2-2.26.13, ad 3. In conjunction with this point I would note that Thomas appends an interesting remark to his response. There will remain, in heaven, reasons for loving one's neighbor not simply in accordance with closeness to God but also in accordance with bonds rooted in honest friendships developed on earth. Here, we have a most beautiful testament to Thomas's deep appreciation for the natural goodness of the created order. Though such reasons will be incomparably surpassed by God as *the ratio*, nevertheless, they will not not be.
[39] Rousselot reads this text as indicating that were God not the good of man, man would have *no* reason to love God. Rousselot, 92. Geiger is right to complain against Roussel-

Towards a Resolution

David Gallagher captures this fundamental point lucidly:

> I love God with the appropriate degree of love, not just because God is the best thing there is. I love God because he is the source of my goodness and because I find in God my own goodness in the highest degree. If, *per impossibile*, there were two or three Gods each with his own created universe, then it seems that I would love my God, the one who created me but not the other Gods, because the goodness of the other Gods would not be mine. In sum, even in the love for God there is an extension of the natural love of my own good, the natural inclination of the will.[40]

Thomas's conception of love of others is thus entirely *relational* and also *realist*, grounded in appreciation of participation in the common good. Thomas does not conceive love as "bending the friend back" towards the self, but he does conceive it in harmony with the way the universe *is* and with the only way that it *could be*, that is, as constituted by beings in communion with one another under God.[41]

Thomas's arguments for the love of God above all things and for His own sake are thoroughly grounded in the metaphysics of participation, in the real structure of the actual universe, according to which created things come from and depend upon God. The participation of the saints in the divine life is an unspeakably more exalted form of this structure. In his approach to the problem of love, Thomas is far from positing a universe of alienated beings in order to study abstractly the ways in which they ought to love. He is far from imagining two things alien to each other, each of which ought to be loved for its own sake apart from any possible perfecting relation to the other.[42] He is far from imagining an a-relational human love to God, even if such a love were to be "added" to the inherently communal nature of the universe and of its participatory relation to God.[43] Thomas's

---

ot's reading (see Geiger, 22 and 120ff). See also Bujo, 175.
[40] Gallagher, "Self-Love," 38.
[41] Thomas reiterates this principle in his treatment of charity. See *ST* 2-2.26.3, ad 2.
[42] Without a proper sense of the common good, we are left with the competing antitheses of (a) altruism and egoism and (b) individualism and collectivism (see Smith, "Common Goods," 599ff).
[43] Nicolas rightly impugns, without naming names, such an a-relational, un-creaturely account of creatures. See Nicolas, 24–26. For the creature, love begins with a natural thirst for beatitude. When there comes the moment of decision, the rational creature must choose his ultimate end. It is at that moment that natural love of beatitude can be

approach may be likened to a physicist's analysis of objects in space in contrast to a merely mathematical analysis of points in spatial configurations. No physicist would ask the stars of heaven to quit their gravitational fields so as to behave as Cartesian points plotted only with an eye to abstract spatial and vectorial considerations. So, too, neither does Thomas conceive love as definable in a-relational or merely objective terms. He grounds the entire analysis in the realism of participation. This analysis, coupled with his conception of the creaturely thirst for God, accords with the poverty of every creature, made for God (Rom 11:36; Col 1:16; Heb 2:10) and needy of fulfillment in Him.

Granted, *per impossibile*, were the beloved to wish the lover to delay or forego consummation of love, the pure lover would offer up this sacrifice. Yet, the act would remain *sacrifice*, and the truer the love, the greater the suffering. Thus, it is clear that the lover would not delight in this sacrifice as such but only insofar as it is ordered to conformity with the will of the beloved, for the sake of His glory. All the while, the lover would necessarily pine for the beloved, and pine everlastingly if the beloved's wish were everlasting. It is impossible to love someone and not to wish to be with him. It is impossible for the holy person to love God and not wish to be with Him. And, indeed, the good beloved would never ask His lover to offer such endless sacrifice. Else, wherefore the gesture of friendship that first aroused the heart's desire? The lover is beloved of the good beloved and so says to the beloved: "Make haste" (Song of Songs 8:14). Precisely because love looks to the Good, it is impossible that love be the ultimate human act: "Although friendship has delights and benefits joined to it, the eye of the lover does not look to these but to the beloved good."[44] Indeed, *the eye looks*: "Thus it is written concerning the Holy Ghost, Who is God's Love, that He *searcheth all things, yea the deep things of God* (1 Cor ii. 10)."[45]

Trinitarian Reduction

We reach a similar conclusion if we return to the Trinitarian analogy. In

---

chosen in precision from love of God above self, although already, incipiently, the very love of beatitude, of man's own proper perfection, anticipates a flowering into the love of God (Nicolas, 24–36). Geiger, by contrast, portrays a love of the whole in precision from any consideration of or relation to the self. Geiger, 26, 32, and 120ff. Olver's criticism strikes at Geiger's particular version of a non-relational notion of the good. Olver, "Bonum," 676ff. See also Osborne, *Love of Self*, 104.

[44] See *Sent*. 2.3.4.1.
[45] *ST* 1-2.28.2.

the order of Trinitarian processions, that by way of intellect precedes that by way of will. The procession of the Word precedes the procession of Love Proceeding. Word comes forth from the Father in an identity of essence and in the mode of likeness or reflection. Love Proceeding, by contrast, comes forth from the Father and the Word and in the mode of impulse or inclination towards.

These processions have analogical correlates in the order of the supernatural virtues. In the genetic order, faith comes first, since we cannot love what we do not know. In the order of excellence, love comes first, since charity is the greatest of the gifts. While the journey towards God has an inchoate status as promise and calling for a believer lacking charity, the integral journey towards God depends on charity (and hope) as well. The believer is fitted to God as supernatural end only when he possesses the infused virtue of charity. Charity quickens the believer so that he begins to live as the Holy Spirit lives. As the Holy Spirit is God from Father and Son in the mode of being towards Father and Son, the justified believer lives towards God. In this sense, charity is the life of the pilgrim, more excellent than faith. Yet the dynamic continues in reverse fashion, following the very pattern of the Holy Spirit's personal characteristic. As the Holy Spirit proceeds from the Father both immediately and mediately (immediately as from the Father and mediately as "also from the Son"), so the Holy Spirit subsists in relation towards the Father immediately, as towards Him, and mediately, as towards Him through the Son. In likeness to His mediate relation towards the Father through the Son, we are made conformed to the image of the Incarnate Word. Charity is thus ordered toward this conformation. As conformed to Christ, the believer relates to the Father as an adopted son.[46] Converted through the power of the Holy Spirit, conformed to the image of the Son or Divine Image, the pilgrim's mind is turned in expectation towards the Eternal Father. Although indeed the blessed see the three Persons and although each divine Person is in the other two, there remains a certain eschatological culmination or termination in the vision of the Father.[47] The Father is ultimate not because He is sheer relation, as though nothing were there but His relationality.[48] How could

---

[46] See *ST* 1-2.43.5 and *Ad Rom* 8.17, par. 647, and 8.29, pars. 702–707.

[47] For a profound meditation on this, see Emmanuel Durand, "A Theology of God the Father," *The Oxford Handbook of The Trinity*, ed. Gilles Emery and Mathew Levering (Oxford: Oxford University Press, 2011), 371–386.

[48] Of course, in the Father, the relation is the substance. But we speak according to the manner in which we know. For us, "relation" is insufficient to express the riches of the Father. For us, "relation" designates the distinguishing mark of the person; by contrast

what *is* not relate? The Father is ultimate because He is Pure Act from no one, Unbegotten Pure Act. In union with this Eternal Father, the soul of the blessed erupts in joy, echoing the Subsistent Joy that is the Holy Spirit. Once again, there is a primacy of intellect in the order of finality, which yet necessarily includes the flourish of joy.

"subsistence" designates the real existence in the infinitely exalted nature.

Conclusion

IF THE ARGUMENT OF THIS BOOK IS ON TARGET, Aquinas holds that the love of happiness is the foundation of human action, while the love of God for His own sake enjoys priority in the order of finality. The love of self implicit in this love of happiness is a starting point, but the end is love of God. In the order of explicit loves, this cannot but be the case. We can love only what we know. Through the senses, we first know creatures, especially things as good for us. The first object of rational consideration is likewise a creature. Hence, by explicit loves, the will first loves creatures. Such loves are by their very structure ordered to love of self, for they reach out to things (health, food, shelter) as good for oneself. One need not know oneself in the manner of adult self-reflection in order to order things to oneself. Discovery of the existence of the Creator allows the rational creature explicitly to love God and thus to order itself to God above all things including itself.

This line of thought does raise a difficulty. That love is perverse which does not order the creature to God above all things. Does the claim that love of self is genetically prior entail this perversion? If so, something has gone wrong in the analysis. Still, Aquinas's claim of genetic priority is discernible and also seems to correspond with reality. Perhaps we should consider this genetically prior stage of self-love to be the stage of the immature dawn of intellectual life. As immature, it would not involve the precise choice of an ultimate end to which to order all things in a definitively final manner. Further, it would bear within it, implicitly as it were, an inclination to transcend to something higher. The very grasp of this or that thing as good already calls out for a grasp of the greater context in which it exists. It is true and truly good precisely in light of the general notion of truth towards which the intellect intends. Similarly, the tendency towards this particular good as instantiating the good in general certainly surpasses this particular good. God is drawing the intellect and will towards their adequate object. Perhaps we can affirm this claim in a different way by consideration of non-chosen loves and the common good.

The order of natural, non-chosen loves is similar to the order of explicit loves, with a subtle and significant difference. A man naturally loves himself and other things insofar as they are one with him. Creatures, taken individually, cannot be more one with a man than he is with himself.

Hence, in the order of intensity, a man naturally loves himself more than any other creature. A man also loves the common good and God Himself insofar as these are one with him; however, this oneness must reflect the structure of being. Because a man has only partially what the common good has in plenitude, and because he has this partial good only from or through his relation to the common good, he is naturally inclined to love the common good more intensely than his own private good. Further, because he has his limited good entirely from God, who has limitlessly, without defect, and simply, whatever is of perfection in the universe, including the man's own perfection, he naturally loves God more intensely than himself. Notwithstanding, this relation of oneness has its orientation from the being of the man loving. Thus, were God an unrelated Infinite Good, the man would not love God more intensely than he loves himself.

In the natural order, then, the movement to explicit love of God above oneself is possible without grace (although not without the divine help proper to the order of nature). In the order of grace, an act of explicit love of God in charity is prepared by the natural order of love and by the infusion of grace and the movements of actual graces. Such an explicit love encounters, in the concrete order, the obstacles of original sin, actual sins, and bad habits. In overcoming these obstacles, God allows to flourish in the human person the natural order of love that emanates from His creative hand.

The foregoing is, as far as this author can discern, the grand vision of Thomas Aquinas. The author also finds this analysis true to reality. If the analysis does accord with reality, depictions of Christian love as requiring the renunciation of genuine happiness are mistaken and dangerous. It goes without saying that false happiness is not to be prized. Clearly, such portraits of love arouse the ire of Christianity's critics. If unfounded, they form no part of the true scandal of the Cross and should be discarded, lest Christianity be needlessly exposed to Nietzsche's correct rejection of self-hatred. On the other hand, there is an ordered development from love of happiness to love of God for His own sake. It goes without saying that the problems of original sin, actual sins, and vice require a conversion that cuts deeply and causes to bleed. Such conversion, however, is rooted in the goodness of existence, of the human essence, and of the cognitive and appetitive powers. Conversion is, on the natural level, the recovery of these for their proper use, against the abuse of sin. On the supernatural level, conversion is reconciliation with the Triune God, who made all things very good and in whom all things hold together. Love of Him is not alienation but communion in the good.

Conclusion

Perplexing questions do remain. It is hoped that that this tour of Aquinas's monumental thought elicits fruitful reflection on what matters most, *real things*.

BIBLIOGRAPHY

Primary Sources by Aquinas

In Latin

Thomas Aquinas. *In Librum Beati Dionysii De divinis nominibus.* Edited by Ceslai Pera. Rome: Marietti, 1950.

———. *In Metaphysicam Aristotelis Commentaria.* Edited by M.-R. Cathala. Rome: Marietti, 1926.

Lectura romana in primum Sententiarum Petri Lombardi. Edited by Leonard Boyle and John Boyle. Toronto: Pontifical Institute of Mediaeval Studies, 2006.

———. *Postilla super Psalmos.* Vol. 14, *Sancti Thomae Aquinatis Doctoris angelici ordinis predicatorum Opera omnia ad fidem optimarum editionum accurate recognita.* Parma: Typis Petri Fiaccadori, 1863.

———. *Quaestiones disputatae*, 2 vols. 8th ed. Rome: Marietti, 1949.

———. *Quaestiones disputatae De veritate, 1–7.* Vol. 22:1, *Sancti Thomae Aquinatis doctor angelici Opera omnia iussu Leonis XIII. P. M. edita.* Rome: Editori di San Tommaso, 1975.

———. *Quaestiones disputatae De veritate, 8–20.* Vol. 22:2, *Sancti Thomae Aquinatis doctor angelici Opera omnia iussu Leonis XIII. P. M. edita.* Rome: Ad Sanctae sabinae, 1972.

———. *Quaestiones disputatae De veritate, 21–29.* Vol. 22:3, *Sancti Thomae Aquinatis doctor angelici Opera omnia iussu Leonis XIII. P. M. edita.* Rome: Editori di San Tommaso, 1976.

———. *Scriptum super libros Sententiarum.* Vols. 1–2. Edited by R. P. Mandonnet. Paris: Lethielleux, 1929.

———. *Scriptum super libros Sententiarum.* Vols. 3–4. Edited by Maria Fabianus Moos. Paris: Lethielleux, 1933–1947.

———. *Sententia Libri Ethicorum.* Vol. 47:1–2, *Sancti Thomae Aquinatis doctor angelici Opera omnia iussu Leonis XIII. P. M. edita.* Rome: Ad Sanctae Sabinae, 1969.

———. *Summa contra Gentiles*. Leonine manual ed. Rome: Apud sedem Commissionis Leoninae, 1934.

———. *Summa theologiae*. Vols. 4–12, *Sancti Thomae Aquinatis doctor angelici Opera omnia iussu Leonis XIII. P. M. edita*. Rome: Ex Typographia Polyglatta, 1888–1906.

———. *Super epistolas S. Pauli lectura*. 2 vols. Rome: Marietti, 1953.

———. *Super evangelium S. Ioannis lectura*. 5th ed. Rome: Marietti, 1952.

In English

Thomas Aquinas. *Commentary on Aristotle's Nicomachean Ethics*. Translated by C. I. Litzinger. Notre Dame, Ind.: Dumb Ox Books, 1993.

———. *On Charity (De Caritate)*. Translated by Lotti H. Kendzierski. Mediaeval Philosophical Texts in Translation, no. 10. Milwaukee: Marquette University Press, 1993.

———. *Summa Contra Gentiles, Book Three: Providence (Part I)*. Translated by Vernon J. Bourke. New York: Doubleday and Company, Inc., 1956.

———. *Summa Contra Gentiles, Book Three: Providence (Part II)*. Translated by Charles J. O'Neil. New York: Doubleday and Company, Inc., 1957.

———. *Summa Contra Gentiles, Book Two: Creation*. Translated by James F. Anderson. New York: Doubleday and Company, Inc., 1956.

———. *Summa theologica*. 5 vols. Translated by The Fathers of the English Dominican Province. New York: Benzinger Brothers, Inc., 1948.

———. *Truth: Questions 10–20*. Vol. 2. Translated by James V. McGlynn, SJ, Chicago: Henry Regnery Company, 1954. Reprint, Indianapolis: Hackett Publishing Company, Inc., 1994.

———. *Truth: Questions 21–29*. Vol. 3. Translated by Robert W. Schmidt, SJ, Chicago: Henry Regnery Company, 1954. Reprint, Indianapolis: Hackett Publishing Company, Inc., 1994.

Other Primary Sources

Albert the Great. *Commentarii in III Sententiarum*. Volume 28, *Opera omnia*. Paris: Ludovicum Vivès, 1894.

Aristotle. *Nicomachean Ethics*. In *The Complete Works of Aristotle: The Revised Oxford Translation*. Translated by W. D. Ross. Revised by J. O. Urmson. Edited by Jonathan Barnes. No. 70.2, Bollingen Series. Princeton: Princeton University Press, 1984.

Derrida, Jacques. "To Forgive: The Unforgivable and the Imprescriptible." Translated by Elizabeth Rottenberg. In John Caputo, Mark Dooley, and Michael Scanlon, *Questioning God*. Bloomington: Indiana University Press, 2001.

Gregory the Great. *Homiliae in euangelia*. Book 1. In Corpus Christianorum, Series Latina, vol. 141. Turnhout: Typographi Brepols,1999.

Hobbes, Thomas. *Leviathan*. New York: Penguin, 1968.

Kant, Immanuel. *Groundwork of the Metaphysic of Morals*. Translated by H. J. Paton. New York: Harper & Row, 1964.

Scotus, John Duns. *Opera omnia*. Paris: Ludovicum Vivés, 1891–95.

———. *Opera omnia*. Vatican City: Typos Polyglottis Vaticanis, 1950–2013.

———. *Scotus on the Will and Morality*. Selected and translated by Allan B. Wolter. Edited by William A. Frank. Washington, DC: The Catholic University of America Press, 1997.

Secondary Sources

Blanchette, Oliva. *The Perfection of the Universe According to Aquinas: A Teleological Cosmology*. University Park, PA: The Pennsylvania State University Press, 1992.

Bourgeois, D. "'Inchoatio vitae eternae.' La dimension eschatologique de la vertu théologale de foi chez saint Thomas d'Aquin." *Sapienza* 27 (1974): 272–314.

Bujo, Bénézet. *Die Begründung des Sittlichen: Zur Frage des Eudämonismus bei Thomas von Aquin*. Vol. 33, Veröffentlichungen des Grabmann-Institutes zur Erforschung der mittelalterlichen Theologie und Philosophie. Edited by Michael Schmaus, Werner Dettloff, and Richard Heinzmann. Paderborn: Ferdinand Schöningh, 1984.

Courtès, Pierre-Ceslas. "La peccabilité de l'ange chez saint Thomas." *Revue thomiste* 53 (1953): 133–63.

———. "Le traité des anges et la fin ultime de l'esprit." *Revue thomiste* 54 (1954): 155–65.

Drost, Mark P. "In the Realm of the Senses: Love, Delight, etc." *The Thomist* 59 (1995): 47–58.

Egenter, Richard. *Gottesfreundschaft: Die Lehre von der Gottesfreundschaft in der Scholastik und Mystik des 12. und 13. Jahrhunderts*. Augsburg: Dr. Benno Filser Verlag, 1928.

Feingold, Lawrence. *The Natural Desire to See God According to St. Thomas Aquinas and His Interpreters*. Naples, FL: Sapientia Press, 2010.

Gagnebet, M.-R. "L'amour naturel de Dieu chez saint Thomas et ses contemporains II," *Revue thomiste* 49 (1948): 394–446.

———. "L'amour naturel de Dieu chez saint Thomas et ses contemporains II," *Revue thomiste* 49 (1949): 31–102.

Gallagher, David. "Desire for Beatitude and Love of Friendship in Thomas Aquinas." *Mediaeval Studies* 58 (1996): 1–45.

———. "Moral Virtue and Contemplation: A Note on the Unity of the Moral Life." *Sapientia* 51 (1996): 385–92.

———. "Thomas Aquinas on the Will as Rational Appetite." *Journal of the History of Philosophy* 29 (1991): 559–84.

———. "Thomas Aquinas on Self-Love as the Basis for Love of Others." *Acta philosophica* 8 (1999): 23–44.

Geiger, Louis-B. *Le problème de l'amour chez Saint Thomas d'Aquin*. Montréal: Institut d'Études Médiévales, 1952.

Gillon, L.-B. "Genèse de la théorie thomiste de l'amour." *Revue thomiste* 46 (1946): 322–29.

———. "L'argument du tout et de la partie après saint Thomas d'Aquin." *Angelicum* 28 (1951): 205–23 and 346–62.

Gils, P.-M. "Textes inédits de S. Thomas: Les premières rédactions du *Scriptum super Tertio Sententiarum*." *Revue des sciences philosophiques et théologiques* 45 (1961): 201–28.

———. "Textes inédits de S. Thomas: Les premières rédactions du *Scriptum super Tertio Sententiarum*." *Revue des sciences philosophiques et théologiques* 46 (1962): 445–62.

———. "Textes inédits de S. Thomas: Les premières rédactions du *Scriptum super Tertio Sententiarum*." *Revue des sciences philosophiques et théologiques* 46 (1962): 609–28.

Hamonic, T.-M. "Dieu peut-il être légitimement convoité?" *Revue thomiste* 92 (1992): 239–66.

Hittinger, Russell. "The Coherence of the Four Basic Principles of Catholic Social Doctrine: An Interpretation." In *Pursuing the Common Good*, Acta 14. Edited by Margaret S. Archer and Pierpaolo Donati. Vatican City: Pontifical Academy of Social Sciences, 2008.

Hoffmann, Tobias. "The Distinction between Nature and Will in Duns Scotus." *Archives d'Histoire doctrinale et littéraire du Moyen Age* 66 (1999): 189–224.

Hoye, William J. *'Actualitas omnium actuum.' Man's Beatific Vision of God as Apprehended by Thomas Aquinas*. Mesenheim am Glan: Anton Hain, 1975.

Jordan, Mark D. "Aquinas's Construction of a Moral Account of the Passions." *Freiburger Zeitschrift für Philosophie und Theologie* 33 (1986): 71–97.

De Koninck, Charles. *The Primacy of the Common Good against the Personalists*. Translated by Ralph McInerny. In *The Writings of Charles De Koninck*. Edited by Ralph McInerny. University of Notre Dame Press: Notre Dame, 2009. 63–108.

———. *In Defense of St. Thomas: A Reply to Fr. Eschmann's Attack on The Primacy of the Common Good*. Translated by Ralph McInerny. In *The Writings of Charles De Koninck*. Edited by Ralph McInerny. University of Notre Dame Press: Notre Dame, 2009. 205–363.

Kwasniewski, Peter A. "St. Thomas, Extasis, and Union with the Beloved." *The Thomist* 61 (1997): 587–603.

Long, Steven. "On the Loss, and the Recovery, of Nature as a Theonomic Principle: Reflections on the Nature/Grace Controversy." *Nova et Vetera* 5 (2007): 133–84.

McEvoy, James. "Amitié, attirance et amour chez S. Thomas d'Aquin." *Revue philosophique de Louvain* 91 (1993): 383–408.

———. "*Philia* and *Amicitia*: The Philosophy of Friendship from Plato to Aquinas." *Sewanee Mediaeval Colloquium Occasional Papers* 2 (1985): 1–23.

Malloy, Christopher J. "De Lubac on Natural Desire: Difficulties and Antitheses." *Nova et Vetera* 9 (2011): 567–624.

———. *Love of God for His own Sake and Love of Beatitude: Heavenly Charity According to Thomas Aquinas*. PhD diss., The Catholic University of America. 2001.

———. "Rahner's Supernatural Existential: What *Is* It?" *Freiburger Zeitschrift für Philosophie und Theologie* 63 (2016): 402–21.

———. "Thomas on the Order of Love and Desire: A Development of Doctrine." *The Thomist* 71 (2007): 65–87.

Manns, Peter. "Absolute and Incarnate Faith—Luther on Justification in the Galatian's Commentary of 1531–1535." In *Catholic Scholars Dialogue with Luther*. Edited by Jared Wicks. Chicago: Loyola University Press, 1970. 121–156.

Mansini, G. "*Duplex Amor* and the Structure of Love in Aquinas." In *Thomistica*. Edited by E. Manning. Recherches de théologie ancienne et médiévale, Supplementa, vol. 1. Leuven: Peeters, 1995. 137-196.

———. "*Similitudo, Communicatio,* and the Friendship of Charity in Aquinas." In *Thomistica*. Edited by E. Manning. Recherches de théologie ancienne et médiévale, Supplementa, vol. 1. Leuven: Peeters, 1995. 1–26.

Maritain, Jacques. "The Immanent Dialectic of the First Act of Freedom." In *The Range of Reason*. New York: Charles Scribner's Sons, 1952. 66–85.

———. *The Sin of the Angel: An Essay on a Re-Interpretation of Some Thomistic Positions*. Translated by William Rossner. Westminster, MD: The Newman Press, 1959.

Mattison, William. "Movements of Love: A Thomistic Perspective on Agape & Eros." *Journal of Moral Theology* 1 (2012): 31–60.

Mohler, James A. *The Beginning of Eternal Life: The Dynamic Faith of Thomas Aquinas, Origins and Interpretation*. New York: Philosophical Library, 1968.

Nicolas, Jean-Hervé. "Amour de soi, amour de Dieu, amour des autres." *Revue thomiste* 56 (1956): 7–42.

Nygren, Anders. *Agape and Eros*. Translated by Philip Watson. Chicago: University of Chicago Press, 1953.

Oesterreich, Peter L. "Thomas von Aquins Lehre von der Liebe als menschlicher Grundleidenschaft." *Theologie und Philosophie* 66 (1991): 90–97.

Olver, Jordan. "*Bonum Nostrum*: Thomas Aquinas and Love of Others for Their Own Sake." *Review of Metaphysics*. 70 (2017): 663–94.

———. "Love of God above Self." *The Thomist* 80 (2016): 97–131.

Osborne, Jr., Thomas. *Love of Self and Love of God in Thirteenth-Century Ethics*. Notre Dame: University of Notre Dame Press, 2005.

———. "Thomas Aquinas and John Duns Scotus on Individual Acts and the Ultimate End." In *Philosophy and Theology in the Long Middle Ages*. Edited by Kent Emery, Jr., Russell L. Friedman, and Andreas Speer. Brill: Boston, 2011. 351-374.

———. "The Threefold Referral of Acts to the Ultimate End in Thomas Aquinas and His Commentators." *Angelicum* 85 (2008): 715–736.

Peter, Carl J. *Participated Eternity in the Vision of God: A Study of the Opinion of Thomas Aquinas and his Commentators on the Duration of the Acts of Glory*. Rome: Gregorian University Press, 1964.

Peura, Simo. "What God Gives Man Receives: Luther on Salvation." In *Union with Christ: The New Finnish Interpretation of Luther*. Edited and translated by Carl E. Braaten and Robert W. Jenson. Grand Rapids: Eerdman's, 1998. 76-95.

Pinckaers, Servais. *The Sources of Christian Ethics*. Translated by Mary Thomas Noble. Washington: Catholic University of America Press, 1995.

Ramírez, Santiago Maria. *De hominis beatitudine: In I–II "Summae theologiae" divi Thomae commentaria (QQ. I-V)*. Vol. 3, *Edición de las obras completas de Santiago Ramírez*. Edited by Victor Rodríguez. Madrid: Instituto de Filosofia "Luis Vives," 1972.

———. *La essencia de la caridad*. Translated by Victor Rodríguez. Madrid: Biblioteca de teologos españoles, 1978.

———. *De caritate: In II–II Summae theologiae Divi Thomae Expositio*. Vol. 12, *Edición de las obras completas de Santiago Ramírez*. Edited by Victor Rodgríguez. Salamanca: Editorial San Esteban, 1998.

Reiner, Hans. "Beatitudo und Obligatio bei Thomas von Aquin: Antwort an P. Pinckaers." In *Sein und Ethos: Untersuchungen zur Grundlegung der Ethik*. Edited by Paulus Engelhardt. Philosophische Reihe, vol. 1. Edited by Wolfgang Kluxen and Dietrich Schlüter. Mainz: Matthias-Grünewald, 1963. 306-328.

Rousselot, Pierre. *The Problem of Love in the Middle Ages: An Historical Contribution*. Translated by Alan Vincelette. Vol. 2, *Collected Philosophical Works of Pierre Rousselot*. No. 24, Marquette Studies in Philosophy. Milwaukee: Marquette University Press, 2002.

Schockenhoff, E. *Bonum Hominis. Die anthropologischen und theologischen Grundlagen der Tugendethik des Thomas von Aquin*. Mainz: Matthias-Grünewald-Verlag, 1987.

Sherwin, Michael. *By Knowledge & By Love: Charity and Knowledge in the Moral Theology of St. Thomas Aquinas*. Notre Dame: University of Notre Dame Press, 2005.

Shields, Daniel. "Aquinas on Will, Happiness, and God: The Problem of Love and Aristotle's *Liber de Bona Fortuna*." *American Catholic Philosophical Quarterly* 91 (2017): 113–42.

———. "On Ultimate Ends: Aquinas's Thesis that Loving God is Better than Knowing Him." *The Thomist* 78 (2014): 581–607.

Simonin, H.-D. "Autour de la solution thomiste du problème de l'amour." *Archives d'histoire doctrinale et littéraire du moyen âge* 6 (1931): 174–274.

———. "La doctrine de l'amour naturel de Dieu d'après le Bienheureux Albert le Grand." *Revue thomiste* 36 (1931): 361–70.

Smith, Benjamin. "The Meaning and Importance of Common Goods." *The Thomist* 80 (2016): 583–600.

Stenberg, Joseph. "Aquinas on the Relationship between the Vision and Delight in Perfect Happiness." *American Catholic Philosophical Quarterly* 90 (2016): 665–80.

Stévaux, A. "La doctrine de la charité dans les Commentaires des Sentences de saint Albert, de saint Bonaventure et de saint Thomas." *Ephemerides theologicae Lovanienses* 24 (1948): 59–97.

Stevens, Dom Gregory. "The Disinterested Love of God According to Saint Thomas and Some of His Modern Interpreters." *The Thomist* 16 (1953): 307–33, 497–541.

———. "The Disinterested Love of God According to Saint Thomas and Some of His Modern Interpreters." PhD diss., The Angelicum, 1951.

Sullivan, Ezra. "Natural Self-Transcending Love According to Thomas Aquinas." *Nova et Vetera* 12 (2014): 913–46.

Toner, Christopher. "Angelic Sin in Aquinas and Scotus and the Genesis of Some Central Objections to Contemporary Virtue Ethics." *The Thomist* 69 (2005): 79–125.

———. "Was Aquinas an Egoist?" *The Thomist* (71) 2007: 577–608.

Trottmann, Christian. *La vision béatifique des disputes scolastiques à sa définition par Benoît XII*. Rome: École française, 1995.

Wadell, Paul J. "Charity as Friendship with God and Form of the Virtues: An Interpretation of the Christian Moral Life according to St. Thomas Aquinas." PhD diss., Notre Dame, 1983.

———. *Friends of God: Virtues and Gifts in Aquinas*. Vol. 76, *Theology and Religion*. American University Studies, series 7. New York: Peter Lang, 1991.

———. *The Primacy of Love: An Introduction to the Ethics of Thomas Aquinas*. New York: Paulist Press, 1992.

Wawrykow, Joseph. *God's Grace and Human Action: 'Merit' in the Theology of Thomas Aquinas*. Notre Dame: University of Notre Dame Press, 1995.

Wippel, John F. "Quidditative Knowledge of God." *Metaphysical Themes in Thomas Aquinas*. Studies in Philosophy and the History of Philosophy, vol. 10. Edited by John K. Ryan and Jude P. Dougherty. Washington DC: The Catholic University of America Press, 1984.

Wohlman, Avital. "Amour du bien propre et amour de soi dans la doctrine thomiste de l'amour." *Revue thomiste* 81 (1981): 205–34.

———. "L'élaboration des éléments aristotéliciens dans la doctrine thomiste de l'amour." *Revue thomiste* 82 (1982): 247–69.

INDEX

A

Act (Commanded act; Elicited act)
Affective expansion (elected love of God; natural love of God): 91–98; regarding natural and elected expansions in love of neighbor: 98–104, 158, 161f;
Amor (Love, passion)
Angelic impeccability: 122–124
Appetite: 9–13
Aristotle: 11n4, 50, 91, 103 (n 74), 138f, 161, 194 (n 5)
Attraction, ecstatic (Ecstatic attraction)
Augustine: 1, 20–25, 28f, 65, 74, 84 (n 44), 148f, 183f, 242
Auxilium (divine help in the order of nature)

B

Beatific charity: 7f, 199–216
Beatific vision (*finis quo*; intellect, attainment as act of intellect): 72–74, 77–86, 136f, 144f, 151, 158–164, 167f, 193–199; and impeccability: 177, 204–207; and intelligible species: 197–199; as perfective of charity: 200–207; loved less than God himself: 222–227; sacrificing the beatific vision: 227–232; uncreated aspect of: 242f; God the Father as ultimate person seen: 248f

Benevolence (love of friendship): 82, 133, 137f, 159–161, 164, 212, 224, 241; misconstrued as disinterested: 64
Bonum proprium and *bonum suum* (Proper good)
Bujo, Bénézet: 54 (n 54), 55 (n 56), 61 (n 82), 66 (n 102), 68 (n 105), 77 (n 21), 110 (n 99), 126f (n 159), 245f (n 39)

C

Charity (commanded act): as friendship with God: 30f, 112 (n 111), 133–145, 152, 164f, 179f, 185f, 204f, 210, 241f, 247; as virtue or created habit: 76, 139–143, 199f, 248; not disinterested: 135f, 164, 184–186, 211–213, 242; love of beatitude as leading to charity: 145–149; threefold relation of self-love and charity: 150–157; and ecstatic attraction: 158–164; charity's imperfections in pilgrimage: 176–190; charity's perfections in glory: 199–216
Commanded act: 15, 154–157, 172 (n 19), 185f, 206f, 216f, 234f (and n 2); charity as commanding: 154–156, 178, 183–186, 206f, 212f, 216, 234f (and n 2)
Common good: 37, 93–96, 98f, 101–103, 106–119; of charity:

135, 156f, 161–164, 182–186, 210–213, 241f, 244–246, 251f; not as alien or unrelated: 93f, 99–103, 117–119, 130f, 158, 243–247, 252

Communion: among men: 60f, 101–103, 118, 244f; with God: 155, 181f, 211, 214, 252

Created beatitude (beatific vision): 77–86, 117, 209f

D

Delight (joy; order of the passions): 9, 16–20, 33f, 57, 65, 82f, 177, 179

Dilection: 7f and 35–70; distinction from sensitive love: 35–41; natural dilection as root of free choice: 41–46, 49–52, 202f; twofold structure of dilection: 53–57

Disinterested love as false notion (Charity, not disinterested): 4–7, 45f, 64, 69, 89f, 99f, 117–119, 130, 136, 161 (n 93), 164, 183–186, 211ff

Divine help in order of nature: 121, 252

E

Ea quae sunt ad finem (things that are for the end)

Ecstasy (Ecstatic attraction)

Ecstatic attraction: 8, 145, 151f (n 59), 157–165, 239–242

Egenter, Richard: 64 (n 91), 92 (nn 17, 18, 21, and 22), 95, 102f (n 70), 110 (n 99), 138f, 143–145, 158 (n 79), 231f, 241 (n 22)

Elected love of God: 119–130, 147

Elicited act: 13–15, 77, 120f, 137, 151, 154–156, 185f, 218, 221f, 234f

Existence-as-substance (second act): 57–63, 70, 71f, 178f, 233f

F

Faith: as disclosing higher end: 85 (n 50), 139–149, 167f, 170–175; lack of vision and: 176–180, 195–199, 242f; as justifying: 4f, 25

Fallen state: 129–130 (and n 172), 133 (n 1)

Finis cui: 80–83, 226

Finis cuius: 72, 77–81, 83f, 226

Finis quo (Created beatitude; intellect, attainment as act of intellect): 72–74, 80, 83f, 219, 221f, 226, 236–238

First moral act: 119, 125–130, 149

Freedom of choice (love of God above self, elected): 46–52, 126; as grounded in love of beatitude: 40–46; as basis for distinction between dilection from *amor* 37–41; and pilgrim life of charity: 176–186; determined to the good in heaven: 200–213; Scotus's opinion and: 87–90, 238f

Friendship (charity, friendship as): 30, 91–104, 110f (n 99), 130f, 161–165, 179f, 204f, 239 (n 17), 247; beatific society of saints: 182 (n 54), 210 (n 61), 212f, 241f, 244

G

Gallagher, David: 39 (n 13), 53 (n 51), 92 (n 23), 98 (n 54), 99 (n 57), 124 (nn 146, 147, and 148), 126, 151 (n 56), 156f, 161 (n 93), 178 (n 42), 246

Geiger, Louis-B.: 7 (n 19), 38, 118 (n 127), 124 (n 146), 227 (n 36), 245f (n 39), 246f (n 43)

Generational priority (passions, order of): of knowledge before love: 45–52, 168–172, 217–219, 242, 248, 251; of love of self before love of others: 69, 91f, 95, 98, 119, 124–130, 146–149, 245, 251

Gillon, L.-B.: 21, 24, 54 (n 54), 55 (n 56), 105 (n 81)

Gils, P.-M.: 22f (n 37), 66 (nn 98, 99, and 100)

Good in general (in universal): 42, 50, 125f, 202f, 211, 251

Grace (divine help): necessary for attaining the supernatural: 75–77, 121, 129f, 139–143, 155, 252; necessary for natural virtue in the fallen state: 120; perfects but does not destroy nature: 85 (n 50), 104, 149, 155–157, 163, 183f (and n 87), 205; and angelic sin: 122–124

H

Habitual referral of love to God: 153, 159, 186–190

Happiness in general: 52

Heavenly charity (beatific charity)

Hoffmann, Tobias: 88 (n 2), 89 (n 6), 124 (n 145)

Hope: 84f, 89 (n 5), 134f, 141, 143, 144 (n 38), 151f (and n 59), 154, 163, 167, 171, 182, 199; as dispositive towards love of the other and charity: 69, 92, 146–149, 151f

I

Impeccability (angelic impeccability): In glory: 200–207, 213–215

Imperated act (commanded act)

Integral nature (fallen state): 74–77, 80f (n 33), 104 (n 76), 120–123, 129–131, 230 (n 45)

Intelligible species: 193–199, 242f

Intellect (beatific vision; light of glory) 36–40, 193–196; naturally affirming first principles: 45–48, 173; absolute priority in relation to will: 218; as presenting appetible objects to the will (generational priority); attainment as act of intellect: 59, 72–74, 79, 222–228, 233–242

Intensity of love (order of love)

J

Joy or intellectual delight (order of the passions): 56f, 72–74, 78–80, 83f (and n 44), 92 (n

INDEX

22), 99–101, 128, 154f–157, 159–164, 179–181, 206f, 215, 238, 241, 247–249; twofold joy: 217, 221–228, 230f, 235f

K

Kant, Immanuel: 5, 239
De Koninck, Charles: 93f (and n 27), 95 (n 35), 102 (n 69), 106 (n 85), 108 (n 92), 182 (n 54), 244 (n 34)
Kwasniewski, Peter: 91 (n 12), 98f, 158 (n 81)

L

Light of glory: 198f, 243
Long, Steven: 74 (n 13), 76, 151 (n 58),
Love: The passion of: 11–13, 16–20
Love of concupiscence (similitude, potential similitude): *ex professo* definition: 53–64, 70, 160, 180; treatment of alternative uses of the expression: 63–70, 97; used with reference to love of another for his sake: 54–61, 68f, 91f (and n 22), 98f, 215; used with reference to love of God for God's sake: 61–63, 124, 133, 226; used with reference to love of attaining one's end: 77–86, 117, 127, 159, 163f, 206f, 215f, 223–228; use of the expression regarding heavenly life itself: 215f
Love of friendship: 19, 53–57, 91f, 96–98, 100f, 179f, 239 (n 17); inseparably connected with love of concupiscence: 57–63, 70, 91, 96, 100, 117, 223–225; love of friendship for oneself: 83, 116f, 127, 225; love of friendship for another bringing ecstasy: 96–103, 158, 222f; love of friendship for God: 80–82, 85f, 114–117, 122f, 127, 133, 137, 158, 207, 215f, 225f, 228; leading to love of beloved's presence: 158–164, 241; in connection with actual similitude: 67–69, 91f, 179f; mistakenly taken as disinterested love of another: 67–69; Ramírez and: 80f
Love of God above self: natural and non-elected: 104–119; natural and elected: 80f (n 33), 119–131, 146–149, 201–203, 229–232, 241 (n 19), 244–247 (and n 43)

M

Malloy: 3f (n 9), 20 (n 29), 74 (n 13), 151 (n 58), 223 (nn 24 and 25)
Mansini, Guy: 53 (n 53), 54 (n 54), 64 (n 92), 65 (nn 96f), 66 (n 101), 74f (n 13), 98 (n 51), 112, 116 (n 121), 133 (n 2), 183f (n 57)
Maritain, Jacques: 124 (n 145), 221 (n 15)
McEvoy, James: 55 (n 56), 96 (n 44), 133 (n 2)
Means (things that are for the end)

Merit: 142f, 167f, 180–186, 191; impossible in heaven: 207–213, 216; Scotus and: 89

N

Natural desire (natural inclination)

Natural inclination (dilection, natural dilection as root of free choice): as non-cognitive tendency: 9–11; regarding the supernatural: 74–77, 122–124, 247

Natural love of God (love of God above self)

Nicolas, Jean-Hervé: 59 (nn 70f), 60 (nn 76f), 61 (n 83), 62 (nn 88f), 80 (n 31), 92 (n 15), 93 (n 26), 110f (n 99), 112, 246f (n 43)

Nygren, Anders: 4, 6 (n 17), 87, 95

O

Olver, Jordan: 57 (n 63), 58, 82 (n 36), 94 (nn 30f), 107 (nn 89f), 109f, 124 (n 146), 244 (n 36), 246f (n 43)

Operative flourishing (second act)

Order of love (generational priority): order of self love and love of others according to intensity of act: 113–117, 180–186, 209–213, 251f; order of self love and love of others according to good willed to the beloved: 113–117, 180–183, 200, 207–213; according to rank of accidental goods: 55–57, 70; order of finality: 91f, 97f, 125f, 146, 149, 242

Osborne, Thomas: 2, 88 (n 2), 92 (n 23), 93 (nn 27 and 29), 103 (n 71), 104 (n 75), 108 (n 91), 120 (n 133), 186–188, 243 (n 32), 247 (n 43)

P

Participation (part-whole): 107–108, 127, 139, 143, 182, 199, 209–210, 233, 243–247

Part-whole: 93–95, 105–116, 120f, 127–130, 231

Passions: 9f, 11–15; order of passions: 16–20; Thomas's development of thought on the order of the passions: 20–33

Phantasm: 194f

Pilgrim charity: 167–191

Pinckaers, Servais: 2 (n 4), 6 (n 17), 239 (n 15)

Possession of the loved object (presence)

Presence of the loved object (union, real): love is of what is had or not had: 16–20, 23f, 68, 143–145, 199, 222, 241

Priority (generational priority, order of love) special priorities of will over intellect: 217–232

Proper good: 87, 91, 95–119, 121–124, 127f, 146f, 153, 158, 162, 185, 203, 211f

Prudence: 156 (n 54), 184f

R

Ramírez, Santiago Maria: 80–82,

INDEX

85 (n 50), 104 (n 76), 158 (n 79 and 81), 159 (n 85), 163 (n 104), 164 (n 109), 222 (nn 20 and 22), 224 (n 26), 226 (n 33), 236 (n 6), 238 (n 14)

Rousselot, Pierre: 1, 54 (n 54), 110–112 (and n 99), 230, 237 (n 12), 238, 245f (n 39)

S

Schockenhoff, E.: 55 (n 56), 56 (n 58)

Scotus: 2, 14, 87–90, 224, 235f, 238 (n 14), 240f (and n 19)

Second act (beatific vision): 57–63, 70, 71–74, 178f, 233f

Self-love (charity, threefold relation of self-love and charity; generational priority): as natural and good: 1, 4f, 55f, 83, 97, 163, 179; as viciously exercised: 91, 179; conceived by some as not basis of love of another: 87–90, 95, 118, 146, 231f; self-love is more intense than love of other created persons: 183, 191; increased by charity: 147–149; perfected in heaven: 204f, 207, 209f, 212, 216; Rousselot and: 110–112

Sherwin, Michael: 27f, 33, 43 (n 26), 50 (n 45), 51f, 56 (n 60), 60 (nn 73, 74, 75), 100 (n 59), 119 (n 131), 125 (n 152), 156 (n 74), 184, 216 (n 70), 237 (n 9)

Shields, Daniel: 13 (n 7), 14, 60 (n 73), 61 (n 84), 75 (n 14), 80–82, 85, 121 (n 139), 124 (n 146), 153 (n 63), 219, 221 (nn 15 and 18), 223 (n 25), 224 (n 26), 226f, 227 (n 35), 239 (n 17)

Similitude: union of similitude: 18f, 91f, 94f, 98–103, 144; similitude as basis of love: 112f, 130; actual similitude as basis of love of friendship: 65, 68f, 92f, 179f; potential similitude as basis of love of concupiscence: 67–69, 91f, 179f

Simonin, H.-D.: 21, 24, 33, 54 (n 54), 64 (n 93)

Smith, Benjamin: 93, 246 (n 42)

Stenberg, Joseph: 73f (n 11), 78f (n 27)

Stévaux, A.: 64, 65 (n 96)

Stevens, Dom Gregory: 107 (nn 88f), 148 (n 51)

Sullivan, Ezra: 109 (nn 94 and 96), 110 (n 98), 112f (n 111), 135 (n 5), 244 (and nn 34f)

T

Things that are for the end: 21, 42–52, 91, 125, 141, 156f, 185f, 202f, 204f, 216, 234f (n 2)

Threefold union of similitude, affection, and real presence treated together (similitude, union of; union of affection; union of real presence of loved to lover): 18–20; Thomas's immature teaching on: 20–30

Toner, Christopher: 6f (n 18), 222 (n 19)

Trottmann, Christian: 199
Twofold end (created beatitude; *finis cuius*; and *finis quo*)
Twofold structure of love (dilection)

U

Union of affection: 93f, 130, 137f, 160f
Union of similitude (similitude, union of)
Union of real presence of loved to lover: 8, 133, 137f, 144f, 157f, 161f, 227–232, 238, 241f

V

Venial sin: 126f, 176, 187–190
Virtual referral (habitual referral of love to God)
Virtue: 2, 53, 55–57, 68f, 76, 154–156, 178, 181–184, 239; theological virtues: 76, 84f, 136f, 139–149, 163, 172–175, 199f
Volitional expansion (affective expansion)
Voluntas ut natura (dilection, natural dilection)
Voluntas ut ratio (freedom of choice)

W

Wadell, Paul: 6f (n 18)
Wawrykow, Joseph: 146 (n 46), 180 (n 46)
Will: 35–41; priority over intellect in order of moving: 79, 218, 221; priority over intellect in relation to things above us: 219
Wohlman: 7 (n 19), 117 (n 125), 124 (n 146), 148 (n 51), 219 (n 9)